THE NATIONAL MALL

NO ORDINARY PUBLIC SPACE

The National Mall in Washington, D.C., is one of the most recognized and frequented urban public spaces in the United States. Considered by many Americans to be "the nation's front yard," the Mall has long been a subject of national interest and debate. Yet little has been written about its role in the twenty-first century.

In *The National Mall*, Lisa Benton-Short explores the critical issues that are redefining and reshaping this extraordinary public space: a legacy of neglect, fragmented management by federal authorities, increased demands for access and security post-9/11, and calls for greater public involvement in the Mall's long-term planning and development. Taking a holistic view of the Mall and its unique history and character, Benton-Short provides a lively and illuminating account of the challenges and opportunities facing America's most important public space.

LISA BENTON-SHORT is chair and associate professor in the Department of Geography at George Washington University and Senior Fellow with the Sustainability Collaborative.

Lisa Benton-Short

THE NATIONAL MALL

NO ORDINARY PUBLIC SPACE

UNIVERSITY OF TORONTO PRESS
Toronto Buffalo London

© University of Toronto Press 2016
Toronto Buffalo London
www.utppublishing.com
Printed in the U.S.A.

ISBN 978-1-4426-3054-3 (cloth)   ISBN 978-1-4426-3055-0 (paper)

♾ Printed on acid-free paper with vegetable-based inks.

Library and Archives Canada Cataloguing in Publication

Benton-Short, Lisa, author
The National Mall : no ordinary public space / Lisa Benton-Short.

Includes bibliographical references and index.
ISBN 978-1-4426-3054-3 (cloth).–ISBN 978-1-4426-3055-0 (paper)

1. Public spaces–Washington (D.C.). 2. City planning–Washington (D.C.)–Citizen
participation. 3. Human security–Washington (D.C.). 4. Mall, The (Washington, D.C.)–
Management. 5. Mall, The (Washington, D.C.)–Planning. I. Title.

F203.5.M2B45 2016   975.3   C2016-902991-3

University of Toronto Press acknowledges the financial assistance to its publishing
program of the Canada Council for the Arts and the Ontario Arts Council, an agency
of the Government of Ontario.

Contents

Tables and Figures

Tables

Figures

Plates

Acknowledgments

I owe a debt of gratitude to many people who have been part of this book's preparation. Thanks to my George Washington University colleagues, in particular Marie Price, who read drafts of several of these chapters. Dorn McGrath suggested the Mall as a potential research topic, and he also introduced me to the National Coalition to Save Our Mall. Thanks also to Nuala Cowan, who crafted the maps for this book. Over the years, other Geography colleagues heard draft chapters given at annual conferences of the Association of American Geographers, and I appreciate their good questions and suggestions.

I also want to thank my editor, Douglas Hildebrand. He was a strong advocate for this book and worked tirelessly with me to improve the manuscript. I also thank him for convincing the University of Toronto Press to include the colour plates.

Some of the material for chapters 5 and 6 were originally developed as journal articles. Some, but not all, of chapter 5 appeared in my 2006 article "Politics, Public Space and Memorials: The Brawl on the Mall," *Urban Geography* 27 (4): 297–329. The journal, published by Taylor and Francis, can be found at http://www.tandfonline.com/?cookieSet=1. Some material in chapter 6 was originally published in 2007 as "Bollards, Barriers and Bunkers: Securing the National Mall in Washington, D.C.," *Society and Space* 25: 424–46. This is a SAGE publication and can be found online at https://uk.sagepub.com/en-gb/eur/pion-journals-published.

Finally, to my husband, John Rennie Short, who has also lived the saga of the National Mall for many years and heard endlessly about this chapter and that: a simple "thank you" seems inadequate. Your support and love have been instrumental.

THE NATIONAL MALL

NO ORDINARY PUBLIC SPACE

Introduction

20 January 2009. They came to the National Mall by the hundreds of thousands. They travelled from around the country and endured frigid weather, security checkpoints, and long lines. They were there to bear witness to history – the inauguration of Barack Obama. The entire two-mile stretch of the Mall was a carpet of nearly two million people – an unprecedented crowd of astonishing size and spirit. That day, the Mall was quite visibly a public stage for and a celebration of democracy. It was an extraordinary day in an extraordinary place.

In his inaugural address Obama proclaimed: "We must ... begin again the work of remaking America. For everywhere we look, there is work to be done." Obama's message was inspirational, but I couldn't help notice as he spoke that around me the grass was trampled, and I could see a scum-filled Lincoln Reflecting Pool, sagging benches, broken water fountains, and crumbling, neglected walls and sidewalks. Fences, barricades, and security details were in abundance. Perhaps, I thought, we should start remaking America here on the Mall, the nation's most important public space.

No Ordinary Public Space

The National Mall in Washington, D.C., is where American society expresses its national ideals of democracy, liberty, and freedom. It is one of the most recognized and frequented public spaces in the United States,[1] hosting

Figure 0.1 On the Mall on the day of the inauguration of Barack Obama. The crowd, pictured here at the east side of the Washington Monument grounds, stretched from the Capitol (almost one mile in the distance) to the Lincoln Memorial. Photo by author.

twenty-five million visitors each year. Many Americans consider the Mall "the nation's front yard." Michael Bednar notes that "America's democratic ideals are exemplified more in Washington, D.C., than in other American cities because Washington is the nation's capital and so is where we encounter the federal government most directly."[2] The Mall is an important place in the formation of national identity and national memory; it physically and symbolically represents layers of national identity, national discourse, and nation building. It is where presidents are inaugurated and where the country has commemorated significant people and events. It is a stage on which citizens act out the meaning of the nation, where protests challenge us to rethink what constitutes citizenship, justice, and democracy. In the twentieth century the Mall became one of the most important national public spaces for public protests and demonstrations, some of which have resulted in enhancing democratic values and practices, such as citizenship (civil rights and women's suffrage), or challenging political policy (on issues such as immigration, labour strikes, and war).

It is on the Mall, perhaps more than anywhere else in the United States, where national discord has been on display, national progress advanced, national wounds commemorated, national celebrations staged. The Mall is no ordinary public space.

A Brief Introduction to Public Space

What is public space? Public space is defined here as space that is open and accessible to the public. There are numerous types of public space: town centres, public squares, parks, beaches, roads, and sidewalks. Public spaces are considered those places held in trust on behalf of the public, for purposes of assembly, communicating thoughts between public citizens, and discussing public questions. Public space is commonly shared and created for open usage throughout the community, whereas, in contrast, private space is individually or corporately owned. It is generally understood that everyone in a community has a right to access and use public space, as opposed to private space that may have restrictions. For example, public space is often where people engage in free speech and assembly; it is where they gather in celebration or protest. The public realm is commonly conceived as an idealized theoretical construct, viewed by many as an arena in which people of different backgrounds, allegiances, and world views may engage in spontaneous encounters and open discussions with one another. Through discourse and debate, public space is generally understood to be a "stage for social learning," a place "accessible to, and used by, all."[3] Public space can be a powerful conduit of economic, social, or political changes.[4]

Scholars have robustly documented public space in urban history – from the agoras of ancient Greece to the forums of Rome, to the marketplaces of Renaissance Florence, where citizens could interact and merchants could sell various goods, to the plazas in Paris and New York. They have noted that, as cities evolved, public spaces began taking on multiple roles, as places of increasing political, social, and economic importance.[5] Jürgen Habermas, whose work remains seminal in this area, argued that the heightened significance of public space originated in Western Europe and the United States during the eighteenth and nineteenth centuries, driven by the growth of democracy, individual liberty, and popular sovereignty.[6] Before this time, notions of the public sphere were highly restrictive.[7] Habermas describes the emergence of a bourgeois public sphere, where all citizens could interact and have rational debates about public matters. Debates of this type were (and still are) crucial to the development of democracy, since they served as counterweights to political authority. Habermas saw an accessible public sphere as essential to a vibrant democracy. Many other contemporary public-space scholars have built on his ideas and argue that urban public space in a democratic society mediates relationships between individual citizens and between these citizens and the state.[8] However, some scholars counter that Habermas and others have tended to idealize the concept of public space. It is important to be wary of idealizing public space, lest it become an unattainable myth. Public space has always operated under some form of restrictions, either formal or informal – for example, even the most open of public spaces prohibit nudity, vagrancy, or other behaviour considered unsuitable. Hence no public space can claim to be completely inclusive.

The bourgeois eighteenth- and nineteenth-century society that Habermas described was in reality exclusionary, requiring as pre-conditions for entry a formal education and property ownership. Feminist theorist Seyla Benhabib has noted that public spaces have excluded significant segments of the population, including women, the poor, migrants, slaves, and criminals.[9] Similarly, Michael Gardiner believes that Habermas's public sphere is characterized by specific regulative mechanisms for rational debate and consensus building, which actively suppress "socio-cultural diversity in constituting an arena inimical to difference."[10] As an alternative approach, Gardiner, drawing on the Russian philosopher Mikhail Bakhtin, proposes the theory of "counterpublics." The Bakhtinian idea of multiple publics within a society, Gardiner claims, is more relevant for contemporary life in America, a society characterized by identity politics and a fragmented but not disunited culture. This recognizes the reality of differences within a population, which in turn leads to a better understanding of the needs of most, if not all, segments of society. Debates about what constitutes public space, the value of public space, what restrictions may mean, and how to balance different kinds of uses for public space underline an important fact: while most scholars agree that public space is vital, there is little agreement on exactly how to measure the quality and the variety of public spaces located in our cities.[11]

Emerging Issues in Public Space

Today there are numerous emerging challenges and opportunities that are reshaping and redefining urban public space in cities around the world. Three such critical issues are particularly evident on the Mall.

One is the management of public space. Political scientists have advanced theories about how to best manage the "commons," a particular form of public space, and have pointed to the degradation of fisheries, parks, and forests as the results of bad management. How to manage and protect "the commons" has been at the centre of local, regional, and international environmental-research agendas for some time.[12] There has been considerable progress in advancing broader theories of collective action and analysing different solutions. Scholars have debated and discussed a diverse range of management regimes; some recommend privatization as the most efficient form of ownership, others stress centralized control, and still others look to alternatives that seek broader representation of stakeholders and users.[13] These debates have been ongoing on the Mall as well, although its management is made even more complex by its status as a federal public space.

The Mall is a public space that, while located in a city, is federally owned and therefore subject to control by Congress and numerous federal agencies. In contrast, most urban public spaces are municipally owned and thus more locally controlled. The Mall has numerous constitutional rules regarding stewardship, budget, and oversight, which have created an unfortunately large and incoherent bureaucracy. This governance structure, I argue, has hindered good management of the Mall.

The Mall is just one unit in the wider national park system. The National Park Service has as its defining mission the protection and preservation of public access for all time. The law also mandates that this public space represent the entire nation, a challenging and perhaps impossible task. All national parks owe the concept of public use and public space to the legislation that created Yosemite in 1864 and Yellowstone in 1872. The language used in both acts is powerful and intentional. The creation of Yosemite called for the area to "be held for public use, resort and recreation that shall be *inalienable* for all time."[14] Similarly, Yellowstone was designated a place "dedicated and set apart as a public park or pleasuring ground for the benefit and enjoyment of the people."[15] Over time, this legislative framework has affirmed that national park units are places where public access is inviolable.

In contrast to many other public spaces, then, the Mall is subject to a more complex federal bureaucracy, something not well understood or analysed in the literature. There are implications to public space under federal control. Like any national park, the Mall is subject to a variety of political pressures on many scales, including Congress, state, and local.[16] However, the Mall, unlike most other national parks in the park system, and most other public spaces in the United States, faces unique political circumstances. It is subject to intense political pressure (for example, continued demands for memorials, museums, and monuments), but it is also a political orphan (its location in Washington, D.C., means that there is no congressman or senator whose constituency includes the Mall; it has no obvious advocate). This political netherworld makes the Mall a very vulnerable urban public space and one without a clear governance structure.

A second emerging issue is the use of and access to public space in democracy in a post- 9/11 context. Many scholars have looked at public space as sites where democracy becomes possible. Geographer Don Mitchell has written on the topic of public space and its relation to democracy, while Gill Valentine has focused on the theatrical component of public space in democracy. Recently, the role of Tahrir Square in Cairo, Egypt, has been examined as the conduit for the Arab Spring democracy movement of 2011 and again in 2013. Restrictions on the use of and access to public space are worrisome to those who have analysed the historically important role of such space as a site for the formation of citizenship and as a vehicle for discussions on civil society.[17]

Many of America's democratic ideals are demonstrated in the public spaces of its cities, where people can participate in social encounters, assemble to protest, or gather to celebrate an event. Public spaces such as the Mall "foster meaningful social relationships by providing opportunities to participate in communal activity. Encounters with strangers in public settings can vitally contribute to people's development of self-identity. Public spaces afford a supportive context in which diverse cultural groups can encounter one another. Stereotypes are diminished, allowing people to respond to others who are different from them, creating temporary human bonds ... Freedom of speech and assembly is witnessed in the countless demonstrations, rallies, parades and festivals held in Washington's public spaces. These all have an implicit or explicit agenda to influence government policy of public opinion."[18]

A century of marches and protests on the National Mall has played a critical role in the evolution and extension of citizenship and freedom of speech.

The Mall provides space for active citizenship, which includes what public-space expert Setha Low calls ritual protest and manifest protest: political protests, national celebrations, and public gatherings.[19] These forms of protest are active in the social production of social and political values, and hence the production of democracy. Active participation seeks to include rather than exclude "undesirables" and often attempts to extend or reinforce notions of citizenship and democracy. In this respect, "active citizenship" enhances the vibrancy of civil society. Americans often refer to the Mall as a "stage for democracy." Not many public spaces in the United States play such a significant role although the Statue of Liberty, Independence Square, and the Freedom Trail are also important stages. The Mall, like many public spaces, acts as a conduit for expressions of social, economic, and political change and contestation.[20] The Mall is more than just a passive landscape, it is also an active agent in the telling of the national story.

The Mall, particularly the area in around the Washington Monument and the Lincoln Memorial, has become an important public space for people to congregate and express ideas. Historian Lucy Barber has documented the emergence of the Mall as a focal point for public protest. She notes that "marching on Washington" has contributed to the development of a broader and more inclusive view of American citizenship and has transformed the capital (and the Mall) from the exclusive domain of politicians into a national stage for Americans to participate directly.[21] Don Mitchell and Lynn Staehli also describe the Mall and Washington, D.C., more broadly as the "national protest landscape."[22] However, in a post-September 11th world, there is the discursive paradox of both freedom and hyper-security reflected on the Mall. Fortification was a trend in Washington, D.C, that pre-dated September 11th, but in the years following security took on a new urgency. Security changes are a fundamental reorganization of physical and symbolic space. Because the Mall represents the fundamental principles of democracy in both form (monuments and memorials) and function (public space), fortification and security is more explicitly at odds with the Mall's symbolism. Debates about security connects to broader planning and management issues about how to balance the competing needs for security and national protest in a public space that embodies the ideals of democracy, freedom, and openness.

The imposition of security measures and restrictions on how public space can be used has led some scholars to decry the "decline" of public space.[23] Michael Sorkin and Mike Davis have declared "an end to public space," noting that modern society has withdrawn from public life. They say this has led to the "destruction of any truly democratic urban spaces."[24] I disagree with their view, because I believe the Mall is a genuine democratic urban space, but I also acknowledge that many of the current challenges confronting the Mall – including the lack of meaningful public participation in planning – endanger this claim.

The decline of public space has occurred in part because of a rise in restrictions on its use. In U.S. cities the most visible restrictions date from the post-September 2001 "War on Terror." Restrictions have resulted from anti-terrorism measures and include security elements like bollards, barriers, and the rise of closed-circuit television (CCTV). These types of restrictions have also happened on the Mall. Other restrictions follow policies that have essentially "criminalized" behaviour such as homelessness, panhandling, or being loud and disorderly. Don Mitchell has explored how capitalism has attempted through homeless laws to make downtowns "safe" for capital by purging what is perceived as disorderly conduct. He argues that public space is important to social change because it provides a venue for representation, and that, by placing restrictions on what can happen there, cities have endeavoured to eliminate activities that can and should occur in democratic public settings.[25]

While heightened security has affected the Mall, so has the demand for new memorials. There are always proposals for new memorials on the Mall, and they, too, change access, use, and meaning in this space. Public space is important to social change because it provides a space for representation. Since memorials on the Mall contribute to a larger national narrative about identity, understanding the pressure for new memorials and opposition to their location or design can expose new meanings of democracy and citizenship.[26]

A third issue is the revitalization and revalorization of existing public spaces and the creation of new ones. In the last several decades, many cities, including Washington, D.C., have redeveloped derelict industrial areas, downtowns, and waterfronts to compete for tourism and business investment. Increasingly, cities have turned their attention to the value of public spaces as part and parcel of redevelopment projects. New redevelopment projects have introduced new forms of public space, such as waterfronts, greenways, pocket parts, and urban gardens.[27] Stephen Carr has documented the proliferation of different kinds of public space that meet the needs of an increasingly stratified society where different subgroups have different priorities. The result, argues Carr, is a renaissance in public space.[28] The District of Columbia, which had historically ignored the Mall as a part of the "city," has plans to reorient development in a way that makes the Mall a centrepiece of residents' everyday lives.

The revitalization and redevelopment of public spaces has led to a wider discussion about how and whether the public is consulted and involved in the planning and development of public spaces. Urban planners are told to engage the community in meaningful participation in planning. Meaningful participation is more than citizens affirming what the planners have proposed: it involves seeing the public as a source of wisdom and information. This recent interest in participatory planning has been in reaction to the undemocratic and top-down nature of the old planning model.[29] Today, planners recognize that the process works better if citizens are actively involved in the creation and management of place. While there are different theoretical approaches to participatory public planning, one key idea is to decentralize the planning process. Participatory public planning assumes that decisions about growth management and future development are highly complex and embedded in the dynamics of the social, economic, political, and environmental systems. It also assumes that, within communities affected by planning decisions, there are various stakeholder groups whose level of power differs and which each have their own values and perceptions.

These issues are evident on the Mall, where there has been a historic absence of public participation in planning. Today, the District is attempting to re-engage the Mall and claim it as part of its urban fabric. Similarly, citizens have asserted their right to determine new uses for the Mall. Recent planning efforts have brought together new stakeholders in dialogue, but more can be done to develop innovative ideas for the future of this public space.

The Narrative

There are numerous books on the history of the Mall and its architecture, but little has been written about the contemporary challenges to the Mall in the twenty-first century. In this book I use current urban scholarship examining debates about public space to understand and contextualize these challenges. Discussing the Mall in such a way contributes to research in urban geography and urban studies that explores the intersection of parks, public space, and capital cities.

The fundamental thesis of the book is that the Mall is a highly significant public space yet suffers from bouts of neglect and disinterest. Its history is one of competing visions and competing interests that have often muddled the narrative and undercut its potential. Two hundred years ago, the Mall was designed to be a grand space; in some respects, it has never achieved this vision. The Mall is a place where many of the most important trends in national discourse are articulated in the form of monuments, memorials, public walks, gardens, and educational institutions like the Smithsonian museums. And yet, as important as the Mall has become, it continues to reflect the dissonance between national visions and experience; it hovers between the ideal and the actual, between political vision and personal experience.[30] There is much that can be done to improve the Mall as a public space.

This narrative is illuminated by examining the three overarching and related themes about public space that form the structure of the book. The first part of the book examines how federal public space is managed and describes the failure of the federal government to maintain and enhance the Mall. Both Congress and the Executive Branch are not doing right by the Mall. The second part considers new pressures for use and development as seen in increased demands for new memorials and heightened fortification and security. These new pressures alter use and development and so raise serious questions about the Mall's future. The third part of the book discusses the role of the public in the Mall's planning and development. Currently, public participation seems an afterthought and is not afforded a meaningful role. This is in contrast to trends in urban planning that emphasize public participation as essential. I examine the consequences of the public being shut out from decision making about the Mall.

These three themes capture timely trends that are reshaping public space in many cities: broader political discourses on citizenship and identity, commemoration, security, planning, sustainability, and the use of public space. These trends are not exclusive to the Mall; many are found in other urban public spaces. Additional challenges to the Mall may also be found in other capital cities where national identity is present and powerful. This book does not examine all of the important trends happening to public space, but it tries to advance our understanding of those trends that have a critical bearing on what the Mall will be for Americans in the next several decades.

Organization of the Book

Chapter 1 sets the foundation by introducing the history of how the Mall was envisioned in 1791 and how it evolved into a national symbolic public space.

While today Americans consider the Mall "the nation's front yard," this was not always true. The Mall has been constructed and reconstructed over time. The significance of the Mall did not just materialize; it was crafted gradually, often intentionally and explicitly, and sometimes through inaction and indifference. Over more than two centuries, various visions and plans helped to transform this "Grand Avenue" of Pierre L'Enfant's 1791 plan into one of the nation's most vital public space. The historical foundation is of critical importance. Two plans – L'Enfant's of 1791 and the McMillan Plan of 1901 – helped to create this public space and remain guiding principles for the Mall's development even today.

An enduring challenge to the Mall as public space is how it is managed. Part One focuses on the complex role of federal agencies for oversight and steward-ship of the Mall. Chapter 2 explores a historical narrative of neglect and indif-ference and how this legacy continues to haunt the Mall even in the twenty-first century. While we might like to think of the Mall as a grand public space, it has not always been treated as such. Cattle roamed the open areas, refuse littered the canals, train tracks once crossed the Mall, and numerous examples of deterio-ration of both buildings and natural features abound. This chapter asserts that Congress has often displayed indifference, ambivalence, and disregard towards the Mall. The narrative of neglect is seen today in disrepair, a lack of amenities and public transportation, trampled grass, and sinking seawalls.

Chapter 3 then builds upon the narrative of neglect to consider more fully the political context in which the Mall is managed. The Mall's development is deter-mined by Congress and the Executive Branch. Congress commissions landscape plans, approves memorials, appropriates funds for new museums, and conducts oversight hearings on development proposals. Agencies of the Executive Branch create comprehensive plans and authorize new memorial designs. Because the Mall is in the District of Columbia, it has, as already noted, no congressman or senator to advocate on its behalf. An examination of the fragmented manage-ment beholden to multiple interests in both Congress and the Executive Branch offers some reasons as to why the Mall over the decades has suffered from decay-ing of infrastructure, a state of affairs that has led many to decry the "Mess on the Mall." The chapter also considers the emergence of public-private partner-ships such as the Trust for the National Mall, established in 2007. The Trust is charged with some educational and programming functions, but its primary task is to raise money for the cash-strapped Park Service. Public-private partner-ships, increasingly common since the 1990s, represent a neo-liberal approach to urban development and have been created to deal with public space, particularly parks. For example, the Central Park Conservancy (a private organization) part-ners with Central Park (city-owned). Its role is to raise money for maintenance and programs. Today, the Central Park Conservancy is responsible for contribut-ing 75 per cent of the park's annual budget. The Trust for the National Mall has been moderately successful at fund-raising. Yet public-private partnerships raise questions, such as whether they are a good solution to management challenges or an appropriate way to support public-space needs.

Part Two examines new developments on the Mall that may change use, access, and symbolism. A major challenge to the form and function of the Mall as public space involves the continued demands and pressures to include new memorials to commemorate events and people, and despite a new congressional law stating that the Mall is "completed" and the lament of others about monument glut, no proclamation or plan or law seems to be able to preserve the central space of the Mall from further buildings.[31] Where will new monuments be located? How will the design and location of new memorials change the meaning of the Mall and the national story? Two chapters examine the debates about design and location of two of the Mall's most recent memorials: the World War II Memorial and the Martin Luther King, Jr (MLK) Memorial.

The MLK Memorial, explored in chapter 4, highlights a national discourse of commemoration that is growing more inclusive: the nation is literally and figuratively making space for the commemoration of civil rights. In this regard, the completion of the MLK Memorial in 2012 addressed one of the most noticeable absences on the Mall: African Americans. Indeed, the silences of the Mall – particularly what is absent in the form of monuments memorials or in the physi-cal landscape – can provide insight into national discourse on public space as much as the monuments that are present. The chapter concludes that memorials have become exorbitant in their costs, and that this may signal a new direction for future memorials on the Mall: corporate sponsorship.

Chapter 5 continues the discussion about commemoration. The controversy over the World War II Memorial reveals an important debate that appeared to pit commemoration on the Mall against the preservation of open space. The chapter also examines the ways in which the World War II Memorial altered the symbol-ism of the Mall and was integral to the debate about the memorial itself.

Chapter 6 discusses the fortification, security, and surveillance of public space. It examines security on the Mall within the broader context of national discourse on the War on Terror and trends in what I call "hypersecurity." In the last decade, our monuments and memorials have been fortified, and on the Mall as in other public spaces, such measures may impede or inhibit active citizenship. Studies by some scholars have shown that both passive and active surveillance significantly curtails personal liberties and freedom of expression within public spaces.[32] How have bollards, bunkers, barriers, and CCTV changed the use and meaning of the Mall? Have they curtailed the access to and use of this valuable public space? What do these security changes reveal about national discourse in a post-9/11 society?

Part Three focuses on the revitalization of the Mall through planning and public participation. Chapter 7 builds on the argument for a greater public voice in Mall matters. Ironically, the Mall has historically lacked genuine public participation. The chapter begins by analysing one of the avenues for public involvement and review, Section 106 of the National Historic Preservation Act, which requires federal agencies to open up the planning process to public review and comment. The chapter documents the epic struggle by members of a citizen's non-profit organization, the National Coalition to Save Our Mall (now the National Mall Coalition), to have a voice at the numerous Section 106 hearings in the past decade.

In addition to individuals and other groups, the District of Columbia government has also undertaken an effort to reintegrate the Mall in its urban-redevelopment visions. Throughout its history, the Mall has had a complex relationship with the capital city. The Mall does not belong to Washington, D.C., only. It is *in* the city but not necessarily *of* the city. It is not exactly an urban park such as Central Park; rather, it is a more liminal space – both national and civic. The city lacks authority over the development of the Mall. As a federally designated public space, the Mall belongs to the nation. In theory, this means that the city has very little say in how the Mall is used, how it is developed, and how it might be improved. Recent efforts by the D.C. Office of Planning to establish a better cooperative working relationship with the Mall's planning stewards, which include the National Capital Planning Commission (NCPC) and the Park Service, can be seen in the context of the city reasserting some claim to the Mall.

Chapter 8 expands on public participation through the concept of "the right to the city." Henri Lefebvre has written extensively on the concept. He says that the right to the city includes the right to access physical urban space; the right to

be social (to express oneself and interact with others); and the right to representation, a sense of belonging. The third right, the right to representation, involves
meaningful access to decision-making channels, the opportunity to participate.
In many cases, citizens have asserted their right, and in many cities partici-
pative democracy at the local level is helping to constitute an "urban citizenship." The chapter begins by discussing a recent effort where ordinary citizens
have asserted their "right to Mall." In 2011 a "flash mob dance protest" at the
Jefferson Memorial challenged the Park Service policy prohibiting dance and
playful expressions at the memorial sites. The chapter then considers the recent
2010–12 National Ideas Competition for the Washington Monument grounds.
The competition, sponsored by a citizen's non-profit organization that I helped
organize, was conceived of as a way to begin a national conversation about
reimagining the monument and grounds for improved public use and education in the twenty-first century. The competition also sought to involve the
public in this process, something that has been lacking throughout the Mall's
history. One purpose of this competition was to show the stewards of the Mall –
like the Park Service – that the public can provide creative and innovative ideas
in design and planning.

A significant number of plans for improving the Mall have been produced in
the last decade. Chapter 9 considers these different plans for the twenty-first-
century Mall. Federal agencies have recently completed several key planning
documents which set out ambitious visions for the Mall for the next one hundred
years. Some have found these plans less than creative, comprehensive, or inspiring. This chapter also looks at alternative ideas for the Mall, ones that allow for a
national narrative that is continuing to extend the story of America.

While several chapters propose ways to move beyond neglect and indifference
to a vision that ensures the Mall is valued as the important public space it is, ultimately the book raises more questions than it answers. It is my aim to stimulate
a public dialogue about how to shape the future use and meaning of this special
public space.

How I Came to Write This Book

As an urban geographer, I study cities, parks, and public space. I am part of a
network of scholars who conduct research and publish work on national parks

and urban public space. One of my first books, *The Presidio: From Army Post to National Park*, published by Northeastern University Press in 1998, examined the planning and politics involved in the conversion of the Presidio Army Post in San Francisco into a new national park in 1994. To explain the challenges of the process, I situated the Presidio within the broader context of the national park system, noting that this system is socially constructed and hence subject to political pressure at the local, state, and federal levels. I argued that the pitfalls and political resistance to the Park Service plan for the Presidio occurred because the Presidio is a non-traditional park site located in a city. As an urban national park, the Presidio did not resonate with the national park ideal, characterized by the expansive wilderness and scenic monumentalism that has informed park ideology. That book highlighted the unique challenges faced by the urban park units in the system, which have been less studied than the so-called "Crown Jewels" such as Yellowstone, Yosemite, and Grand Canyon.

When I joined the faculty at George Washington University, I realized that my office was just blocks away from another urban national park, the National Mall. My commute to work took me past the Washington Monument, which was then under restoration and wrapped in scaffolding. A few years later, the grounds of the Washington Monument were fenced off for the construction of a new security project. I saw these highly visible changes to the Mall as another opportunity to explore the important role of national parks in cities, thereby building on some of the ideas in my previous book. Like the Presidio, the National Mall is a national park and a highly visited urban public space. Unlike the Presidio, however, the National Mall has some unusual political constraints. I began to examine some of the contemporary issues on the National Mall, initially conceiving of one or two short articles. For many years I attended meetings and public symposiums while also following debates in the media (including the emergence of websites and blogs on D.C. planning). A few years turned into ten years and what started as one or two articles became a book project.

When I first started researching the Mall, I assumed that the one or two articles I had in mind would be published in journals for a predominantly scholarly audience. But the more I continued to research, the more I became convinced that this story needed to reach a wider readership. I began to include the ideas presented in this book in my classroom and on field trips, challenging students to engage with the issues and to tell me what they experienced when they took friends and family to the Mall. Slowly, I realized that I wanted this book to inform, but I also wanted to encourage a broader public discussion about how to shape the use and meaning of the Mall. I wanted the American public to pay more attention to the Mall and, ultimately, to participate more fully in its future development.

In the time I have been researching the book, the National Mall has been transformed. New security measures, memorials, and restoration projects have been visible transformations. There have also been the not-so-visible transformations: some changes to the Mall have generated debates about long-term planning, public involvement, and access to this public space. These issues resonate with wider research in urban geography and urban studies that explores the intersection of parks, public space, and cities. I hope scholars will appreciate that understanding the challenges to the Mall advances an understanding of public space.

Readers will find that my analysis tends to be critical of the federal agencies in charge of the Mall, particularly the Park Service. This was unexpected. I have long admired the national park system and believe that the role of urban national parks is undervalued and under-resourced. My work has tried to illuminate the challenges and importance of urban national parks and the success stories; indeed, in my earlier book, I applauded the efforts of the Park Service in planning the transformation of the Presidio in San Francisco in 1994. I expected when I began this project that I would find similarly positive developments on the National Mall. However, after many years of attending meetings, hearings, and forums, of poring over public documents, and of private conversations, I arrived at a more critical position on the role of the Park Service in the Capital Region. In some cases, federal employees have admitted (usually off the record) that they are frustrated and constrained by their own bureaucracy.

My research included a mixed-methods approach of archival work, some interviews, participant observation, and personal involvement in two citizen's groups. I have done extensive reviews of the literature, reading through hundreds of public documents, newspaper articles (local and national), archival records, and plans. I've relied on a wealth of books on the history of the Mall. I have mined websites of the Park Service, the Smithsonian, the Committee of Fine Arts (CFA), the National Capital Planning Commission (NCPC), the Trust for the National Mall, and numerous memorial associations to document memorials and other planning projects.

In addition to in-depth primary and secondary source material, I became involved with a citizen's organization, the National Coalition to Save Our Mall.[33] This group formed in opposition to the location of the World War II Memorial. The Coalition included architects and planners who had spent a good deal of their careers in Washington, D.C. It also included historians, architectural historians, and World War II veterans, many of whom were life-long residents of the Capital Region. In 2004, a few years after I began my research, I attended several Coalition events, including a public forum that was held at George Washington University. I became more involved with the organization and grew to appreciate its expertise and insight on many planning issues. Several of its members were also associated with the Committee of 100 on the Federal City, a non-profit organization dedicated to responsible planning in Washington. In 2005 I was invited to join the Board of Directors for the Coalition. Since then I have attended numerous meetings with my Coalition colleagues. These include our own board meetings, strategy meetings with Coalition members, and dozens of meetings with community leaders, congressional staff, and congressmen and senators. Along with Coalition colleagues, I've met with White House staff, federal agencies, and other non-profit citizen groups. I have also attended many meetings of the Park Service, the Commission of Fine Arts, and the National Capital Planning Commission (all of these were open to the public).

A significant debt of gratitude goes to the members of the National Mall Coalition. Judy Scott Feldman and Neil Feldman, Jay Brodie, W. Kent Cooper, Charles Cassell, Ellen Goldstein, George Idelson, George Oberlander, Gordon Binder, Tom Jensen, Joe West, and Kay Murphy are tremendous individuals who have devoted a decade of their lives to providing an alternative voice on National Mall matters. They have been tireless in their work and I am humbled by their energy, resolve, and tenacity.

In the spring of 2010 several Washington area scholars and architects formed the Steering Committee for the National Ideas Competition for the Washington Monument grounds. Besides me, the committee consisted of: James Clark, Steering Committee director, a principal at MTFA Architecture and then president of the Virginia Society of the American Institute of Architects (AIA); Adele Ashkar, vice-chair of the Steering Committee, an associate professor of the Landscape Design Program at George Washington University; Kenneth Bowling, a nationally recognized scholar on the presidency of George Washington and an adjunct associate professor of history at George Washington University; W. Kent Cooper, a retired architect whose projects included the Korean War Veterans Memorial and the Vietnam Veterans Memorial; Judy Scott Feldman, an art historian and chair of the National Coalition to Save Our Mall; Ellen Goldstein, who has had a long career in public policy, public affairs, and government relations; and

Richard Longstreth, professor of American Studies at George Washington University. This group of scholars and professional architects and landscape designers came together because we believed that the Park Service had consistently demonstrated a lack of creativity in providing for public involvement in planning and that a public competition could launch a conversation that would engage the public in reimagining the Mall's future. The committee aimed to encourage Americans of all ages to develop innovative and creative ideas for making the Washington Monument grounds more "welcoming, educational and effectively used by the public." I owe a debt of gratitude to all the individuals on the Steering Committee, who, with their wealth of experience and knowledge about the Mall, the workings of the federal government, and planning in the nation's capital, showed the potential of thinking outside of the box.

This book is thus informed by rigorous scholarly research as well as my personal experiences over the last ten years. My service on the board of the Coalition and on the WAMO Steering Committee (WAMO being the Park Service abbreviation for the Washington Monument) exposed me to numerous perspectives on and experiences in Mall planning, design, and politics. Certainly, some may hold that it is inappropriate for academics to engage actively in advocacy work and to integrate it into their scholarship. In my case, the scholarly interest preceded my involvement in either non-profit organization, but this book was greatly enriched because of my participation in the Coalition and in the WAMO Competition. While I incorporating this experience in the pages that follow, I have tried wherever possible to support my ideas, arguments, and interpretations with direct quotes from Coalition or WAMO position papers, newsletters, annual reports, list-serve e-mails, and website resources, nearly all of which are publically available. I did this because I wanted to balance my recollections and notes with documents that others could access. Ultimately, my opinions are my own; sometimes, but not always, they are shared by many members of the Coalition or the Steering Committee. I owe a great debt to members of the Coalition board as well as the WAMO Steering Committee. Their substantial professional expertise in planning, history, architecture, and real estate development was an invaluable contribution to this book.

CHAPTER 1

From Grand Avenue to Public Space: A Brief History of the Mall

In January 2009, when nearly two million Americans filled the expanse between the Capitol and the Lincoln Memorial, the inauguration of President Barack Obama reaffirmed the National Mall as the symbolic centre of American public life and a stage for the expression of national identity. How did the Mall become such a vital public space? To answer this important question, we must first examine the historical intentions that set the foundation for the Mall to become the symbolic space it is. While we might be tempted to see the Mall as an immutable embodiment of the America's highest democratic ideals, its meaning and purpose today has emerged because of many layers of intentions and implementations of plans, designs, and uses. The capital city and the city's grand public space, the Mall, reflect a discursive struggle to create a space representative of American ideals and aspirations. L'Enfant's Plan intended the Mall to be a Grand Avenue and public walk, one rich in the physical and symbolic expression of democratic ideals and a reflection of the formulation of American national identity. Later plans developed in the nineteenth and twentieth centuries refined and expanded the Mall's function as well as its symbolism, allowing it to evolve into the most important public space in the United States.

L'Enfant's Plan for the Federal City and the National Mall

The shaping of the National Mall begins in 1791 with a man, a map, some notes, and a grand vision. This grand vision was of a spacious urban stage upon which the promise of the new democracy could be born.[1] It began on a rainy Tuesday, 29 March, 1791, when thirty-six-year-old Major Pierre L'Enfant stopped on a ridge with a view south to the Potomac River. On this ridge would rise a house for the president. The mounted party rode another mile to Jenkins Hill. "This place," said L'Enfant, is a "pedestal waiting for a monument."[2] It would become the U.S. Capitol, a visual anchor and hub for the city. The space in between these two points would become the Grand Avenue, or National Mall. The day marked the start of a visionary plan that would be revised several times by L'Enfant, under President George Washington's watchful eye. They had embarked on a monumental task: the capital of a new country was to be set down in a quiet, sparsely inhabited territory of hills, forests, and farms.[3] There was no design competition, and no budget. Before there was a National Mall or even a federal city, the area around the Potomac was forests, plantations, and farmlands. The origins of the Mall and the city are the same: both were planned and designed long before the city was home to enough people and buildings to make it worthy of the name National Capital.[4]

Pierre "Peter" Charles L'Enfant was born in France and trained as an artist and painter under his father at the Royal Academy of Painting and Sculpture in Paris from 1771 to 1776.[5] In 1777, at the age of twenty-three, L'Enfant came to America to volunteer in the Continental Army. He was wounded at Savannah, fought on crutches at Charleston, and was at Valley Forge with Washington.[6] He rose to the rank of major by the end of the Revolutionary War, despite his lack of military schooling. Washington knew of L'Enfant's artistic skills from the sketches and portraits of officers he had done while at Valley Forge.[7] After the war, L'Enfant established himself as an architect and worked in New York and Philadelphia. He designed the Federal Hall in New York, where the early government operated, and his architecture and aesthetics gained recognition among those in the government. Washington appointed L'Enfant as the designer of the nation's capital and sent him to the Potomac to study the topography and design the city.

L'Enfant arrived at Georgetown in March 1791 intent on designing a capital that would befit a great new country. It was a unique opportunity in that it was the first national capital ever established by law and comprehensively designed. In a letter to Thomas Jefferson, with whom he would regularly correspond, L'Enfant noted that "to change a wilderness into a city, to erect and beautify buildings ... to that degree of perfection necessary to receive the seat of Government of a vast empire the short period that remains to effect these objects is an undertaking vast as it is novel."[8]

The concept of a planned city was not new. European and American examples were well known to Washington, Jefferson, and many other of L'Enfant's contemporaries. L'Enfant himself knew of the plans for Annapolis, Savannah, Williamsburg, Philadelphia, and New York.[9] He was also well versed in European city planning. In another letter to Thomas Jefferson, L'Enfant requested plans of several European cities, not to use as templates, but as inspiration. Jefferson provided L'Enfant with plans of Lyons, Bordeaux, Orleans, Milan, Turin, and Frankfurt. Before he began the project, L'Enfant had perceived that "the plan should be drawn on such as scale as to leave room for that aggrandizement & embellishment which the increase of the wealth of the Nation will permit it to pursue at any period however remote."[10] On this he and Washington were in agreement: a grand setting would help elevate the aspirations of a new nation's citizens.

The neo-classical spatial-order tradition from which the capital city was created was partly inspired by monumental-planning trends in France. Within this milieu the creative spirit in planning was expressed through an atmosphere where Baroque gardens and hunting forests were a quintessential archetype for an informed city planner.[11] Also common in France was the use of radial patterns imposed upon orthogonal streets, which offered an urban typology for expedient circulation, enchanting entry vistas and open spaces for defining neighbourhoods.[12] Within these monumental plans were symbolic spaces (from which emanated the radial streets). Designing celebratory public spaces in squares and semi-circles gave the city an air of grandeur, delight, and edification.[13] L'Enfant was familiar with these planning elements and he incorporated many of them into his design. Yet, while there were European influences, his plan is generally considered notably American. It displayed "all the sophistication of the European baroque in combination with a good dose of George Washington's republican sensibilities."[14]

In 1791 L'Enfant drafted a majestic and comprehensive plan for the new city of Washington, D.C. It only took him fourteen days from the time of his arrival at Georgetown to complete the draft of his idea for the federal city.[15] The plan consisted of both a large map and a series of descriptions (Figure 1.1). L'Enfant's broad vision of a capital of magnificent buildings, public squares, and promenades reflected the new country's optimistic outlook.[16] It was a design intent on celebrating a ceremonial city, the centre of national government and culture. The plan was on an immense scale, far beyond the size or even expectation of

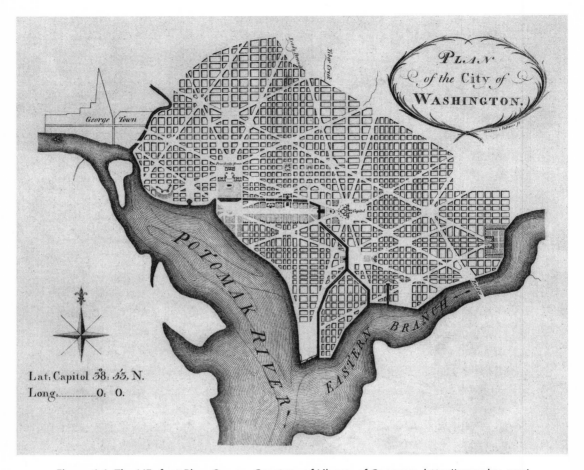

Figure 1.1. The L'Enfant Plan. *Source*: Courtesy of Library of Congress. http://www.loc.gov/item/88694120/.

the government at the time.[17] While Jefferson rejected the idea of a lavish capital in principle (that was what monarchies did), L'Enfant argued that, if this new capital was to succeed, it needed to give concrete evidence of the great empire the country would become, not the fledgling nation as it was.[18] Two of the more unique characteristics of L'Enfant's Plan were its grand scale and the fact that it was laid out so as to utilize to the fullest extent the natural topography. The plan encompassed five thousand acres, comparable at that time to the footprints of Paris and London and as large as New York City, Boston, and Philadelphia *combined*.[19] Historian Sara Luria has commented that the "boldness of the original plan for the Federal City is particularly striking if we consider how paltry a thing the nation was in 1791. It was financially crippled by the Revolutionary War, run by a disputatious Congress that was deeply ambivalent about centralized power, and peopled by a citizenry spread across a vast area who travelled little and so had no reason or chance to develop a national consciousness."[20] Such a grand plan appealed to Washington because he saw it as a concrete model of what was then an ambiguous political experiment called the "republic"; in contrast, when Jefferson saw the plan, he was displeased that it "glowed with an iconography of federal supremacy."[21] Yet Washington perceived in architecture and monuments a way to foster a national identity and character and was eager to ground the constitution quickly in political habit.[22]

L'Enfant's Plan was a combination of both nation-centred federalism and state-centred republicanism.[23] The city was shaped as a diamond, tilted on its point. It was based on a template of a grid system of streets on a square-block pattern, within which broad diagonal avenues would link the main hills. The diagonal avenues were named after the states. Each street suggested a ray of light emanating from the Capitol and radiating outward towards every part of the country; at one point it was proposed that the prime meridian of longitude be established through the Capitol to replace that of Greenwich, thus sanctifying the city as the centre of a new order.[24] The intentional relationship between the plan and the constitution is apparent – the street plan embodied the early organization of the federal government and translates the constitution into physical space.[25] For example, the avenues created the paths legislated by the constitution between the different branches of government. By reinforcing the balance of power in this way, the city would physically help fulfil the constitution, serving as home to the national government and the stage where the abstract concept of the nation could be experienced as a physical reality. The extent to which Washington, Jefferson, and other "framers" believed that the physical landscape could alter political behaviour might seem improbable to us today, but it was an outcome of the legacy of the Enlightenment.[26]

The north/south/east/west street pattern was used as a framework for the more dramatic elements of his plan: the diagonal avenues and spaces superimposed on that framework.[27] This lattice established a network of public spaces of great variety linked together by broad, diagonal avenues.[28] The resulting circles and squares provided public "reservations" or public space throughout the city.[29]

Some of the spaces were seen as sites for civic institutions such as academies, courthouses, markets, or a city hall; others were designated as the social centres of neighbourhoods; and still others were given no specified function but were to evolve according to the future needs of the city.[30] Some of the squares and circles were to be filled with public monuments of national self-representation. The vast expanse of boulevards did not set up a closed vista terminating in a large building, nor an open vista leading to infinity; rather, the radial boulevards would lead from one vertical landmark to another.[31] The vast integrated system of public open spaces expressed the democratic ideals of the new nation. L'Enfant wrote of his designation of squares as public open spaces:

> The squares colored yellow, being fifteen in number, are proposed to be divided among the several states in the union, for each of them to improve, or subscribe a sum additional to the value of the land ...
>
> The center of each square will admit of statues, columns, obelisks, or any other ornaments such as the different states may choose to erect; to perpetuate not only the memory of such individuals whose counsels, or military achievements, were conspicuous in giving liberty and independence to the country; but also those whose usefulness hath rendered them worthy of general imitation; to invite the youth of succeeding generations to tread in the paths of those sages or heroes, who this country has thought proper to celebrate ...
>
> This mode of taking possession of, and improving the whole district at first, must leave to posterity a grand idea of patriotic interest which promoted it.[32]

An important design element was the axial alignment of the city, eloquent in its balance and symmetry. L'Enfant envisioned a primary east-west axis stretching from the Capitol to the banks of the Potomac. The secondary north-south axis would be perpendicular, crossing from the President's Palace (later called White House) to the river to the south. Where the two axes crossed, the convergence point, L'Enfant intended to place the statue of President Washington on horseback.[33] The westward view from the front of the Capitol was also a statement about American destiny. Central to the plan were two hills. One was Jenkins Hill, which would be the site of Congress House as L'Enfant called it (since no one had yet settled on a name for the building that would house the Senate and the House of Representatives).[34] "The home of Congress was to be a kind of national temple to the secular religion of democracy, a physical counterpart to the Constitution, a civics lesson in stone as it were."[35] On the other hill to the west would be the President's Palace. L'Enfant intended the two critical government buildings to be the geographic anchors of the city; they would be separated by space, a metaphor for the need to separate the branches of government. L'Enfant explained that presidential messages should be delivered to Congress with decorum, thus requiring time and therefore distance.[36] Equally important, L'Enfant's innovation was the way in which the sightlines do not converge on one single point, thus eschewing a centralized point of power common in many European Baroque plans. The many avenues, squares, and various focal points assert the physical possibility of *E pluribus Unum*.[37]

L'Enfant's design is both an art form and a response to social, economic, and political conditions. The plan reinforces the newly founded nation's iconography of democratic ideals. It is also a diagram of political equilibrium. L'Enfant expressed in physical form key political ideologies in the new republic: the separation of powers, the balance between the federal and state governments, and the optimism of a new and expansive nation. Architectural historian Pamela Scott has noted that the separation of the branches was explicit and intentional. Noticeably absent from this plan is the third branch of government, the Supreme Court, although L'Enfant did designate a judiciary court north of Pennsylvania Avenue near the Capitol. The lack of a prominent position for the Court reflects the uncertain form and function of the "third branch" of government at the time. It was not seen as equal in political status to the other two branches of government. The Supreme Court was organized during the First Congress (not in the Constitutional Convention), and it had very different powers and procedures from what would evolve. In the first decades, the justices did not "sit" in the capital but rode about the country, assigned to preside over one of three circuits (eastern, middle, and southern).[38] There would have been no reason for L'Enfant to have included a Supreme Court building in his plan, since there was no need for it at the time; no one could envision how important and powerful the Court would become two centuries later. In 1791, for example, the justices sat for only two days in Philadelphia over the entire year. Gradually, the court's powers, initially enumerated only vaguely, were established by actual practice.[39] The Supreme Court did not move to the capital permanently until after 1800 and even then did not reside in its own building until 1935.[40]

The placement of streets and avenues honoured the historical forces that created the republic and acknowledged the importance of states within the union.[41]

L'Enfant's Plan is not only geographically sensitive, moulding the design to the existing topography, it is also geographically symbolic by including physical representation of the thirteen states that then comprised the union. The north-eastern states were located in the northern segment of the quadrangle, the southern states in the southern quadrangle, and the mid-Atlantic states in the centre, reflecting not only the country's geography but its regional, political, and social alignments. Pennsylvania Avenue is given pre-eminence, passing through the Capitol and the President's Palace, both to honour Philadelphia's role as the site of the signing of the Declaration of Independence and of the Constitutional Convention of 1787 and to placate the state that had clamoured to be the centre of government.[42] Delaware Avenue crosses the Capitol, acknowledging it as the first state to ratify the constitution. New York Avenue is also given prominence, passing through President's Square, in part for its large financial role during the Revolutionary War and because Washington took the presidential oath in New York City in 1789.

The delicate balance of power between the federal and state governments is also reflected in the overall grid system. L'Enfant's Plan honoured the states both in the naming of the grand diagonal avenues and in the design of circles and squares where states would commemorate residents who had become national heroes. "Each street is an emblem of the rays of light which, issuing from the Capitol, are directed toward every part of America, to enlighten its inhabitants respecting their true interests."[43] These squares would provide a diversity of civic places – for churches, fountains, memorial columns, residences, and embassies.

Finally, the plan takes advantage of the city's topographic setting and its river location through grand vistas that help create a monumental federal precinct. The broad diagonal street connecting the two was designated Pennsylvania Avenue. The two elevations were to be linked also by two large parks. One would stretch south from the President's Palace, and from the Congress House westward would be another termed the Grand Avenue, which we know today as the National Mall.[44]

The National Mall

In his notes, L'Enfant described the Mall as a "Grand Avenue, 400 feet in breadth and about a mile in length, bordered with gardens, and ending in a slope from the houses [of diplomats] on each side. This Avenue leads to Monument A [an equestrian figure of George Washington], and connects the Congress garden with the President's park."

L'Enfant's Grand Avenue or "public walk" was referred to as a "vast esplanade in the center of which, and at the point of intersection of the sight from each of the Houses, would be the most advantageous place for an equestrian statue, which with proper appendages and walks artfully managed, would produce a most grand effect." The Grand Avenue would be composed of a tree-lined walkway perhaps planted in the natural, picturesque style of landscape gardening then gaining popularity in France and Britain or in the more formal landscaping that was common in European cities.[45] L'Enfant noted that the stretch of land would become the "sort of places as may be attractive to the learned and afford diversion to the idle." His proposal that the major axis of the new city should be two great parks meeting at a central point (the statue to George Washington) was unusual in that most cities were built around commercial streets. Historian Kirk Savage has remarked that "nowhere were L'Enfant's elegantly interlocking metaphors more evident that at Point A, reserved for the most important monument of all – an equestrian statue of George Washington."[46] Several years later, Jefferson would set the meridian line through point A, which today is marked by the Jefferson Pier (a monument poorly sign-posted and hence overlooked by most tourists). Figure 1.2 shows the Mall up close.

While some believe that Versailles was a prototype for L'Enfant's Grand Avenue, there is a major difference between the two: Versailles was a greensward that could be visited only with the king's permission, while L'Enfant's Grand Avenue was designed to express the democratic accessibility of American government and act as an open invitation to all.[47] It was, at the time, a peculiarly American idea to conflate political freedom with open space. As a "people's park," the Mall would be lively and ensure that the city would fill with people, not just buildings. These public grounds, said L'Enfant, would "give to the city from the very beginning a superior charm over most of those in the world." The President's Park, Capitol Square, and the Mall were explicitly intended as national civic spaces, places where the democratic political ideals of the new nation were to be realized.[48]

L'Enfant's Plan for the Mall also featured a canal forming the northern boundary of his Grand Avenue, then known as Tiber Creek or Goose Creek (present-day Constitution Avenue). The Tiber, a shallow, languid tributary, was an important

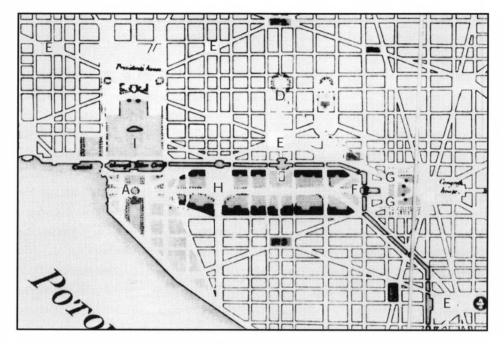

Figure 1.2. L'Enfant's plan for the Mall; point "A" is where L'Enfant placed the statue to George Washington. Courtesy of Library of Congress.

feature that bisected the key axis of the plan. To the north of the Tiber would sit the President's Palace. The land to the south would frame the massive public open space. At the eastern end, near the place reserved for the Capitol, L'Enfant envisioned the waters of the Tiber cascading into the Washington Canal, which paralleled the Grand Avenue bordered by gardens and diplomatic residences.[49]

L'Enfant had been explicit in locating the Mall as the primary axis of the city, a vast open space that comprised roughly 175 acres.[50] This feature made the plan unique from other European or American cities. That the Mall dominated the capital's central composition also reflects L'Enfant's vision that a democracy should have public grounds. The placement of the Mall as the centerpiece of the design represents the fact that open space conferred visible power and strength and symbolized an open, not closed, society. These were important values in the fledgling republic, which sought to distinguish itself from the British monarchy. It was intended that the presidency be viewed physically and symbolically as "open" and accountable to the public. The Mall was central also as a large open space that reflected the vast openness of the continent. Even as early as the 1790s, it was generally accepted that the nation would expand westward, adding new territories and then states to the union. The orientation of the Mall as open to the west symbolized the future growth of the country.[51]

Although L'Enfant describes the Mall's function and form in only a few sentences, we can infer three important roles that he intended for it : first is the role of open space and vista; second is the role of the public forum and public promenade; and third is the role of ceremonial space, exemplified by L'Enfant's placement of the Washington Monument at the cross-axis. Although the Mall would evolve and mature over time, particularly as twentieth-century ideas about public space developed, these three roles are present to some degree in L'Enfant's original vision. The use and meaning of the Mall, first articulated by L'Enfant, laid the foundations for the concept of public space, which would be significantly advanced some one hundred years later by the McMillan Plan of 1901.

From Grand Avenue to Premier Public Space

In 1900, as the capital's centennial approached, political and intellectual leaders called for an initiative to capture the dignity and prominence originally intended for the city and the Mall. It had not become the Grand Avenue and public walk envisioned by L'Enfant. Parts of the Mall had deteriorated into scraggly, overgrown fragments of parks and areas overlain with train track and cattle pens. There were even brothels nearby. The Mall was a mess. There was growing interest in revitalizing and redefining the public spaces of the L'Enfant Plan and completing a patriotic program of national sites and monuments.[52] And there was a consensus that the capital city needed a comprehensive plan for the development of the District, and particularly for the location of public buildings since there were increasing demands that accompanied an expanding federal workforce. A report to the Senate acknowledged that "now that the demand for new public buildings and memorials and reached an acute stage, there has been hesitation and embarrassment in locating them because of the uncertainty in securing appropriate sites."[53]

The foundation for a comprehensive plan was already there in L'Enfant's design. Many civic groups, leaders in architecture and planning, and members of Congress agreed that this was an opportunity not only to re-emphasize the architectural values of the city but also to return to some of the basic long-range ideas of L'Enfant.[54] The new plan, known as the 1901 McMillan Plan, would be the most significant event in the capital's and the Mall's development since the original design of L'Enfant in 1791. It would reimagine the form and function of the Mall and redefine it as a national public space.

The McMillan Park Commission

In December 1900 the American Institute of Architects held its annual convention in Washington. Distinguished architects and planners presented a series of papers on civic improvement. Keynote speaker Fredrick (Rick) Law Olmsted, Jr noted that the Mall was a "great opportunity thrown away through disregard of the large meaning of the original plan [L'Enfant's Plan]."[55] Glenn Brown, secretary of the AIA in Washington, was an advocate of quality architecture and lobbied for a greater role for private architects in federal projects.[56] He along with several architects and planners then formed a committee to impress on Congress the need for a professional commission to study the improvement of the city. They also consulted with the Senate Committee on the District of Columbia. Michigan Senator James McMillan, chairman of the Committee, was interested in the opportunity to study the "Monumental Core" (the National Mall and surrounding federal buildings) and all of the surrounding parks within a larger master plan. In March 1901 he commissioned architects Daniel Burnham and Charles McKim, the landscape architect Fredrick Law Olmsted, Jr, and the sculptor Augustus Saint-Gaudens to submit to the Senate a comprehensive plan for developing the entire Washington park system, which included the Mall. Daniel Burnham of Chicago was well known for his work as director of the World's Columbian Exposition held in Chicago in 1893. Olmsted, Jr, whose famous father had designed Central Park in New York, was considered one of the most outstanding young men in the profession of modern landscape architecture. McKim was recognized as the dean of American architects and Saint-Gaudens was in the first rank of American sculptors.[57] Burnham would serve as chairman and Charles Moore, clerk of the Senate Committee on the District of Columbia, acted as secretary. Each of the men served without pay, for they considered this a matter of national importance. John Rep's book *Monumental Washington* thoroughly documents the planning process and its results.[58]

These experts would comprise a commission called the Senate Park Commission, in later years known as the McMillan Commission. The Commission was given the authority to create a new master plan for the city and the Mall. The Commission intended to build on L'Enfant's Plan and the Baroque tradition from which it had emanated, while updating these historical precedents in response to the contemporary needs of the federal government and the federal city.[59] Burnham believed that L'Enfant's Mall existed only on paper; in reality, the vision had been eroded over the course of the nineteenth century. Burnham had long lived by his motto "Make no little plans, for they have no magic to stir men's blood. Make big plans." Consistent with this thinking, the plan would evolve into a far broader and more elaborate design for beautifying the capital than anyone had initially conceived.

The McMillan Commission began its work by making a visual survey of the District and examining the topographical features in and outside of the city. Its members ventured up the Potomac River as far as the Great Falls, studying the character and quality of the water supply as well as the scenery along the river.[60] They visited the hills surrounding the District, Arlington, and Alexandria and even several of the old estates in Virginia that had influenced Washington and Jefferson in their planning ideas for the federal city back in 1791 in order to "familiarize ourselves with the very source of the original inspiration."[61] They noted that "the very fact that Washington and Jefferson, L'Enfant and Ellicott, and their immediate successors, drew inspiration form the world's greatest works of landscape architecture and of civic adornment made it imperative to go back to the sources of their knowledge and taste in order to restore unity and harmony to their creations and to guide future development along appropriate lines."[62]

The commissioners then toured Europe to visit the cities, civic spaces, and gardens that would have been well known to L'Enfant – London, Paris, Vienna, Budapest, Venice, Versailles, and Rome – taking notes on the features they considered to be outstanding examples in architecture, landscaping, and public grounds. In Rome, where the hot climate reminded them of Washington, they decided that water fountains should be included in their plan for the Mall.[63] The pilgrimage to Europe reflected the reverence for the Old World classicism and monumental planning, which had also influenced L'Enfant. The more they studied and discussed, the more they became convinced that "the greatest service they could perform would be done by carrying to a legitimate conclusion the comprehensive, intelligent, and yet simple and straightforward scheme devised by L'Enfant."[64] When they returned, they spent the remainder of the year completing the report, which included an exhibition of maps, models, drawings, and paintings, and presented it to the Senate Committee in 1901 and then the full Senate in January 1902.[65]

The McMillan Plan

Underlying the plan was a consensus that the capital city should inspire awe at the history and promise of the nation; the city should be a work of civic art. As with other City Beautiful plans, the McMillan Plan referenced nineteenth-century Europe but also positioned the twentieth-century United States as a peer of Europe's old imperial powers.[66] Despite the notable European connections and models, the McMillan Commission created a distinctive American paradigm in its plan for Washington, D.C. It was notable in that it integrated monumental civic spaces into the overall fabric of the city, while also incorporating formal and informal natural landscapes.[67] The plan embodied a new mature American identity – celebrating the capital as a monument to freedom and liberty, a symbol of a nation that would continue to flourish and inspire as the American people made their mark on the world.

The plan covered the design and layout of several aspects of the District. One of its major parts focused on the city's system of parks, open space, and recreational areas. The proposed park system included neighbourhood recreation centres for various sports, with playgrounds for small children; a circumferential parkway joining the remains of the old Civil War forts; and the extension of the small city parks planned by L'Enfant. It suggested that the Civil War forts, which ringed the city, be developed as parks and unified in a system with the additions of pathways and the acquisition of small parcels of land. The Mall would be connected to a city-wide system of parks, parkways, and shores throughout the District and into Maryland and Virginia. This suggestion is noteworthy in that it is the first attempt at creating a regional park system in an American city. Historian Kirk Savage has noted that the fact the plan articulated a "system" of parks was indicative of a modern transformation in how to view parks and indeed space. To view parks as "system" came from a belief that they should be integrated and thus ordered. Space now had an integrative power to knit together disparate parts into a unified and compelling whole.[68]

Revisioning the Mall as Public Space

The McMillan Plan called for the Mall to become a "undulating green mile and half long and three hundred feet wide" with elm trees planted four abreast on either side. Bordering this *"tapis-vert,"* park-like roads would provide a walk or drive protected from the sun by the trees, thus framing the axis visually through vegetation. The "Mall would afford variety and refreshment to those going and coming and the other sections of the city."[69] Gone would be the dense and tangled Victorian plantings that had characterized the nineteenth-century Mall; the large broad lawn would restore the Mall to L'Enfant's intentions.

The concept of a *tapis vert* is French, meaning an unbroken expanse of green space that is the centrepiece of a landscape design. Undoubtedly, the McMillan Commission was inspired by Versailles, for example, but it was also incorporating many of the English estate garden designs as well. Critics have argued that the planners were too caught up in a romantic ideal of nature that was largely devoid of life. Elbert Peets decried the grassy centre of the Mall and charged that the McMillan plan created a Mall that was not for walking on.[70] In fact, the scheme deviated from L'Enfant's vision of a Grande Avenue significantly because the "Grand Avenue" ceased to be an avenue at all and became instead a greensward. Sara Luria has noted that the McMillan Plan moved away from L'Enfant's original vision of an avenue by proposing a broad green lawn modelled after the *tapis verts* of Europe.[71] Instead of redefining the Mall as an all-purpose street with all kinds of traffic (pedestrian, commercial, and residential), the Mall became a place to circulate tourists. Critics of the plan argued that the greensward actually "sealed off" rather than connected the monument space from the rest of the city.[72] As a result, the Mall became something difficult to define: it was not quite an avenue and not exactly an urban park such as Central Park. It became a new space: something between a park and a boulevard. But the Mall would lack amenities such as stores and cafés that create an everyday flow of civic space, perpetuating its disconnect from the city and its residents.

Kirk Savage has also noted that the planners replaced the *public grounds* of the nineteenth century with the new term *public space*, thus creating a "new spatial order that unified the geographic center of the capital and promised to overcome the fragmentation of both landscape and nation."[73] Savage sees the creation of public space as a step in the modern spatial turn that profoundly changed cities in the twentieth century.

The most important aspect of the plan was the extension of the Mall westward nearly one mile on the new landfill dredged from the Potomac River. The dredging of the Potomac River and the creation of the East and West Potomac Parks were initially an engineering solution to a flooding problem that had nothing to do with expanding the Monumental Core. Yet the new "real estate" opened the door to the possibility of a number of significant changes to the original city plan. The McMillan Commission capitalized on this opportunity by expanding on the L'Enfant legacy and altering the character of the city to reflect early-twentieth-century visions of the country and the city. These changes were not a minor tweak; they meant a major shift of the city westward,[74] as well as creating new spaces for symbolic structures.

The McMillan Plan geographically extended L'Enfant's north/south and east/west axis of the Mall by integrating the land dredged from the Potomac River. The new land added to the west of the Washington Monument became the present-day Lincoln Memorial grounds, and new land to the south formed the Tidal Basin and would later become the site of the Jefferson Memorial. The plan thus built upon L'Enfant by re-establishing the axial relations between the Capitol, the Washington Monument, and the White House. The commission spent considerable attention on the Mall's cross-axis – the imaginary line that connects the Capitol, the Washington Monument, and the White House with the Jefferson Memorial. The secondary axis (north/south) had largely been ignored and the Commission proposed that a pantheon honouring American heroes be located on the Tidal Basin south of the White House.[75] The vision was to complete the four cardinal points of the two axes and to place a monumental classical structure at the end of each of the four points (today the Capitol, the Lincoln Memorial, the Jefferson Memorial, and the White House) (see Figure 1.3).

Many believe that what gives the Mall its power today is that the axis is anchored by three elements – the Capitol, the Lincoln Memorial, and the Washington Monument. To the east is the Capitol, a "monument to democracy," and the Washington Monument, a "monument to freedom and independence"; and to the west is the Lincoln Memorial, a "monument to unity and equality." The east-west axis of the Mall represents a sort of national backbone formed by the themes of the country's founding and codified in the twentieth century by the implementation of the McMillan Plan.[76] These are seen as timeless, embodying democratic ideals associated with the founding, preservation, and governance of the republic.[77] It may sound abstract but

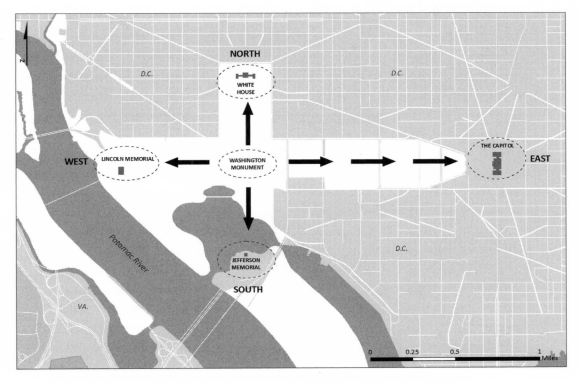

Figure 1.3. The north-south, east-west axis of the Mall. Map by author.

many visitors pick up on it, turning back and forth to admire the visual connection among these key elements.

Public Space Uses

With these twentieth-century additions in the McMillan Plan, the Mall's axes have come to represent fundamental principles of democracy in both form (monuments and memorials) and function (public space). Consider: the National Capital Planning Commission (in charge of planning and design in the District) asserted that the city's broad avenues and expansive public spaces "are reminders of America's democratic values, and the Monumental Core is the symbolic heart of the nation and the physical expression of our Constitution with its three separate branches of government."[78]

By the second half of the twentieth century, the Mall had evolved into what we know it as today: a public space for purposes both grand and solemn, popular and political.[79] The Mall has become an expression of democracy, freedom, and the ideology of equal access. As architectural historian Pamela Scott has noted, the Mall is a landscape that contains a story, and visitors "read" the Mall as a physical expression of national identity.[80] Not everyone who comes to the Mall is seeking a deeper engagement with history and meaning, however. Some come to relax, to play, to picnic. As public space, the Mall has evolved to have both formal and informal uses. The last half of the twentieth century saw the Mall mature into a premier public space with three critical functions: recreation, protest space, and national commemorative space.

Commemorative Space

The McMillan Commission rededicated the Mall to L'Enfant's original ideals of openness and patriotic pageantry, and by physically altering the Mall to create the present-day East and West Potomac Parks and the Tidal Basin, it also helped to redefine it symbolically by adding the Lincoln Memorial. It thus codified the Mall's role as a place for national commemoration. While L'Enfant designated the role of the Mall as a Monumental Core with the placement of the statue to Washington, the memoralization of the Mall coalesced in the twentieth century. During that century, Americans' sense of their own history changed; they began considering the legacy of slavery and racism, the fate of the American Indian, the role of women and others who help to construct the country but who had been largely absent in the story of American identity. By the 1980s, many groups were making compelling demands for memorials or museums to many of these diverse stories and important events. The Vietnam Veterans Memorial, completed in 1982, reinvigorated the role of commemoration on the Mall and ushered in a new era of civic pilgrimage. Daily offerings – drawings, letters, military uniforms, flowers – assert the "right to leave tokens" as part of the process of commemoration (see Figure 1.4). Since the Vietnam Memorial, six other memorials have been built on the Mall, and a host of new ones have been proposed. As chapters 4 and 5 will argue, the tension between commemoration and the other functions of the Mall continues to be a significant challenge in the twenty-first century.

Figure 1.4. Leaving tokens at the Vietnam Wall has become part of the process of commemoration and a visible sign of the power of memorials to speak to society. Photo by author.

Protest Space

In addition to the Mall's role in national commemoration, events throughout the twentieth century codified its role as one of the most important national public spaces for public protests and demonstrations. Thus, the Mall as a public space has fostered social resistance and challenges to democratic values. Along with commemoration, the Mall has served as an active agent in national discourse and the reformulation of national identity. It has been the stage for critical debates that underlie the health of a civil society. Protests on the Mall tend to capture the public's attention.

The Mall, particularly the area in around the Washington Monument and the Lincoln Memorial, has become an important public space for people to congregate and express ideas. Historian Lucy Barber has documented the emergence of the Mall as a focal point for public protest. She notes that "marching on Washington" has contributed to the development of a broader and more inclusive view of American citizenship and has transformed the capital (and the Mall) from the exclusive domain of politicians into a national stage for Americans to participate directly.[81] An 1894 protest led by unemployed civil worker Jacob Coxey, whose band of supporters "marched on Washington," marked the first time ordinary citizens came to petition their elected leaders directly. In 1913 women suffragettes descended upon Washington to demand the vote, and showed that demonstrations in the city could be both dramatic and respectable. Nineteen years later, in 1932, "Bonus March" veterans called on Congress to honour its promise of payment for service during World War I. Civil rights leaders saw the Mall's open space and monuments as the ideal setting to air their grievances. Critical public protests such as these have made a powerful claim to the public spaces of this capital and have linked democratic ideals with public space. Although the iconic image of Martin Luther King, Jr delivering his "I Have a Dream" speech from the Lincoln Memorial steps remains powerfully associated with the Mall's tradition of public protest, there have been more recent protests and marches as well, such as the March for Gay Rights (1993), the Million Man March (1995), the Million Mom March (2000), and annual marches such as the March for Life and annual celebrations such as Earth Day – all of which reaffirm the importance of the Mall as a place to express visions of national politics and identity.[82] If the Mall has become democracy's stage, citizens are the players.

This is not to argue that any or all protests are equally important for extending democratic values. The civil rights marches of the 1960s, the anti-Vietnam War demonstrations, women's rights marches, and perhaps, most recently, immigration protests have been highly influential in articulating or at the least reflecting a social-political movement of considerable strength. Other protests or marches do not necessarily rewrite civil society – for example, the Million Mom March or the annual Rolling Thunder motorcycle parade. Nevertheless, the Mall and Washington, D.C., is a public space of articulation, a "national protest landscape" where national identity is celebrated and political/social change is both demanded and, sometimes, achieved.[83]

Open Space and Recreation

With the completion of many of the landscape projects envisioned by the McMillan Plan, along with increasing attention to the value of recreation and play in American society in the first part of the twentieth century, the Mall became an public place of recreation. Some elements of recreation and park use in the Mall echo general trends found in many U.S. parks. Urban Park historian Galen Cranz has noted that there have been several "park movements" that have influenced both use and design at specific times in the twentieth century. Parks have constantly shifted both use and design characteristics: activities once popular in the parks during the 1920s, such as fishing from rowboats and vegetable gardening, disappeared by the 1940s.[84] The Mall has also seen activities come and go. Until the 1970s, the Lincoln Reflecting Pool was used by ice skaters during the winter and by children floating toy boats during the summer, but these practices ended as concerns about the pool's safety and water quality trumped play.

Starting in the 1930s and continuing through the 1960s, park planning became more practical and pragmatic in ideology, with a focus on promoting parks as recreation facilities. Many recreation facilities were built using federal monies during the Depression as Works Progress Administration (WPA) programs. Today, recreational facilities and open space on the Mall have become a central part of the Mall's function. Recreation occurs on the water (paddleboats at the Jefferson Memorial, for example), on formally organized recreational fields, and in informal recreation and open-space areas. Trails accommodate running, walking, and bicycling. Formal recreational fields are available for baseball, soccer, sand volleyball, rugby, and even polo. Some of the most visible recreational activities on the Mall, however, take place not on designated facilities but informally on the vast open spaces. There are numerous recreation leagues for softball, rugby, kickball, lacrosse, Frisbee, and even Australian Rules Football (which requires one of the largest fields of any sport). For example, kickball and softball games are often played in the grassy open space around the Washington Monument. Ice skating is available during the winter months at the open-air skating rink at the National Gallery of Art. East Potomac Park has a vast recreational complex including a Tennis Center with some twenty-four courts and golf facilities consisting of three golf courses, a miniature golf course, a driving range, and a pro shop. Recreation on the water includes kayaks and canoes and rowing, along with fishing at both the East and West Potomac Parks and the Tidal Basin. In addition to formal recreation, the Mall has many places for relaxation reading and picnicking – these include some of the gardens around the Smithsonian museums, the benches that line Mall walkways, and the picnic grounds at East Potomac Park.

Because of the Mall's expansive open areas, it hosts numerous public events, including July 4th fireworks, the Smithsonian's Annual Folklife Festival, candlelight vigils, Memorial Day concerts, and the annual Smithsonian Kite-Flying festival. Figure 1.5 highlights the public-gathering function of the Mall. The site's recreational role contrasts with the sacredness and solemnity of the commemorative landscape. Scholars who have critiqued the McMillan Plan note that the expansive green space was intended not necessarily for play and recreation but rather for the more imperial and triumphal grand space of reflection. In this regard, the rise of recreation and play has been an important public assertion of the right to redefine "public space" and the Mall itself. One public-space challenge on the Mall is the unresolved tension between play and recreation, on the one hand, and solemn commemoration, on the other.

Washington, D.C., and the Mall have become a landscape of civic pilgrimage. It is where people come to reclaim the past, celebrate the foundations of community, and witness historical re-enactments. It is where monuments and memorials prompt thoughtful discussion, healing, spiritual renewal, and reconciliation. Sometimes the Mall is just a place of the mundane, but it can be a place of transcendence. The Mall has become the *axis mundi*, the great stage for American secular worship.[85] It is a place where we worship not a particular figure or hero but democracy itself. As Robert Stern and Ray Gastil have said, the Mall has become a "temenos for a democracy."[86] It is a setting for American rituals, from picnics to

Figure 1.5. The Mall has become a place of public gatherings. Shown here is the July 4th celebration, where people picnic during the day waiting for the firework display. Photo by author.

funerals, rallies to football. The Mall has become multifunctional, existing as play space, sacred space, and utilitarian space. And yet, despite its generally accepted role as the nation's premier public space, it remains challenged by many contemporary pressures, many of which are examined in the remaining chapters.

PART I   MANAGEMENT
CHALLENGES

The chapters in this section document the way in which the Mall as a public space has been managed (or mismanaged).

Chapter 2 examines the legacy of neglect that has been omnipresent on the Mall since L'Enfant's grand vision of 1791. It focuses on the history of that neglect, schemes to sell off parts of the Mall, and attempts to improve it (some successful, others abandoned). The purpose is to set the context for understanding public-space management challenges in the present day. When pressed, Congress is more concerned with solving immediate needs for infrastructure or other uses than with thinking comprehensively about the Mall and its long-term needs. Two centuries of problematic decision making and management established a discourse of neglect or indifference that continues today.

Chapter 3 details the management structure and management challenges that now confront the Mall. The Mall is federal public property; hence management and oversight fall under the purview of federal agencies including the National Park Service. Unlike most urban public spaces, however, national legislation mandates that the Mall ensure public access in a way that makes this space simultaneously common property (a right not to be excluded from its uses and benefits) and public property (governed by federal agencies that determine the same uses and benefits). A challenge for effective public-space management is that, unlike municipally owned public space such as city parks or public squares, the Mall is a federally designated public space because it is a unit in the national park system. But it is also a public space over which other federal agencies also claim jurisdiction. The result is a combination of disjointed management structure and poor management policies that have created conditions in which both the use and the environmental quality of the Mall are under threat. Such challenges are not unique to the National Mall; Independence Square, the Statue of Liberty, the Presidio in San Francisco, and Boston's Freedom Trail are other examples of national parks that function as urban public space and have similar management challenges.

Added to the management-structure problems are the challenges of a chronically underfunded public space. The Mall, as is true of the many units within the national park system, suffers from a backlog of maintenance. Estimates are that the Mall has $350 million in deferred maintenance, leading to ongoing issues of disrepair and neglect. While the Park Service does what it can with its limited resources, Congress has failed to appropriate resources for the Mall.

I conclude chapter 3 by looking at public-private partnerships for parks and other types of public spaces. The growing trend of public-private partnerships has been lauded as a solution to chronic underfunding for many public spaces. The establishment of the Trust for the National Mall created a private partner tasked to raise money to support and restore the Mall. But the emergence of public-private partnerships in public space raises as many questions as it answers: Why should a public space require a private partner? Is it not the role of government to provide the necessary money in the first place? Are we letting Congress off the hook for its financial neglect by raising the money privately?

The failure of the federal government to maintain the Mall and to manage it effectively has exacerbated other problems such as how to deal creatively with development pressure and new uses and how to be innovative and transparent in planning – issues explored in the rest of the book.

CHAPTER 2

Neglecting the Mall

In 2006 the D.C. Preservation League named the small, often overshadowed World War I Memorial, situated on the Mall, as one of the ten Most Endangered Places in the District of Columbia (see Figure 2.1). The memorial, a circular temple, was built in 1931 to honour local heroes who served the nation in World War I, and is tucked in a shady grove of trees. The marble is deteriorating, the structure is crumbling in places, and the names of those who gave their life are weathering away. By placing the memorial on the Most Endangered Places List, the Preservation League hoped to remind the public about the significance of the site and to compel the Park Service to place it at the top of their list for minor upgrades such as lighting, landscaping, and benches and to secure funds for the restoration of the memorial to its historic grandeur.[1] The Park Service admitted that it was confused. It thought it had responsibility for the grounds, but not the structure. This confusion over stewardship is a result of the unclear jurisdiction and the fact that multiple agencies coordinate poorly with each other. But it also represents an important discourse that has played out consistently throughout the history of the Mall: neglect and indifference. This history is worth considering.

The Nineteenth-Century Mall: A Narrative of Neglect

L'Enfant envisioned making Washington "a splendid inviting capital," but, for nearly a half-century following, it was merely a "contemptible hamlet."[2]

Figure 2.1. The neglected D.C. World War I Memorial in 2006. Photo by author.

Historian Scott Berg relates: "A bird's eye view of the city of Washington in 1800 would not have revealed L'Enfant's gridiron arrangement of streets crisscrossed by dramatic diagonal avenues, but rather a rural region of forests, pastures, open fields, and produce gardens interrupted here and there by brick kilns and barracks, the entire picture dominated by two gargantuan construction projects ... L'Enfant's squares were nearly empty and in some cases nearly impossible to find ... In the absence of any progress on the Mall, Pennsylvania Avenue was the city's only true axis."[3]

Historical geographer Donald Meinig observes that the formation of the city of Washington was both a national and federal process with powerful implications for the shaping of the republic.[4] The evolution of the city and of the Mall was deeply enmeshed in the national politics of the time and the capital both symbolically and literally exposed the realities of political conflict and economic instability. Both the city and the Mall were hampered in their development because of political unwillingness or indecisiveness to implement L'Enfant's plan, poverty in the city coffers, and unexpected calamities such as wartime destruction. Whatever the causes, the result was a congressional attitude of indifference that led to what can be characterized as haphazard development.[5]

For the Mall, the nineteenth century started with indecisiveness and unrealized visions. It is not that nothing happened. L'Enfant's plan was neither forgotten nor ignored, but it was often compromised and altered with seeming indifference.[6]

In the early 1800s, the term "The Mall" was gaining currency as the name for swath of land L'Enfant called his Grand Avenue, but that land had barely been touched.[7] It bore little resemblance to an elegant promenade. The nearby Center Market meant that geese, pigs, and other livestock freely roamed the Mall. It was little more than a barren, unkempt area along the ragged bank of the canalized Tiber Creek. Hundreds of acres around the Potomac flats were covered with marshes breeding the malarial mosquito. The proposed equestrian statue to honour George Washington, introduced by L'Enfant seventeen years earlier, was nowhere to be seen.

The lack of civic conveniences was due to several factors. First, the city lacked its own financial muscle to create a vibrant commercial centre. The real-estate bubble Washington had hoped for to make the plan work had never materialized.[8] For most cities, economic fortunes are somewhat determined by taxing their businesses. But Washington's only business was federal government, and the government refused to be taxed.[9] Secondly, Congress was reluctant to support the costs of local development outright. This was because there was considerable concern that the appropriations of federal funds would be perceived as favouring a single city, causing an outcry from others and generating jealousies or resentment. This reluctance was also connected to a general hesitance to expand federal authority. For example, until 1817, most presidents refused to allow Congress to provide permanent funds for roads, canals, and internal improvements of any kind anywhere in the nation, fearing that this would lead to an escalation in federal authority. Congress's lack of financial commitment to the city meant that it remained underdeveloped. Because the city did not develop into a great commercial centre with a strong tax base, development projects and civic improvements lagged behind other cities of the Atlantic, exactly what L'Enfant predicted would happen in the absence of a significant influx of public cash.[10] Compared to Philadelphia, which boasted paved streets, bridges, turnpikes, and public parks, the federal city sadly lacked urban amenities befitting a nation's capital.

A third problem that exacerbated the lack of civic development was structural. Under article 1, section 8 of the constitution, Congress was given the power to govern the District, but it did not specify the form that local government should take. Debates over the form and power of the local government prevented urban development from occurring in any meaningful measure. The exclusive jurisdiction of Congress over the affairs of the city proved to be a primary obstacle for commercial development.

When in 1804 the Irish poet Thomas Moore sarcastically called the capital city "The City of Magnificent Distances," he was referring to the fact that so little had been built that the journey from one building to another was magnified by tremendous open distances. But his moniker could equally apply to the fact that the realization of L'Enfant's vision was literally and figuratively miles away from completion.

By the 1820s, Congress remained uncertain as to what shape and function the Mall should play and this is best exemplified by several ill-planned efforts to dispose of the Mall as a federal responsibility. In 1822 Congress authorized the city of Washington to drain the low grounds on and near the Mall and to take this land and sell it as building lots (about nineteen acres in the area between 3rd and 6th streets).[11] Several years later, the federal government reacquired these sites. Congress next sold an area of the Mall between 6th and 15th streets to the mayor of Washington, but Congress reconsidered its action at its next session. These were awkward attempts to divest of parts of the Mall, and "fortunately, cooler tempers eventually prevailed in Congress, so that the mistake of destroying the original concept of the Mall were rectified before the effects reached fatal proportions."[12] The reasons behind these efforts to break up the Mall are puzzling and unclear. Perhaps federal officials had lost sight of the L'Enfant Plan, or perhaps they were eager to be rid of land that needed considerable investment. Regardless, the attempts to parcel out the Mall were emblematic of ambivalence by federal officials who were uncertain as to the function or symbolic importance of this space.

These early actions did not have a permanent impact on the shape of the Mall as we know it today, but they did establish an enduring legacy of inconsistency with regard to the value placed by Congress on the Mall. Sometimes Congress affirms the importance of the capital city and the Mall by commissioning new plans and improvements; other times, its actions and attitudes range from indifference to disregard.

Cleaning Up the Mall

By the 1840s, the capital city had emerged as a border city balanced between a sharply demarcated North and South.[13] The antebellum years were particularly noteworthy as the city and the Mall embodied the great debates over citizenship, equality, slavery, and succession. Washington, D.C., had an active slave trade and slave market, which appeared to some as a federal endorsement of the practice. The Mall itself was home to two large slave pens.[14] The right to buy and sell slaves (which had been present since the origins of the city) came to symbolize to anti-slavery activists the "dominance" of the South in the national government.[15] Others saw the uncomfortable juxtaposition: in a place where government prided itself on freedom, it was commonplace to see manacled slaves being led through the streets by a trader with a whip. The federal government could not afford to alienate either the North or the South and tried hard to maintain neutrality through symbolic gestures. But the reality of slave pens on the Mall made neutrality impossible.

Congress passed the Compromise Act of 1850, which outlawed slave trading in the District of Columbia. The act transformed the District into an island of neutrality surrounded by southern states. The political manoeuvring over several years to achieve this compromise underlines the capital city's symbolic importance on the matter of the slave trade. Challenges to the federal city generated a desire to strengthen the physical symbols of the national identity and project an image of republican strength and unity.[16] The reaction to the growing crisis of slavery and succession was to display an *image* of democracy and national achievement. Political elites sought to make the city resemble a strong agent for centralism over sectionalism: one solution was to focus on creating national symbolic spaces. Congress attempted to provide symbolic unity by establishing the Mall as a ceremonial core for the city, but obviously the slave pens had to be removed.[17] Several improvement projects for the Mall were commissioned. No doubt, such actions were a substitute for genuine equality; cynics might view the "improvements" as a smokescreen to distract attention from the more serious issues of the day.

The Mall was a shambles. It was covered with trees and criss-crossed by railroad tracks. According to one account, the Mall was a large inhospitable common with zigzag meanderings.[18] It was home to a slaughterhouse, a tannery, a paper mill, a nickel-plating facility, a glass-eye workshop, a brewery, a tinsmith's, a petting zoo, a glue factory, a tuberculosis sanitarium, and not one, but two, opium dens. Brothels were within sight of the Capitol dome, including the notorious "Mollie's on the Mall."[19] On the other hand, the Mall had become a well-used public grounds and was integrated into the city to a greater extent than it is today.

Over the next several years, there were efforts to establish public gardens in the Mall as a way to counteract the city's reputation as an unimproved capital and the centre of slavery. After a half-century of haphazard development, the Mall appeared to be a priority. In this regard, the Mall benefited from a national discourse of anxiety. Improvement projects such as art galleries, public libraries, and botanical gardens reflected a national discourse that sought to highlight common values on which all political factions could agree. Civic improvement was seen as linked to full participation in the democratic system and was part of a movement for popular education during the 1840s and 1850s.[20] As the expansion of government operations accelerated in Washington, and as the city grew under the umbrella of more sophisticated concepts of urban and landscape planning, the realization took hold that the city and the Mall symbolized national identity.[21] Yet poor decisions, indifference, and neglect would continue to characterize the rest of the century.

The Shadow of War

The start of the Civil War cast a long shadow over the city and the Mall. Congressional appropriations ceased, and it became impossible to preserve the landscaping work that had been started on the Smithsonian grounds and the Mall. In 1860 Lincoln delivered his inaugural address from the Capitol, with the Mall as the visual backdrop and the city bristling with bayonets for his protection.[22] The Mall served as a stage for rival speculations as to the direction the nation would go. Would the union remain intact? Not long after Lincoln's inauguration, South Carolina succeeded from the union. By February 1861, Mississippi, Florida, Alabama, Georgia, Louisiana, and Texas had followed suit. The Union was disintegrating.

The Civil War meant visionary plans gave way to basic needs for survival. The city stood poised on the front lines of war. The summits of the city hills were transformed into Fort Reno, Fort Stevens, Fort Totten, Fort Lincoln, and other strong points to protect against invasion.[23] In 1855 Congress authorized the secretary of war to select a site for an armoury on the Mall where the volunteers and militia of the District could drill and where arms and ammunition could be stored in case of emergency.[24] The proximity of the Washington Canal made the southeast corner of the Mall an ideal site. Farther east on the Mall near the Capitol, Thaddeus Lowe, then chief of the Aeronautic Service, Balloon Corps, conducted experiments with balloons for air reconnaissance.[25] The reconnaissance balloons were first used in 1861 on the Potomac where Confederates tried to shoot them down.[26]

The war had a tremendous impact on the city of Washington. The city was never invaded, but it never felt safe. Its geography meant that it was a strategic pivot point in the war as well as an activity centre. To quote historian Carl Abbott: "The winds of war swirled around the city in vast clockwise turns as if it were the eye of a great storm system."[27] Long lines of army wagons and artillery continually rumbled through the streets. Cavalry, mule trains, and herds of cattle made their way through the city, destroying streets and sidewalks. Schools, churches, and homes became hospitals. Anxiety was pervasive. By 1861, the need for troops to defend the city transformed the Mall into an area to quarter troops in tents. To feed its troops, the army opened a bakery in the basement of the Capitol and slaughtered cattle on the Mall only a few blocks from the White House. The grounds of the Washington Monument were used for units temporarily stationed in the city and also became the site of the Washington National Monument Cattle Yard (Figure 2.2). The yard contained extensive stables for horses, cattle pens, corn houses, a slaughterhouse, a forage house, hay sheds, and mess quarters for officers and men.[28] Cattle and horses brought into the city were driven to

Figure 2.2. Union slaughterhouses on the Mall. Courtesy of Library of Congress, http://www.loc.gov/item/2004680190/.

the monument yards, where the cattle were slaughtered to feed Union troops in and around the city.

During the war, tens of thousands of recruits passed through the city. "In hospitals, offices, forts and camps on both sides of the Potomac, they waited and recuperated in the shadow of the Capitol and the half-finished Washington Monument."[29] Walt Whitman, who was in Washington in March 1863 working as a hospital orderly, wrote of this interesting spectacle: "I ... see spread, off there, the Potomac, very fine, nothing pretty about it – the Washington monument, not half finished – the public grounds around it filled with ten thousand beeves, on the hoof – to the left the Smithsonian with its brown turrets."[30]

Wartime Washington did not resemble a stately federal capital of a strong, united republic. The area around the Washington Monument became known as "murderer's row" during the war because it was a gathering spot for Civil War deserters and derelicts.[31] In April 1865, with the news that the Confederate capital had fallen, the population poured into the streets, laughing, yelling, and weeping with joy. Several days later, President Lincoln, in order not to disappoint those who had been led to expect him there, reluctantly attended a performance of *Our American Cousin* at Ford's Theatre.

By the end of the Civil War in 1865, the city had been forever altered. On the eve of the conflict, Washington had still been a collection of small towns separated by woods and fields. While the war had enormously enlarged its population, nothing had been done to improve its quality. Washington was now a city, and one that revealed starkly the effects of careless development. This neglect continued in the years that followed. One of the more ill-advised changes to the Mall occurred in 1872 when Congress granted fourteen acres of public grounds on the Mall to the Baltimore and Potomac Railroad Company. The "invasion" of the Mall was part of an effort to attract passenger and freight railroad in the District. The grant authorized the railroad company to cross the Mall from south to north and to construct a depot at the corner of 6th and B streets (today the National Gallery of Art). Trains soon chugged across the Mall at 6th Street, where empty freight cars sometimes stood in the yards for days. Unsightly train sheds and the sooty trains defaced the Mall and generated public protest but to no avail. This time Congress did not revisit its decision and reacquire the land – at least not in the nineteenth century. It is noteworthy, however, that the protests against the train tracks on the Mall can be traced to the maturation of the city as more of its residents became civic-minded and as the nation and city grew in affluence and prestige. Would the twentieth century right a hundred years of wrongs?

The Twentieth Century: Unfulfilled Visions, Continued Disregard

By 1900, the Mall had not achieved the grandeur of L'Enfant's design as a great park-like vista but it had made improvements since the early decades of obvious neglect and the Civil War years of slaughterhouses and tents. The Mall had endured a century of disinterest and little investment, while numerous grand plans had languished. Parts of the Mall had deteriorated into scraggly, overgrown fragments of parks and areas overlain with train tracks and cattle pens. In the words of historian Scott Berg, the Mall in 1900 was result of a century of bad luck, bad taste, and bad advice.[32]

The lack of a long-range plan for the location of government buildings had allowed the government to postpone many decisions or make compromises that marred the beauty and dignity of the National Capital, such as the scar of railroad tracks across the Mall.[33] The McMillan Commission summed up the results of the nineteenth century: "During the century that has elapsed ... the great space known as the Mall ... has been diverted from its original purpose and cut into fragments ... thus invading what was a single composition ... The demand for new public buildings and memorials has reached an acute stage, there has been hesitation and embarrassment in locating them because of the uncertainty in securing appropriate sites."[34]

Although the 1901 McMillan Plan was generally accepted, it, like the L'Enfant Plan before it, faced many hurdles and saw unfortunate deviations from its vision as the years passed. It was not until 1929 that Congress passed legislation that formally acknowledged its acceptance of the McMillan Plan. And it would take almost another thirty-five years to bring into existence a landscape that bore any resemblance to that of the plan. Even then, Congress would continue to make decisions that would disregard the symbolic importance of this public space. That the McMillan Plan was never completely implemented speaks to the persistent inability of political elites in Congress to value and support the Mall throughout the twentieth century. But it wasn't just Congress. Architects would fight over what architectural forms – neo-classical, Victorian, modernist – should define the Mall.[35] Insensitive planners still built uninspired, disconnected federal buildings. Politicians and planners let other pressing demands encroach on the Mall. In many ways, these trends continue today.

The 1920s and 1930s were marked by a decline in generosity and civic spirit, particularly with the onset of the Great Depression. Some parts of the city continued to progress simply because the federal government needed them. The large parcel of land whose long sides are Pennsylvania Avenue and the Mall was purchased by the government to construct a complex of buildings known as the Federal Triangle, which included the departments of Commerce, Labor, and Justice, the Post Office, and the Archives. The Great Depression, which began in 1929, is considered by many to the one of the worst experiences American has ever endured. During this period, the capital became a city of despair. In 1933 Congress refused to vote the city a budget as part of an effort to reduce government spending in order to end the economic recession. Despite the continuation of some federal building, unemployment in the capital began to rise and inaction or lack of policy led to acts of disregard. For example, throughout much of the 1920s people parked wherever they could, even on the White House grounds and the Mall.[36]

An element in Franklin D. Roosevelt's New Deal was to distribute money to people through public works. These programs included the Civilian Conservation Corps, which gave jobs to more than 300,000 youths to work on conservation projects around the country; the Tennessee Valley Authority, which constructed a series of dams across the Tennessee valley and supplied electric power where it had not existed before; and the Works Progress Administration, which employed millions to carry out public-works projects, among them the construction of public buildings, parks, and roads.

Under the WPA, some improvements to the city helped to revitalize and beautify the Mall. Construction of the National Gallery of Art started in 1937. The public-works program also improved the Mall via a federal grant to the Park Service. In 1933 Congress authorized an initial grant of $600,000 for various landscape projects that included grading the Mall, paving several drives along the greensward, removing the Victorian gardens, and planting the rows of elms as the McMillan Plan outlined. With the picturesque Victorian landscaping removed, the east-west axis became clearly visible and one of the most important components of the McMillan Plan was finally implemented. The grant also supported the development of Union Square in accordance with the McMillan Plan. The rehabilitation of Union Square at the foot of the Capitol grounds enclosed the Mall at its east end and opened the vista between the Capitol and the Washington Monument. In addition, several roads and walks were constructed and lawns and ornamental trees and shrubs were planted (or transplanted). The areas bordering the outer roads to the north and south of the Mall were planted with more than 300 American elms in four-parallel rows, as envisioned by the McMillan Plan.[37] In the centre panel of the Mall a lawn area was seeded to create the greensward we see today, some three feet in width and approximately one mile in length between the Capitol and the Washington Monument, complete with an underground sprinkling system.[38] Another project involved the installation of fluted bronze lighting posts twenty-one feet in height.

The area formerly occupied by the Botanic Garden had deteriorated owing to a lack of funds for proper maintenance, and its sad appearance – overgrown vegetation hid from view two memorials, one to Ulysses Grant, the other to George Meade – coupled with its prominent location made it the focus of particular criticism.[39] In the 1930s, run-down buildings were demolished, the area was landscaped, and the memorials were restored. And yet, for every good decision, there continued to be bad ones that negatively affected the Mall.

The Case of the Not-So-Temporary Tempos

Despite two grand plans, the Mall was periodically subject to disheartening deviations from those visions. The outbreak of World War I interrupted improvement projects on the Mall. With the city preparing for war, thousands of defence workers poured into the capital. Many of these workers came to support the war effort: they were clerks, administrators, and other logistical personnel who helped procure material, oversaw shipping and delivery, and coordinated troop recruitment. The Navy Yard in the southeast of the city was where weapons were designed and built for the Great White Fleet. The fourteen-inch naval railway guns used in France during World War I were also manufactured at the Navy Yard. As a result of wartime labour, the city population increased from 350,000 to 526,000 within several months. The McMillan Plan began to falter under pressure. The Mall, only recently cleared of railroad tracks, was filled with endless rows of concrete buildings, many clustered between 4th and 9th streets, to accommodate federal agencies. The new plaza in front of Union Station was filled in with dormitories for the new government workers to live

Figure 2.3. The tempos on the right remained in place until the 1970s. To the left of the buildings are parked cars on what is today Constitution Gardens and the Vietnam Veterans Memorial. Courtesy of Navy Archives #NH 92386, http://www.ibiblio.org/hyperwar/OnlineLibrary/photos/pl-usa/pl-dc/nav-fac/mn-mun-c.htm.

in. The temporary buildings became known as "tempos," although there was nothing temporary about them. By the end of the war, the squat tempos with their tall, narrow smokestacks cluttered the Mall grounds between the Capitol and the Washington Monument. Even after construction began on the Lincoln Memorial and the long Reflecting Pool in 1919, the tempos remained in place. The original McMillan Plan called for transverse arms on the Reflecting Pool, but the presence of the tempos blocked the full realization of that part of the plan. Discussions began on removing them from the Mall area, but as the capital again prepared for war in early 1940, plans to dismantle the tempos were put on hold. More tempos were built to accommodate defence needs again during World War II (Figure 2.3). Unlike the temporary buildings of World War I, which were concrete, these were built of wood. They, too, stayed after the war was over because the demand for office space remained high during the Cold War years. The tempos were a persistent eyesore and a testament to lingering disregard for the Mall.

In 1966 the National Park Service issued a Mall Master Plan, known as the "Skidmore, Owings and Merrill Plan," after the principal author, the architectural firm of the same name. It was designed to reassert the principles of the 1901 McMillan Plan and to improve and enhance the Mall given its new uses and increased number of visitors. Perhaps in reference to the tempos, the plan noted that "the national monuments be set off and protected from *alien inroads of convenience.*"[40] The plan also directly and specifically called for "the Mall to be cleared of temporary and non-conforming facilities as soon as possible." Yet, three years after the publication of the new Master Plan, the tempos remained in place and many of the design proposals remained unimplemented.[41] In 1968 the Lyndon Johnson administration, in one of its last acts, called for the beautification of the Mall, noting that "there is need to carry forward the plans to develop the Mall, so that it may be a place of life and beauty, of pleasure and relaxation."[42] Johnson, too, asked that the temporary buildings be removed from the great sweep of open space. But in fact the tempos were not completely removed until the presidency of Richard Nixon.[43] Nixon's original idea was to replace the tempos with an amusement park, which would include two levels of underground parking. That idea was functionally inappropriate and, thankfully, Nixon was instead persuaded to endorse a plan to construct Constitution Gardens to coincide with the Bicentennial in 1976. A memorial island in the middle of an artificial lake, the Gardens contain stones bearing the names and signatures of the fifty-six men who signed the Declaration of Independence. At last the "temporary" buildings on the Mall – which had stood for more than fifty years – were removed.

Revisiting the Neglected Memorial

In March 2008 Frank Buckles, the last surviving American veteran of World War I, visited the District of Columbia War Memorial on the Mall. He observed that this peaceful, secluded memorial, dedicated in 1931 as a memorial to the 499 residents of the District of Columbia who gave their lives in World War I, sat neglected and in extreme disrepair. The memorial was not even listed on the Park Service map of the Mall. Buckles issued a call for the restoration and rededication of the memorial as a National and District of Columbia World War I Memorial.[44] In 2008 the World War I Memorial Foundation was formed to this end. Money was raised to rescue the memorial from neglect. Perhaps chastened by the negative press, in 2009 the National Park Service announced that it would dedicate $7.3 million of "stimulus funds" (American Recovery and Reinvestment Act) to the full restoration of the memorial. That sum was later reduced to $2.3 million. Throughout 2010 and 2011 contractors cleaned and restored the stone and addressed drainage issues. In addition, the vault hatch cover in the memorial chamber was replaced to specifications based on historical documentation. The electrical system and lighting were replaced, the landscaping restored, and new paving stones reflecting the historic pattern of the 1930s installed. The "makeover" also called for the memorial to become a venue again for concerts and other public events. "This project will ensure the memorial and its surrounds remain in excellent condition," said John Piltzecker, superintendent of the National Mall and Memorial Parks.[45] By late fall 2011, the restoration of the War Memorial was completed.

While we might be tempted to think of the Mall as a public space reflective of the nation's highest democratic ideals, in fact its history has been a complex story of action, inaction, indifference, and controversy. Two centuries of problematic decision making gave the Mall a cattle yard, slave pens, train tracks, tempos, and the forlorn and decaying World War I Memorial. That Congress allowed or even undertook these developments seems contrary to the embrace of the Mall as "the nation's front yard." Indeed, Congress has often displayed indifference towards the Mall, sometimes outright disregard. When pressed, the federal government is more concerned with solving immediate needs for infrastructure or other uses, trumping the historic plans and intentions for the Mall. Several centuries of planning, or failure to plan, or insensitivity to plans have created a variety of buildings that often say little to each other, reflecting instead the episodic and ad hoc development that has characterized the Mall's evolution. The periodic need to reassert commitment to L'Enfant's original design is, I argue, a testament to the federal government's persistently ambiguous relationship with the Mall. One result was the deterioration of the World War I Memorial. But the endangered memorial is but one example of a growing mess on the Mall that can be traced back, in part, to the historical discourse of ambivalence, indifference, and neglect. In the next chapter, I look at how the Mall is managed in both the Executive Branch and Congress.

CHAPTER 3

Managing the Mall

Seen from afar, the National Mall looks grand and monumental. Just don't look too closely. The grass has been trampled to dust. Latches are missing from the stall doors in public restrooms. Paint is peeling from the benches that line the walkways. The Lincoln Memorial Reflecting Pool walls were recently crumbling and the stagnant water was full of muck. There are broken or missing light fixtures. Algae choke the lake at Constitution Gardens. There are insufficient food and beverage concessions and not nearly enough restrooms. The Mall looks run down, worn out, and abandoned (see Figures 3.1, 3.2, and 3.3).[1] Senator Craig Thomas complained, "I've noticed on my drive into work early in the morning that some of the memorials occasionally have no lights or only some of the lights are working. This seems to be the case for weeks at a time."[2] In a congressional hearing, Delegate Eleanor Holmes Norton, D.C.'s non-voting member of the House of Representatives, admitted that there was "no site more neglected, more undervalued. The Mall is a disgrace. We need to rescue the Mall from neglect."[3] How did one of the nation's most important public spaces become such a mess?

The mess on the Mall is partly due to the legacy of neglect explored in the last chapter, and partly the outcome of the complexity of managing the Mall as both an urban public space and a national park in the twenty-first century. A closer look reveals that Mall management is confusingly fragmented. Congress, the Executive Branch, and numerous federal agencies all have some stewardship of the Mall. The management, planning, and development of the Mall, whether it

Figure 3.1. The Mall in disrepair; trampled grass at the Washington Monument. Photo by author.

Figure 3.2 Benches in need of repair. Photo by author

Figure 3.3 Sinking floodwalls around the Jefferson Memorial. Photo by author.

is the construction of a new building or memorial or the installation of benches or security bollards and bunkers, only occurs with federal approval and oversight. Even the day-to-day management of the Mall, such as cutting the grass, collecting garbage, organizing annual events such as the Smithsonian Folklife Festival, and ensuring public safety, is the outcome of management policies and coordinated efforts that occur under the jurisdiction of a dizzying array of multiple federal agencies. Several federal agencies in the Executive Branch and numerous committees and subcommittees in Congress have different roles and responsibilities, but there is no single agency with sole stewardship and ultimate authority. The Mall belongs to no one and everyone. As a consequence, management and policy does not always serve the best interests of the Mall and the public. Until very recently, there has been a curious silence on how decisions shaping the Mall's physical form and symbolic meaning are made, and on who makes them. In this chapter I explore the role of management and stewardship. Who runs the Mall? How is it managed? How are decisions that affect this important public space made?

The Critique of Government Bureaucracy

One of the enduring discourses of the late twentieth and early twenty-first centuries is the debate over the effectiveness and accountability of government. Conservatives have criticized "The Government" for becoming bloated, ineffective, and unwieldy. Liberals agree that government is often ineffective and there is much to improve, but they also contend that the public good is served by public agencies and that deregulation and private interests may not be the solution. Since the Reagan era, a critique of big government has permeated our culture, and there is a general belief that government is "the problem." Charles Goodsell says that it has become fashionable to mock bureaucracy, a word often uttered in contempt, which is considered bloated in size, inefficient compared to the private sector, indifferent to ordinary citizens, and, in short, the problem rather than the solution. He notes that there has been a "war" of rhetoric against American government and the result is a deeply embedded mistrust of public administration. The actual workings of government seem mysterious to most Americans, and yet the mandates given to federal agencies as well as how they interact and cooperate have had a critical bearing on management of the Mall.

In this chapter, I situate some of the management issues in the context of two interrelated debates: one that critiques the effectiveness of government and another that examines how public space (the Mall) is challenged by management practices and policies. I do not want to perpetuate a set of negative assumptions or attitudes about the Park Service. According to many public surveys, the parks and wildlife agencies rank highly with regard to satisfaction, behind only the Post Office and public institutions such as fire and rescue services.[4] However, we can and should cast a critical eye at how the Park Service and other key federal agencies manage and protect the Mall. Ultimately, it may be more accurate to critique these federal bureaucracies not for being "too big" but for being too disjointed and poorly coordinated.

Managing "The Commons"

The classic reference of "tragedy of the commons" was popularized in 1968 by an essay in *Science* written by Garret Hardin.[5] The commons refers to any shared resource such as water, air, and land. Hardin cites the parable of an open and unmanaged common (such as Boston Common in the nineteenth century). Individuals are motivated to add to their flocks to increase personal wealth. Yet every animal added to the total degrades the commons a small amount. Continued overgrazing – the result of apparently rational decisions by numerous individuals to maximize their own gain – will ultimately destroy the resource. The tragedy of the commons model has been used to explain a variety of contemporary problems including the depletion of fisheries, congestion on urban highways, climate change, and the accumulation of foreign debt.

Today, scholars use the term "common pool resource" (CPR) and further study has expanded our understanding of the many types of commons.[6] One class of common is the public good. Public goods are resources that are not owned by any single individual, household, community group, or firm and the use of these by one individual or firm does not exclude others from using or enjoying them. "A public good allows collective use and consumption and the use of that resource does not reduce the value or utility for others by using it at the same time."[7] A public park is an example of a public good. So too are many types of public spaces, including town centres, squares, and beaches. As with many commons, environmental problems associated with public goods include overcrowding, pollution, and overuse. But most of the empirical studies have tended to focus on more traditional CPRs such as fisheries, forests, and grazing pastures and there have been far fewer studies looking at the urban commons or public space.

The Mall is a public space that meets the definition of a common/public good. Public property is owned by a government authority that holds the property on behalf of a larger constituency (i.e., the American public). Government officials have the right to determine who has access to such resources.[8] The Mall is federal public property, hence management and stewardship fall under the purview of federal agencies like the National Park Service. The Park Service has long used the term "stewardship" to describe its resource management responsibilities for the various properties under its jurisdiction. It considers resource management not simply as a task that is technical in nature but rather as one involving an ethic of stewardship that focuses on passing the parks unimpaired to future generations. Stewardship is defined as "an ethic that embodies the responsible planning and management of resources." Park stewardship is a pre-eminent duty of the Park Service.[9] Unlike most urban public spaces, however, national park legislation mandates that the Mall ensure access in a way that makes this space simultaneously common property (a right not to be excluded from the uses and benefits) and public property (governed by, in this case, federal agencies that determine its uses and benefits).

As a public good, the Mall serves multiple functions and multiple users. The use of the Mall for protest or recreation does not necessarily threaten the quality of the Mall. Certainly, with more than twenty-five million visitors annually, the Mall's physical condition is affected by use. But high use does not solely explain the neglect and disrepair.

Many academic studies on common pool resources focus on resources that can be depleted through use. In this chapter I show that it is a combination of disjointed management structure and poor management policies, rather than overuse and depletion, that have created conditions in which both the use and the environmental quality of the Mall are under threat. The chapter will examine the rules and governance system and also the behavioural patterns, norms, and values of the stewards of this public space.[10]

How to manage and protect "the commons" has been at the centre of local, regional, and international environmental research agendas for some time.[11] There has been considerable progress in advancing broader theories of collective action and analysing different governing solutions. Scholars have debated and discussed a diverse range of management regimes; some recommend privatization as the most efficient form of ownership, other stress centralized control, and still others look to alternatives that seek broader representation of stakeholders and users.[12] CPRs may be owned by national, regional, or local governments or by communal groups, by private individuals, or corporations; or they may be used as an open-access resource by whoever can gain access. Yet, after much theoretical and empirical development, there are still gaps in our understanding of the array of problems associated with governing and managing the commons. In part this is because there are a diversity of resources that are characterized as CPRs and an equal diversity in institutional arrangements that govern their use.[13] Public goods are often treated as state property. The public-good regime places CPRs into the custodianship of national, regional, or local governments. The Mall is a resource managed under federal control. Although many public goods that are owned by the state are treated as resources for revenue, in this case the state is only acting as a custodian and hence its role is limited to "policing" and management duties. In situations where CPRs can be overused or depleted, the management task is to handle the problem of access to the resource; however, in other situations, such as cultural landscapes or urban public spaces like the Mall, management tasks are to regulate access, ensure maintenance, and plan for new public uses. As a unit in the national park system, the Mall has as its primary custodian or steward the National Park Service.[14] Urban national parks, like the Mall, the Statue of Liberty, or Independence Square in Philadelphia, are inherently different from municipal public parks or public spaces – they may be *in* a city, but not *of* a city, since these spaces are controlled *not* by municipal governments and planning departments but by Congress and numerous federal agencies. In the case of the Mall, however, the "local community" (the city and local residents) has been excluded as a primary stakeholder, a theme I explore in greater detail in the last section of the book.

Although the Mall is under the jurisdiction of the Park Service, there is actually no single owner – since the Park Service must also report to Congress and other federal agencies. Thus, the Mall's management structure is somewhat unique to its location. The Mall has numerous constitutional rules regarding stewardship, budget, and oversight, all of which has created an unfortunately large and incoherent bureaucracy. It is this governance structure that I argue has hindered good management of the Mall.

Political scientist Elinor Ostrom asserts that, when the commons fails, it may often have to do with the lack of capacity for communication, an inability to develop trust, and a lack of sense of sharing a common future.[15] This chapter will document how all of these "failures" are present in the management of the Mall by its custodians. The current condition of the Mall validates these observations; its management structure consists of numerous bureaucratic stakeholders (congressional committees, Executive Branch agencies and commissions, and other stakeholders) that often have competing or divergent interests and appear unable to manage the commons for the collective good. The Mall's management is as complex as that of any CPR, and most of the conditions for successful common-property resource management as established by scholars are absent with regard to the Mall.[16] The failure of the federal government to maintain the Mall, to deal creatively with development pressure and new uses, and to be innovative in planning raises serious questions about the Mall's future. I offer the term "bureaucratic tragedy of the commons" to characterize the broader political/bureaucratic context which affects the Mall's day-to-day management as well as long-term development.

The problem illustrated by the commons of the Mall is not overdevelopment of a resource but poor development and maintenance neglect. It is not the case that the Mall is highly ecologically degraded (although the quality of many areas is poor). Rather, it is that neglect of the Mall in terms of investment, aesthetics, and a vision for long-term development has resulted in a public space that fails to meet the needs of the people it is intended to serve: the public. The Mall is threatened most by those who govern it.

A Geographically Divided Mall

In terms of authority and accountability in government, the Mall is geographically divided. By law, six federal and local government agencies have been given jurisdiction and authority over specific areas on the Mall. These agencies include the Park Service, the Architect of the Capitol, the Smithsonian Institution, the National Gallery of Art, the General Services Administration, the D.C. government, and various memorial funds (see Figure 3.4 and Table 3.1). A 2005 report by the Congressional Research Service confirms that jurisdiction is primarily vested by law in the National Park Service and U.S. Park Police, acting

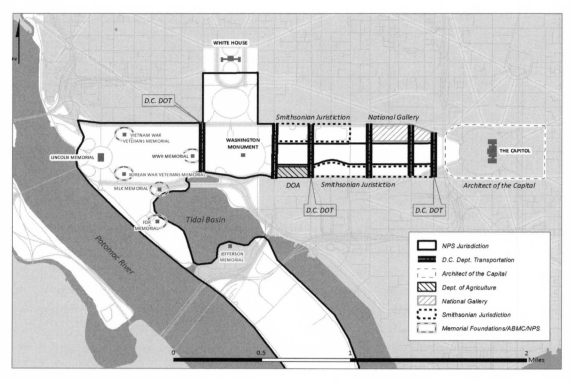

Figure 3.4. A geographically divided Mall. Note the various federal agencies in charge of different areas of the Mall. Map by author.

on behalf of the secretary of the interior. However, the report also states that certain jurisdiction is vested in the secretary of the Smithsonian Institution and several other agencies, who have claim to the grounds around the buildings. According to the National Park Service, it manages 90 per cent of the 725-acre National Mall; the remaining 10 per cent is managed by the Smithsonian Institution, the Department of Agriculture, and the National Gallery of Art.[17] The responsibility for policing and security of the various areas of jurisdiction also involves the U.S. Park Police (in charge of Park Service areas), the D.C. Metro Police (in charge of patrolling the streets around the Mall), the Secret Service (in charge of security at the White House), and the Capitol Police, who coordinate security on the Capitol grounds. This geographic fragmentation is mirrored administratively as well.

Table 3.1 Mall Jurisdiction by Agency

National Park Service	Has jurisdiction over the Mall but has had a history of conflicting definitions that often exclude the Capitol, the Smithsonian, and White House grounds.
Architect of the Capitol	Has jurisdiction over the Capitol and grounds surrounding the Capitol, the Supreme Court, House and Senate Office Buildings, and the Botanic Garden.
Smithsonian Institution	Has jurisdiction over buildings and grounds in front of the Smithsonian museums.
General Services Administration	Has jurisdiction over the Department of Agriculture building, located on the Mall at Maryland Avenue.
National Gallery of Art	Has jurisdiction over the building and grounds around the National Gallery of Art.
D.C. government	Has jurisdiction over the roads that cross the Mall (1st, 3rd, 4th, 7th, 14th, 15th, 17th, 23rd).
Park Service in conjunction with memorial funds	Memorial funds exist for the Vietnam Veterans Memorial, the Korean Memorial, the World War II Memorial, and the FDR Memorial. The funds raise all monies needed for the construction of the memorials and are in charge of maintaining and repairing them, although the Park Service cares for the surrounding grounds and the day-to-day maintenance issues (example: many are administered by the American Battle Monuments Commission).

Fragmented Management: The Legislative Branch

Answering the question "Who is in charge of the Mall?" is difficult when examining the role of Congress and the Executive Branch. Figure 3.5 shows the complex political terrain in which decisions are made that affect the Mall.[18] Many House and Senate committees have jurisdiction over the Mall in some capacity. In the Senate, the Committee on Energy and Natural Resources has jurisdiction over all national parks and historic sites.[19] This committee is routinely involved with issues concerning the Mall. But there are others. The Senate Committee on Environment and Public Works has jurisdiction over public buildings and grounds of the United States generally, including federal buildings in the District of Columbia.[20] The Senate Committee on Governmental Affairs has jurisdiction over the District of Columbia – and hence the Mall; and the Senate Committee on Rules and Administration has jurisdiction over the United States Capitol and the Smithsonian Institution, both of which are located on the Mall.

Mall Management in Congress

House Committees   Senate Committees

Appropriations	Resources (National Park Service)	Appropriations	Environment & Public Works (Federal buildings in DC)
Government Reform (DC municipal affairs)	House Administration (Smithsonian)	Rules & Administration (Smithsonian)	Energy & Natural Resources (National Park Service)
Joint Committee on the Library (Library of Congress)	Transportation and Infrastructure	Homeland Security & Governmental Affairs (DC municipal affairs)	Joint Committee on the Library (Library of Congress)

Figure 3.5. The various House and Senate committees with oversight of the Mall. Compiled by author.

In the House of Representatives, the Committee on Resources has jurisdiction over national parks and all parks within the District of Columbia. This committee plays a primary role in issues concerning the National Mall, but there are others too. The Committee on Government Reform has jurisdiction over the municipal affairs of the District, and the Committee on House Administration has jurisdiction over the Smithsonian Institution. Issues concerning Mall management and policy can be decided within these committees as well. Finally, the Committee on Transportation and Infrastructure has jurisdiction over the construction, reconstruction, and maintenance of the buildings of the Smithsonian.

The multifaceted management structure of oversight and appropriations in both the House and Senate is fragmented and uncoordinated at best. Yet there is no one committee that oversees all Mall issues. In the management structure of the Mall, there are several competing committees in both houses of Congress.

The Mall is a national park that must negotiate numerous Senate and House committees. The Park Service likes to say that "this grand open space has been jointly nurtured and guided by the Executive, Congressional and Judicial branches of government for over two centuries."[21] Others see fragmented, poorly coordinated management that occurs within a multitude of agencies and organizations.

As a result of such "Balkanized" oversight, Mall issues are considered in piecemeal fashion. House and Senate committee and subcommittee hearings usually focus on a specific bill or legislative mandate particular to an area of the Mall under the appropriate jurisdiction. There are no real opportunities for discussion of an overall vision that involves all stakeholders, or for oversight of comprehensive long-term management and development. Paradoxically, the Mall is a political orphan with many parents; it lacks a voting member of Congress to act as its champion, yet at the same time members of Congress constantly interfere, threaten to cuts budgets, and filibuster bills the Park Service has an interest in.[22] As former National Park Service Director James Ridenour remarked: "Imagine my surprise when I got to Washington and found that the National Park Service wasn't in the executive branch of government ... Instead I found Congress, and worse yet, congressional staffs running it. I was absolutely amazed to find staffers on Capitol Hill trying to decide whom I would hire and when I would hire them. They are into micro-management big time."[23]

The relationship between agencies such as the Park Service and Congress is not a one-way street, since members of Congress and their staffs have been known to defer to the judgment of the leaders of agencies. Influence runs in both directions, but the relationships are not symmetrical and many agency staff members and appointees believe it is imperative to avoid Congress's displeasure.[24] The complex management structure, concomitant with the challenge of pleasing public officials who occupy powerful oversight and authorizing positions, has often resulted in inconsistent and shifting mandates for the Park Service to negotiate. It also means that accountability, too, is difficult to pinpoint. Public accountability is often defined in terms of "persons with public responsibilities" being answerable to "the people" for the performance of their duties.[25] The ability to clearly identify stakeholders is a critical task for increasing the efficiency, accountability, and success of any agency,[26] yet, in the case of Mall management, this is difficult if not impossible. However, not all the blame for confusing and fragmented management rests with Congress. The Executive Branch has equal responsibility.

Fragmented Management: The Executive Branch

In addition to the fragmented character of Mall management at the congressional and level, there are also numerous Executive Branch commissions, councils, and offices that review specific planning issues and proposed development on the Mall (see Figure 3.6).

In the years following the recommendations of the 1901 McMillan Plan, it became apparent that there was a need for advice on plans for future public buildings, bridges, parks, sculptures and paintings, along with other elements

Mall Management: The Executive Branch

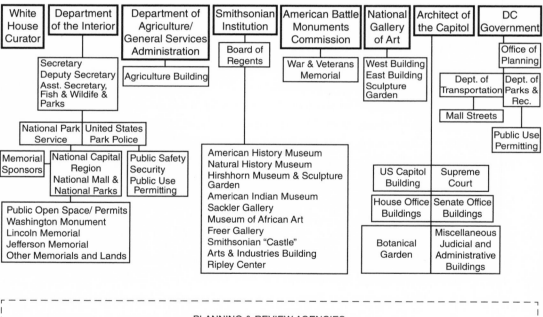

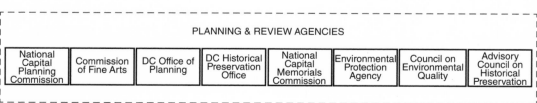

Figure 3.6. The complexity of Mall management in the Executive Branch. Compiled by author.

of city planning such as traffic, water supply, sewerage, and housing. Congress and the Executive Branch created several commissions and agencies to advise on Mall development (why they created several different commissions instead of one remains a mystery). Currently, eight Executive Branch agencies have the power to review and approve development, environmental impacts, planning, and design. These include the Commission of Fine Arts, the National Capital Planning Commission, the National Capital Memorials Commission (NCMC), the Environmental Protection Agency (EPA), the Council on Environmental Quality, the Advisory Council on Historic Preservation, the D.C. Office of Planning, and the D.C. Historic Preservation Office (see Table 3.2). These review agencies were created in the twentieth century as a response to shifting cultural and ecological imperatives in American society. Each new agency or commission represents a political moment of momentum and public pressure. For example, the National Environmental Protection Act (NEPA) of 1969 created the EPA and opened the door to a much more public process of assessing environmental quality. Today, the mandates of NEPA affect the Mall because any proposed changes to the land – such as the construction of a new facility – must include an environmental-impact assessment (EIA), to be reviewed by the EPA. Similarly, any proposed changes to existing historic structures on the Mall must consider and detail the impacts of these changes on the historic character of the Mall under the guidelines of the National Historic Preservation Act. Of the eight agencies, three are worthy of more in-depth discussion since they have exercised significant authority over the Mall.

The National Park Service

In 1790 the president appointed a superintendent to direct the federal district and its lands. In 1849 Congress approved and created a new executive department, the Department of Interior. The secretary of interior was to claim and preserve, within its Office of Commissioner of Public Buildings, certain properties in the United States, including the federal reservations of Washington, D.C. The supervisory power of the secretary of the interior continued until 1867 when Congress abolished the office and transferred the duties to the chief engineer of the Army. In 1898 Congress passed another act that transferred the parks in the District of Columbia, which included the Mall and also Rock Creek Park and Potomac Park, to the control of the chief of Army engineers. Other small

Table 3.2. Planning Review Agencies

Planning and Review Agency	Origin	Role
Commission of Fine Arts	Boards, commissions, and committees of the Executive Branch	Guide the development of the capital city; advise upon the location of statues, fountains, and monuments, as well as the selection of artists for the execution of same; advise on plans for any public buildings erected by the government in the District of Columbia.
National Capital Planning Commission	Independent agency in the Executive Branch	Review all federal development in the Capital Region on a wide range of plans and projects from memorials and museums to new federal office buildings to communications towers and perimeter-security projects; review District of Columbia public projects, proposed street and alley closings, and Zoning Commission actions; responsible for preparing a "comprehensive, consistent, and coordinated plan for the National Capital."
National Capital Memorials Commission	Secretary of the interior in the Executive Branch	Review and approve the design and site selection of memorials and certain museums within the nation's capital; play an advisory role with the secretary of interior and the administrator of general services (as appropriate) on policy and procedures for establishment of, and proposals to establish, commemorative works in the District of Columbia.
Environmental Protection Agency	Independent agency in the Executive Branch	Protect human health and safeguard the natural environment; review the EIAs assessments required when developing or making changes to federal land.
Council on Environmental Quality	Executive office of the president	Coordinate federal environmental efforts and work closely with agencies and other White House offices in the development of environmental policies and initiatives; ensure that federal agencies consider the effects of their actions on the quality of the human environment; report annually to the president on the state of the environment; oversee federal agency implementation of the EIA process; act as a referee when agencies disagree over the adequacy of such assessments.
Advisory Council on Historic Preservation	Independent agency in the Executive Branch	Primary federal policy adviser on preservation to the president and Congress, with power to recommend administrative and legislative improvements for protecting the nation's heritage; advocate full consideration of historic values in federal decision making; and review federal programs and policies to promote effectiveness, coordination, and consistency with national preservation policies.
D.C. Historic Preservation Office	Local	Determine the appropriateness of changes to historic landmarks and historic districts; review proposals that affect existing historic landmarks and buildings. Federal agencies are required to "consult" with local Historic Preservation Offices.
D.C. Office of Planning	Local	Assess and review plans that affect the District of Columbia; to date it has played limited role in planning on the National Mall.

Source: Compiled by author based on information from these government agencies.

park areas at the intersection of streets (such as the circle and square parks) were made part of the park system of the District and placed under the control of the chief of engineers at that time. While the chief engineer may seem a curious steward, the Park Service did not yet exist. It would be created several decades later, in 1916. For some years after the establishment of the Park Service, the Mall remained under the jurisdiction of the U.S. Army. In 1933 Franklin D. Roosevelt's penned Executive Order No. 6166,[27] section 2 of which brought the administration of the Mall under the Park Service and created an administrative unit called the National Capital Parks.[28] Park Service historian Cornelius Heine observes:

> While the office of National Capital Parks is a unit in the National Park System of the United States, it occupies an unusual place with respect to all other field units in the National Park Service. It is older than the National Park Service, since its legal continuity can be traced back to 1790. At the same time many of its functions are entirely different from other field units in the National Park System. In addition to performing work similar to other National Parks and National Monuments, the office supervises a vast system of municipal parks and parkways, which in itself differs from all other National Parks. Not only does the office supervise a municipal park system, but it supervises the park system of the Nation's Capital, established for the enjoyment of the people of the United States.[29]

The great task of the Park Service upon assuming jurisdiction was to unite and manage the scattered holdings of the Mall, which included the former Botanic Garden site (today Union Square), the section between the Garden and the Smithsonian grounds (known as Reservation 3B), the area north of the buildings of the Department of Agriculture (which became known as Seaton Park East and Seaton Park West), and some small parcels of land owned by the Treasury Department.[30] These required years of negotiation between the Park Service, the Architect of the Capitol, the Department of Agriculture, the Smithsonian, and the Treasury Department. Park Service historian George Olszewski notes that the acquisition of the former Botanic Garden site (some 490,000 square feet of land) allowed the Park Service to establish its jurisdiction over the head of the Mall at the foot of the Capitol.[31] With the acquisition of these lands finally under Park Service jurisdiction, the Mall was united and controlled by a single federal agency. Or was it?

The Park Service has assumed that it has sole jurisdiction, and has said so often enough that many forget the Mall itself consists of other federal agencies that occupy the land and can claim some jurisdiction. Today the Park Service has a significant management challenge in the Mall. It must accommodate some twenty-five million visitors annually and supervise approximately thirty permitted events each day. Maintenance crews pick up more than three tons of daily. More than 444,000 vehicles travel the roads daily around and through the Mall. As both an urban park and a public space, it is one of the most heavily visited urban national parks in the United States.

Commission of Fine Arts

In 1910 Congress created the Commission of Fine Arts under Public Law 181 to preserve and implement the concepts of both the L'Enfant and McMillan Commission plans. Implicit in this charge was the mission to guide the development of the capital city "to reflect, in stateliness and grandeur, the emergence of the United States as a world power."[32] The Commission would be composed of seven "well-qualified judges of the fine arts" appointed by the president who would serve without compensation for four-year terms. The chair and vice-chair are elected by the members. Daniel Burnham was appointed as chair of the original CFA; he was joined by several others including Frederick Law Olmsted, Jr and Charles Moore (who had been secretary to Senator James McMillan and was also closely associated with the McMillan Plan). Perhaps for this reason, the CFA became the "custodian" of the McMillan Plan – essentially the successor to the Park Commission. The McMillan Plan, which had been stored for several years in the basement of the Library of Congress, was moved to CFA building. Meetings were held monthly, as they are today. Many Commission members were and are architects, planners, landscape architects, sculptors, and painters. Among the duties of the CFA was to advise upon the location of statues, fountains, and monuments and to review the execution of these by the selected artists. Subsequent executive orders enlarged the scope of the CFA duties to include advising on plans for any public buildings erected by the government in the District of Columbia. Congress has also enacted legislation to allow the CFA to regulate the height, exterior design, and construction of private and semi-private buildings in certain areas of the capital. Importantly, the CFA approves and advises and reviews the aesthetic quality of designs but it does not actually design; in effect, it "acts as a quality check for design purview."[33]

The CFA's first project was to review the location and the design for the Lincoln Memorial. While today the building is considered beautifully sited and universally admired, minutes of CFA meetings disclose that many months of deliberation were necessary, more with regard to the site than to the design of the building itself.[34] What is noteworthy, however, is how involved the CFA was in inspecting the models and drawings and even working closely with architects on the selection of materials (such as the type of marble or granite to be selected) and other details including the spacing of trees. Its work on the Lincoln Memorial included the memorial itself, the landscape development of the area including the approaches to the memorial from parks and parkways, and the building of the long rectangular Reflecting Pool.[35] Such involvement helps explain why the design and construction of memorials on the Mall can take decades. Similarly, the Jefferson Memorial took several decades to be approved and built. It was first proposed in 1914, but no action was taken. A proposal came before the CFA again in 1934 when President Roosevelt asked the Commission members to study the possibility of locating a statue of Jefferson at the apex of the Federal Triangle. A second suggestion was also made that the statue be placed on the Mall at 7th Street; a third site mentioned was to the south of the Washington Monument, which, according to the McMillan Plan, was to be dedicated to the founding fathers. Commission members at the time assumed that, if they selected this third site, the Jefferson Memorial would be only one of several memorials erected there.[36] They approved the site where the Jefferson Memorial stands today; however, Jefferson stood alone for many decades until the memorial to fellow Virginian George Mason was completed in 2002.

The projects reviewed by the CFA since its formation number some ten thousand (in 1911 there were forty-one submissions; today there are four to five hundred each year).[37] Sometimes projects involve the realities of the Mall's urban setting: the construction of cross roads and lighting, for example. Above all, the CFA has been guided by the McMillan Plan, to which it tries to adhere as much as possible. Often the CFA will make a decision to do nothing until they there is a plan it can approve enthusiastically.[38] Susan Kohler, historian to the CFA, has shown that each of the projects involved considerable discussion, debate, compromise, and revision. CFA commissioners were very attuned to issues of expense and politics, and while they often would have preferred to implement the design as originally articulated, they also realized that there were limited funds available.

National Capital Planning Commission

In 1924 Congress established the National Capital Park Commission, which in 1952 was renamed the National Capital Planning Commission. The NCPC consists of twelve members (three appointed by the president, two appointed by the mayor of Washington, and seven ex-officio representatives from Executive Branch agencies, such as the Department of Interior, the chairmen of the House and Senate committees with D.C. oversight responsibility, the mayor of Washington, and the chairman of the Washington city council. Initially, the NCPC was mandated to acquire lands to complete a regional park, parkway, and playground system for the national capital, which was a major step in realizing the objectives of the 1901 McMillan Plan.[39] Congress later extended its responsibilities to include comprehensive planning, designating the NCPC as the central planning agency for the federal and D.C. governments.

One of the first projects undertaken by the NCPC was to coordinate the grading of the entire length of the Mall and to plant the formal rows of elm trees. In 1928 the NCPC produced a study of the Mall area that included subtle adjustments to the cross-axis through the White House at the Oval. By 1929, the Lincoln Memorial was completed and Arlington Memorial Bridge that linked the memorial to Virginia and Arlington Cemetery was under construction.

By law, no new development on federal land in Washington, D.C., including the Mall, can proceed without commission approval. The NCPC reviews and approves federal and District of Columbia master plans and construction proposals, approves the location and design for commemorative works (in conjunction with the CFA), and evaluates and adopts an annual Federal Capital Improvements Program. It also reviews local, state, and regional plans and policies, including local proposed zoning and site-plan applications, for their impact on the federal establishment. It prepares regional plans and deals with highways, airports, sewerage, and drainage and water-supply issues. Examples of recent agenda items include the installation of perimeter-security cameras, plans for modifying entrances in buildings, and the revision of zoning regulations to allow the siting of the new Washington Nationals Baseball stadium on South Capitol Street.

The Politics of Federal Agencies

When either the CFA or NCPC receives a project submission, the planning and design staff analyse the proposal, consult with submitting agency planners, and prepare a recommendation. The CFA or NCPC may either accept or reject the project or make minor or major adjustments to it. At the NCPC, for example, the final Commission action on a proposal is usually a report to the submitting agency based on the executive director's recommendation and incorporating any Commission changes to that recommendation.[40] Importantly, the last step, the monthly meeting, is the *only* avenue for public comment and observation. However, some citizens groups claim that the public meeting is merely a formality since the Commission has already made its decision beforehand.

There have been long and extended debates about the appropriate architectural style for buildings and memorials on the Mall. In general, for the first half of the twentieth century, most of the members of the CFA and the NCPC agreed the Mall should remain fundamentally classical in character. This is not to say that the Mall never experienced radical modernist or abstract design: it did, beginning in the 1960s. The Hirshorn Museum and the National Air and Space Museum and the emergence of radical modernism were linked to the changing perception of Washington as an international or global city and America's unquestioned global leadership.[41]

Sometimes these agencies disagree. The CFA, for example, "waged a long battle with the Park Service reminding them that the trees [around the pool at the National Sculpture Garden] are to grow together finally as an architectural band."[42] Sometimes the disagreements are more substantial. Inter-agency conflict occurred with the design for the Vietnam Veterans Memorial. The CFA felt that Maya Lin's original design was complete; but the secretary of the interior (on behalf of the Park Service) had endorsed a compromise that included new elements such as a sculpture and flagpole. The chairman of the CFA at that time, J. Carter Brown, recalled that "if we refused to compromise, there was the risk that whole design would be discarded."[43] Months of discussions ensued about the location of flag and statue and about at what scale they should be. Wrote Brown:

> Proponents of the changes wanted the flagpole on top at the apex [of the Wall], which I felt would look a little like a flag on a golf course. I knew we could always find a place for an American flag, as long as it did not become a precedent for having them scattered all over the Mall above every monument. They also wanted the

sculpture place in front of the apex ... I did not think it was fair to the piece, on its own merits, to place it in the middle of a great space. It would be diminished, and it would compromise the very essence of Lin's design. Furthermore, this use of axiality was absurd, because one approaches the memorial either from the east or from the Lincoln Memorial and the southwest. So in the letter to the secretary we hinted at a solution incorporating both pieces as part of the entrance.[44]

The key agencies – the CFA, the NCPC, and even the Park Service – are highly politicized. The politicization of these agencies begins in the appointments process. That process involves two steps: first the selection and nomination by the president (and White House staff); and second, the confirmation by the Senate.[45] Many administration jobs are still regarded as an important part of the elections-rewards system. These selections provide the president with an opportunity to reward those who have supported him in the past and to broaden his base of support within his own party, with interest groups, and in Congress.[46] Appointments are an occasion to establish the character and direction of the administration. Members of the CFA and NCPC (and other planning and review agencies) are composed of members who are appointed by either Congress or the Executive Branch. The members of the CFA are all presidential appointments of four-year terms. At the NCPC the president appoints three ex-officio citizens, one from Maryland, Virginia, and the District. Executive Branch agencies are represented on the Commission by ex-officio representatives from the secretary of interior, the secretary of defense, and the General Services Administration.

The CFA and NCPC have ambiguous and somewhat contradictory roles. Neither of these agencies thinks that it really has any power. They have a history of not taking the initiative and of backing down to Congress. Some believe that Congress has disdain for the CFA and NCPC, casting them as scapegoats for ineffective plans and design controversies and as the impediments to change.[47] Rather than standing up to Congress, these agencies tend to validate through the sin of omission. They also tend to act deferentially towards other federal agencies, often ignoring the input of citizens or even respected professional organizations. One reason for this may be inherent to the review process. Those in federal agencies who want to accomplish things will scratch each other's backs in order to ensure that their future projects are also approved. This is also reinforced by the "cross pollination" effect – where many members serve ex officio on other boards. For example, as the designee of the secretary of interior, John Parsons, then associate regional director for the National Capital Region of the National Park Service, sat on both the CFA and the NCPC for many years.

Together, three key federal agencies, the Park Service, the CFA, and the NCPC, are the most important planning and review agencies for the Mall. All three are typically involved in any major changes to the Mall. Even the construction of a new food-concession stand near the Lincoln Memorial required the approval of all three agencies, each of which holds its own review meetings and consultations. But because the original 1791 Mall plan is open to interpretation, there can be multiple and competing ideas. This can occur within the agencies, between the agencies and Congress, and sometimes between the public and the agencies. As a result, nearly every memorial or building's design and location has been disputed. And Mall development proceeds slowly or contentiously, if at all.

Nothing happens on the Mall without the involvement of both branches of government. No building is placed on the Mall without legislative approval, agency review, and, in some cases, federal appropriations.[48] And yet the fragmentation of management into numerous House and Senate committees does not necessarily dilute political power. A single powerful politician can affect the development of the Mall. For example, Senator Joseph Cannon of Illinois was able to delay the construction of the Lincoln Memorial for almost a decade because he believed that the memorial was being "relegated to a swamp" by the Potomac; similarly, Secretary of Treasury Andrew Mellon personally chose the architectural consultants for the Federal Triangle. Congress has a history of simultaneous indifference and interference. The Executive Branch, too, has contributed many layers of bureaucracy in the form of commissions, agencies, boards, and advisory councils. Through political appointments to important commissions and agencies such as the Park Service, the CFA, and the NCPC, it, too, exerts power. For some political appointees in agencies such as the CFA and NCPC, their primary concern is with higher political leadership, not necessarily the public at large. The end result of such fragmented management has led to the "the mess on the Mall." This neglect underscores the tragedy of the commons.

(Mis)managing the Mall?

The Mall is a complex public place under the confusing jurisdiction of numerous House and Senate committees as well as federal and local agencies.

As a result, it faces numerous planning and public-use challenges explored throughout this book, including the pressure for new memorials, the issue of security, the quality of public use and access, public transportation, and comprehensive planning.

Because the Mall is a geographically divided and administratively split among many agencies, the dissemination of public information is not well coordinated. Events at the Capitol are not always coordinated with events near the Washington Monument. Frequently, the agencies do not speak to each other or coordinate their use of the Mall. One glaring absence is that the Park Service has not yet digitized the permit process for First Amendment demonstrations. Like many federal agencies and bureaucracies, the Park Service confronts a combination of insufficient information-technology resources and a lethargic bureaucracy that has lagged behind. Perhaps worse, there is no comprehensive "National Mall" web page on the Internet. A glance at the National Park Service web page features a calendar of events, including bike tours and walking tours but only those offered by the Park Service. To find out what is happening on the Mall with regard to the various Smithsonian museums and their outside courtyards, a visitor must access the Smithsonian calendar. And still other events are listed on web pages for the National Gallery, including its popular summer free jazz concerts in the sculpture garden. In the Internet age, online calendars, podcasts, and interactive maps could offer an exciting and novel way of experiencing the National Mall. However, WiFi exists only sporadically on the Mall and there is no consumer-friendly portal for access to Mall-related educational and informational materials that include event calendars, historic materials, or self-guided walking tours. The fact that no such "one stop" website and WiFi access exists reinforces the lack of coordination and inter-agency cooperation. It also underscores that there is no mechanism for the various jurisdictions to talk to one another and that there is no common purpose among the jurisdictions in treating the Mall as a unified whole.

The jurisdiction of multiple House and Senate committees also means that there is no unified financing of the Mall. Although the Park Service is the recipient of most of the appropriations, there is no overall funding scheme that covers maintenance, planning, and development. Perhaps because of this fragmented management and funding, the Mall lacks a vision. The last time a long-term comprehensive plan was developed for the Mall was the McMillan Plan of 1901.

A poorly managed Mall has generated a long list of important public-use needs that are currently not met. For example, it is hard to imagine, but until 2010 there was no comprehensive recycling program on the Mall. Park Service officials estimated that nearly twelve hundred tons of trash were collected daily on the Mall, half of which could be recycled but was not. In the summer of 2009 the Park Service studied the issue and in the fall of 2010 the Coca-Cola Company donated $1.1 million dollars to provide 320 recycling bins, along with recycling trailers for special events. While the program is to be applauded, it is appalling that it took forty years after the first Earth Day celebration (on the Mall, ironically) to install permanent recyclable containers on the Mall. The recycling program also highlights a new trend that many parks are embracing: public-private partnerships, where the "public" is the park and the "private" are individuals or corporations. I will explore this in more detail later in the chapter.

More problematically, there is no unified management of the Mall. Simply, there are too many House and Senate committees for Congress to have a complete picture of the competing demands and needs of the Mall. This is absolutely central: while many management structures are complex, there is usually one person or group of persons poised at the top. The Mall, in contrast, is treated as a collection of federal fiefdoms, and each custodian (Park Service, Smithsonian, NCPC, etc.) plans for the benefit of its separate interests. As scholars have noted, CPR problems can occur because of a fragmented institutional setting that necessitates cooperation between a considerable number of actors with highly varying norms, interests, and powers to act.[49] Problems related to organizational fragmentation exist between tiers of government. One possible consequence of institutional fragmentation may be that no one "owns the problem, and therefore no one takes responsibility for solving it."[50] The consequences are significant, as the following examples illustrate.

Contested Boundaries

As we have seen, the Park Service assumes that it has jurisdiction over the Mall. However, in reality, "the exact boundaries of the Mall may be subject to dispute."[51] The National Coalition to Save Our Mall claims that there is no statutory definition of "the Mall" and various managing agencies define it differently. Until recently, the Park Service asserted that the National Mall did not include the Capitol or Smithsonian grounds or the White House.[52] In some definitions, the Park Service called the Mall "the area west of the US Capitol between Madison and Jefferson drives from 1st to 14th street NW/SW" (this is essentially the grass area only and does not include the Washington Monument, the Lincoln or Jefferson memorials, or the Smithsonian and other museums).[53] Another definition of the Mall references the area "bounded on the north by Constitution Avenue, on the south by Independence Ave, by the Capitol on the east and 14th street on the west, prior to reaching the Washington Monument."[54] Thus, Park Service appeared to distinguish between the "National Mall" and "The Mall." It defined "The Mall" as only the strip of grass and trees in the centre panel of L'Enfant's original plan, the area called Reservation 1 (it is worth noting that, at that time, there was little land west of current-day 17th Street). However, to most Americans, the "National Mall" is the entire area stretching east to west from the Capitol to the Lincoln Memorial and north to south from the White House to the Jefferson Memorial. Yet for many years the Park Service published documents with different and even contradictory definitions of the Mall.[55] In part because of public discussion about uncertain boundaries, and the 2007 launch of an extensive planning effort to create a fifty-year comprehensive plan for the National Mall, the National Park Service refined its definition of the National Mall[56]: "Today, the term National Mall includes the area historical referred to as the Mall (which extends from the grounds of the U.S. Capitol to the Washington Monument), the Washington Monument, and West Potomac Park (including the Lincoln, Jefferson, Vietnam Veterans, Korean War Veterans, World War II and FDR memorials). The White House and President's Park, a unit of the national park system, is within the Reserve, but it not within the National Mall."[57]

These semantic subtleties are not insignificant, but rather indicative of a lingering uncertainty as to boundaries and hence jurisdiction. It may also be reason the Park Service has not been pressured to better coordinate with other federal agencies that share the Mall – the Park Service says that these agencies are not on the Mall as they define it. The Park Service assertion that it alone has jurisdiction over the Mall appears to be based on a definition that limits the Mall to the strip of grass and memorial parks under its jurisdiction but that excludes the Smithsonian museums, National Gallery of Art, the Capitol, and other nearby areas. In addition to confusion over the exact boundaries of the National Mall, official acreage is also uncertain. Official statements to Congress and in the press refer to the Mall as 650 acres, 700 acres, and even 725 acres.[58]

Unclear Directives

In 2003 the National Football League (NFL) held its season kick-off celebration, known as the NFL Extravaganza, on the National Mall. The season opener coincided with the introduction of a new soft drink by Pepsi-Cola. For three days, the NFL and Pepsi event obstructed much of the Mall and included football activities on the grass (that required a ticket) such as the Coors Light "Field Goal Kick" and the Pepsi Vanilla "Let If Fly" and widespread signage by corporate sponsors. A pre-game concert featured Britney Spears, Aerosmith, and Mary J. Blige. Jumbotron screens displayed various events, as well as the football game and its commercials. Was this event just a big commercial for the NFL and its sponsors? According to the National Park Service, the usual rules that prohibit commercial marketing on the Mall did not apply because the promotional aspects were "sponsor recognition," not advertising.[59]

The NFL's arrival on the Mall generated immediate and stinging criticism. Allowing the Mall to be used for commercial purposes has long been problematic and this event appeared particularly crass. One critic noted, "To be turning the Mall into a billboard is, I think, what all the people would recognize as a violation of the stewardship of the Park Service."[60] Then CFA Secretary Charles Atherton remarked, "I would say there's not a trace of any dignity to that space." The National Coalition to Save Our Mall argued that the NFL and television stations appeared to be making the decisions about how the Mall is to be used, that this set a dangerous precedent, and that the episode highlighted the urgent need to have a much broader discussion as to what the true parameters of the use of the Mall ought to be.[61]

Letters to the editors of both the *Washington Post* and *Washington Times* called for Congress to demand an explanation of who was responsible for allowing this event. One letter stated, "What can we expect to see next? A pitch for McDonald's at the Lincoln Memorial?"[62] Another, in the *New York Times*, noted that "Abe Lincoln's view down the National Mall should not include pop singer Britney Spears gyrating at a Pepsi-sponsored concert."[63] As outrage over the "NFL/Britney Spears Extravaganza on the Mall" continued, members of Congress demanded a hearing on the issue. Delegate Eleanor Holmes Norton said that the "spectacle crossed the line on balancing the use of treasured public spaces over commercialization."[64] Another member described the event as "the most extravagant misuse of the nation's front lawn in history."[65] Within two weeks, the Senate had taken up the issue. Senator Jeff Bingaman (D-New Mexico) condemned the Park Service and the Department of Interior for the "NFL fiasco on the Mall." He said: "There has been broad public agreement both in Washington and around the country [that] to allow the type of activity that occurred at these commercial events is a new low point in the storied history of the Mall. We need to act to prohibit increased commercialization in our national parks, and a good place to start is acting to protect the Mall."[66] Bingaman declared that the event "persuaded me that there is a real disconnect between what the Park Service and Interior Department is saying about not wanting commercial activities on the Mall and what they actually permit. I thought I would try to get something in the law that more specifically states the policies of the government."[67] He offered an amendment to the Interior Appropriations Bill (HR 2691) that would prohibit future commercial advertising on the Mall, and, in a 92 to 4 vote, the Senate backed his measure. The response is telling. This marked perhaps the first time since the 1901 McMillan Commission that the Senate had made policy specifically related to the Mall. It is also noteworthy that bad press and a publicity crisis can and does trigger quick political resolution. However, I am not convinced that the solution to confused or imprecise directives should be met with more laws and hearings and more bureaucracy.

Violating Public Interest: The Tourmobile Monopoly

A key component for any national park unit is to provide transportation services that allow visitors to move to and from and within the park. Although the story of the Tourmobile is now history, the Park Service's relationship with Tourmobile until 2012 underscores a long record of decisions that can arguably be described as bad for the public. Starting in 1969 and lasting until 2012, the Park Service allowed and encouraged a single-source contract for public transportation and interpretation on the National Mall, Landmark Service, Inc. (Tourmobile). Tourmobile provided an interpretive shuttle service that included the National Mall, the Capitol, Union Station, Arlington Cemetery, the Kennedy Center, the Frederick Douglass Home, and the George Washington Home, located about fourteen miles south of D.C. in Mount Vernon, Virginia.

In 2011 Tourmobile fares ran $32 for adults and $16 for children (aged 3–11) per day. For a family of four with two teenaged kids, a one-day tour of the Mall would cost about $128. An elderly or disabled war veteran who wished to visit several memorials faced the choice between walking or paying $32 to Tourmobile. These were not reasonable rates for visitors to the Mall, nor were these reasonable public-transit options. Although the Park Service had final approval over the rates charged by Tourmobile, there was not much incentive for the Park Service to keep the costs low. This was because the Park Service received a certain percentage of the revenue generated by Tourmobile. It is estimated that the Park Service received $330,000 a year in concession fees.[68]

Given the Mall's urban location, it would be reasonable to assume that there were a variety of public-transportation options to getting to the Mall and getting around it. However, an independent transportation study by George Mason University's School of Public Policy in 2008 found that the western portion of the Mall (between the Washington Monument and the Lincoln Memorial) was not accessible by public transit, nor was it easy to use public transit to circulate around or through the area.[69] Access to the Mall from the greater Washington region via public transit on weekends was very limited and inadequate. Even parking was inadequate and inconsistent for private automobiles as well as for tour buses. In short, there were few public-transit options, and accessibility remained a challenge for most visitors.

Prior to 2012, public-transit options were limited because the Park Service had in effect prevented Mall access to both public and private operators. The Park Service operated under the assumption that, because it had an exclusive contract with Tourmobile, Tourmobile should be the only transit service for the public within the Mall and surrounding areas. Because the Park Service manages parking lots and street parking within the Mall area, it created a de facto zone of exclusivity for Tourmobile. This negatively affected many other private-tour operators, including the L'il Red Trolley, the Old Town Trolley, D. Ducks, and the D.C. Downtown Circulator. The latter is worth noting. The D.C. Circulator is a *public* bus system that began operating in 2005 to provide additional means of mass transit in the area of the National Mall and the city core. It was conceived as a way to encourage visitors to the Mall to venture downtown. Fares range from $1 per ride to $3 per day (compared to the $32 Tourmobile fares). The Park Service prevented all of the private operators and also the D.C. Circulator from posting signs about their shuttles on the Mall or moving through it (they are forced to move around the Mall on its perimeter streets, Constitution and Independence, but may not stop on cross streets). For example, the D.C. Circulator Red route, which went between the Convention Center and the Mall, could stop only on

7th street outside the Mall. 7th Street is about one-half mile from the Washington Monument and one-half mile from the Capitol. This is was as close to the major visitor destinations as the Circulator was allowed to go – it was forbidden from the western area of the Mall near the Lincoln Memorial. Restricting public transit in such a way is also a violation of contract, since government rules state that concession contracts cannot be an exclusive right to provide all or certain types of visitor services in a park area (36 C.F.R. §51.77.) And yet public statements by a Park Service official suggest that the Park Service viewed the contract with Tourmobile as an exclusive one: "It's an awkward situation ... We have a concessionaire who by law has full rights within the park. It's not allowed for anyone else by Metro [at its Smithsonian station] to collect fares ... It's not our intent to have an insular park in the center of the city ... But currently, Tourmobile views the Circulator as competition."[70]

Although the D.C. Office of Planning and the D.C. Downtown BID (supporters of the D.C. Circulator) were frustrated with the lack of public transit and could have filed a lawsuit against the practice, they were advised that they had no jurisdiction over the Mall (it is not clear that this is true, but the D.C. government assumes it is). Too bad, because by April 2011 D.C. Downtown BID had pulled the plug on the D.C. Circulator Mall route, citing weak revenue and poor ridership. Though private operators could have made a case that the Tourmobile monopoly had caused "harm" in the way of revenue, few of them appeared willing to take the matter to court. This may be in part because, in the long run, challenging the Park Service might make their situation worse. As a result, Tourmobile remained the unchallenged sole provider of transportation. An investigation by the law firm of Gibson, Dunn, and Crutcher concluded that the Tourmobile monopoly was a violation of government laws regarding contracting procedures in two ways: first, the lack of a competitive bid, and second, the cumulative term of the contract.[71] Its report noted that in 2009 the Park Service renewed the Tourmobile contract without a competitive bidding process because the Park Service claimed that it could be renewed "upon satisfactory performance," although the Park Service was unable to provide documentation of performance. This is not the only report to cast a highly critical eye on Park Service practices: in 2008 a report by the Office of the Inspector General, U.S. Department of Interior, concluded that the department (and by extension the Park Service) had a "culture that values expediency in contracting over protecting both *the best interest of the public* and the accountability, integrity and transparency in Departmental acquisition practices."[72] The report noted that there was a marked preference across the agency towards sole-source contracting that circumvented competition; that justifications for such contracts were inadequate or non-existent; and that small businesses were not given opportunities to compete. One of the park units evaluated was the National Capital Parks, which include the Mall.

The example of Tourmobile highlights that the Park Service often blatantly disregards the "competition selection process" mandated by the National Park Service Concessions Management Improvement Act of 1998. This act stipulates that concessions contracts, including renewals or extensions, must be awarded through a public solicitation process. Most federal agencies award contracts for ten years or less; Tourmobile had its contract in place for several decades. The Gibson, Dunn, and Crutcher investigation concluded that allowing Tourmobile to offer sole transportation at the Mall was not in the best interest of the public.

While the Park Service may say the right things about being "cooperative," it tends to ignore studies such as those by Gibson, Dunn and Crutcher and George Mason University that show otherwise.[73] That the Park Service continued to allow Tourmobile to operate as the only shuttle service on the Mall despite these findings reflects either management incompetence regarding the contract or wilful disregard of the public's transit-options needs. Each of these possibilities supports the claim that, despite the Park Service's best efforts, it does not always act as a good steward or custodian of the Mall.

This type of bureaucratic mentality also initially led the Park Service to prohibit Capital Bikeshare, a low-cost public bike-share program ($5 a day), from installing a station on the Mall. Park Service spokesman William Line explained that a bike station on the Mall would violate the National Historic Preservation Act because it would be seen as going against the historical purpose of the Mall and its monuments. Weeks of scathing editorials in the *Washington Post* made the Park Service rethink this decision and allow Bikeshare stations to be installed. Two stations were completed in 2012. Today, hundreds of visitors and residents ride Bikeshare bikes on the Mall. But the resistance to public transit and Bikeshare shows that the Park Service has difficulty recognizing the vastly different role that parks play in urban settings.[74]

As demands for other transit options – such as Capital Bikeshare, the D.C. Circulator, and pedicabs – continued to increase, the Park Service finally terminated its contract with Tourmobile in late 2011. The bizarre forty-two-year Tourmobile monopoly finally ended. Four years later, in the spring of 2015, the D.C. Circulator revived its low-cost service.

The "Mess" on the Mall Revisited

The Park Service announced in June 2008 that the Mall had more than $350 million in deferred maintenance.[75] With some twenty-five million visitors each year (more visitors than the Yellowstone, Yosemite, and Grand Canyon parks combined), the decay on the Mall from wear and tear was massive and ongoing.[76] As one Park Service official noted, "if you had 25 million people coming through your front yard, it might not look so nice either."[77]

The Mall's disrepair has been evident for years, but it generated heightened publicity in the spring and summer of 2008 following a congressional inquiry. This hearing also produced several follow-up stories the *Washington Post*, one of which, prominently placed on the front page, called the Mall "America's Unkempt Front Yard."[78] The *Washington Business Journal* featured an eight-page cover story called the "Mall of Shame." By July, as the issue became more widely discussed and debated, CBS News had aired a story on the Mall called "Gone to Seed," CNN had broadcast an item titled "National Mall in Monumental Disrepair," and other newspapers around the country had also run stories on the subject.[79]

Some attribute the Mall's decline to a massive increase in usage and an inadequate maintenance budget; limited resources have plagued the Park Service for decades. For the Park Service, a "restoration wish list" for the Mall includes $50 million for turf renovation, $5 million to replace bathrooms, $25 million to make repairs to the Lincoln Reflecting Pool (where the stone walls are crumbling), $3 million to replace the Washington Monument visitors' tent, and $7 million to move and restore the Lock Keeper's House at 17th and Constitution streets. D.C. Delegate Eleanor Holmes Norton decried the state of Mall, noting that it "got this way through complete and total inattention. You've got to keep the lawns mowed. But if nobody's looking, you don't have to do much more than that."[80] Few Washington insiders seemed to care and until recently there hasn't been a vocal enough constituency for the Mall at either the local or the national level.

What are the reasons for this maintenance backlog? Part of the problem is related to system-wide issues for the entire national park system. National parks scholar Lary Dilsaver explained that congressional interference makes budget appropriations complex; for example, a congressman or senator may request that the Park Service carry out research or undertake a project for which it had not planned or budgeted. The result is that the Park Service feels pressured to deplete or shift maintenance resources to congressional pet projects to satisfy the oversight committees.[81] During the Reagan administration, for instance, the Park Service sometimes received a bigger budget than requested, but this often included "add-ons" that were earmarked for projects or new parks or even local economic development projects, something former Park Service director James Ridenour wittily called "park barrel politics."[82] He noted that in 1993 Congress actually cut the operating budget by $47 million but added on more than $90-million worth of construction funds the Park Service didn't request.[83] "You might think the Park Service would welcome all that extra money, but most of it was earmarked for a congressmen's pet project and couldn't be used for things the parks needed most."[84] Despite the oftentimes conservative budget requests, the Park Service does fairly well in securing funds for new projects, but not as well in getting money to take care of what it already has. The budgetary cutbacks of recent years have compelled many agencies to "trim the fat" but after a while they are not trimming the fat but hitting the bone and marrow.[85] Budget add-ons can also subtly undermine the budget process itself since they encourage playing games with the process.[86] Dwight Rettie, a national park expert, notes that appropriations are inadequate in most agencies, and that the growth of programs budgets or staffs for any agency is often met with dismay, particularly because the political climate during the last several decades has been highly critical of a "growing government."[87] He says that, while appropriations for the national park system have increased overall, many within the Park Service believe that real needs have far out-distanced appropriations and that large gaps continue to exist and even grow.

Another reason for the maintenance backlog involves the politics of creating the budget in the first place. Once the Park Service director has prepared a budget, it is reviewed and modified by the secretary of the interior; from there it is reviewed by the Office of Management and Budget (OMB). The numbers often change as the process wends its way from the initial Park Service request to the Department of Interior request and to the official presidential budget. Once the budget reaches Congress, it is often used to make the Executive Branch look bad for requesting so little (or too much), and yet there isn't enough money to take care of the true and total needs of the Park Service. It is rare that the Park Service receives the entire budget requested and inadequate funding has been an ongoing issue. Because the Park Service has no inventory or program documenting long-range needs, no long-range budget program has ever been done for the national park system.[88] In the last twenty years, new mandates have emerged for hazardous wastes, species management, safety and working conditions, and access for people with disabilities – all of which has increased operating expenses. The Park Service notes that budget increases have not occurred at a rate high enough to meet the backlog of needs.

Once the Park Service receives the funding, it must allocate it to the various park units, another chance for institutional politics to enter the process. Dwight Rettie has argued that many park superintendents believe that the allocation of funds is often based not on outlined criteria but on personal networks or the pleading of people on friendly terms with the regional director.[89] Others believe that new units added to the system "scavenge" funds and staff from existing park budgets.[90] Former Park Service director James Ridenour has referred to this as "thinning the blood" of the park system.[91]

Another reason for the maintenance backlog for the Mall specifically is that it is often the stage for many unforeseen and unbudgeted activities that deplete funding resources and delay the ability of the Park Service to complete projects and programs. Unanticipated events and parades, accommodating group activities such as political demonstrations, and overseeing the arrivals and departures of world leaders all cost the Park Service money. To meet these immediate expenses, the Park Service takes from the maintenance budget. Lastly, unlike some national parks, the Mall generates little revenue of its own. There are no "gate fees" as there are at some national parks. Nearly everything on the Mall – from visiting the memorials and monuments to taking guided tours – is free.

One reason for the inability to allocate money to Mall is that shortfalls in the appropriations process in general are often made up through the regrettable process of earmarks. Yet, in the case of the Mall, which lacks a powerful representative or senator, earmarks are difficult to achieve. Earmark data is nearly impossible to discover; only since 2008 has Congress begun disclosing earmark recipients. Still, some familiar with the system say that they do not remember any congressional earmarks for the Mall in decades. An analysis of congressional spending since 2005 found that the Mall has been at a disadvantage in competing for extra funds doled out by lawmakers, compared with sites that are represented by powerful members of Congress.[92] A few examples tell the tale.

In 2008 the Senate killed a $3.5-million earmark for Mall maintenance but did approve $123,000 to restore a Mother's Day Shrine in West Virginia (home to then Senator Robert Byrd, chairman of the Senate Appropriations Committee). Another 2008 bill to appropriate $100 million for Mall repairs also failed. In January 2009 the long-neglected backlog in maintenance seemed to be over. The White House and Congress were paying attention to the need for Mall restoration and the Obama administration had included $200 million in funding for renovation of the Mall as part of the American Recovery and Reinvestment Act (the "stimulus package"). However, at the last minute, the funding was pulled. Opponents sneered that the proposal was excessive. Republican Representative Jeb Hensarling of Texas stated that Mall funding wasn't an emergency and House Republican whip Eric Cantor of Virginia criticized efforts to "help upkeep the grass on the lawns of Washington."[93] In fact, the money would have been used to repair the crumbling walls of the Lincoln Reflecting Pool, to restore the World War I Memorial, and to shore up the sinking seawall around the Jefferson Memorial. Republicans refused to vote for the funding.

A few months later, in April 2009, the American Recovery and Reinvestment Act authorized a $750-million outlay of stimulus funds for the entire national park system, which the Interior Department claimed would help create or retain about 30,000 jobs.[94] Ultimately, Congressman Jim Moran, a Mall advocate and, importantly, chair of the House Appropriations Committee, was able to secure $58 million in stimulus for the Mall. It was speculated that, because of Moran's position on the House Appropriations Committee, he had enough power and authority to get at least *some* stimulus money approved. Interior Secretary Ken Salazar instructed that $58 million be directed to the Mall for three projects: the rehabilitation of the Lincoln Reflecting Pool; the restoration of the once-elegant D.C. War Memorial; and repairs to the sinking seawalls near the Thomas Jefferson Memorial plaza. Although the money did not come close to meeting the more than $400 million in deferred maintenance, it was a start.

New Solutions: A Public-Private Partnership

Years of deferred maintenance place the Park Service in no position to restore the Mall with its current budget. Continued political indifference, or even hostility, has killed appropriations legislation and resulted in only a small fraction of the needs being funded. A new solution has emerged. The Park Service has embraced the discourse of public-private partnerships as the answer to the money problem. There are public-private partnerships in numerous national parks, including Golden Gate, Grand Canyon, and Yellowstone. In 2007 the Trust for the National Mall was created and designated the "official private partner" of the Park Service. Its mission is to:

- support the National Park Service;
- raise the funds to maintain and restore the National Mall;
- connect visitors to the National Mall's rich history; and
- develop engaging programs and events that will educate and inspire current and future generations.

To date, the most important function of the Trust for the National Mall has been to raise funds for restoration, revitalization, and maintenance. In short, the Trust is raising money that *should* have been allocated by Congress. Projects have included new signage, improving grass and general irrigation, new recycling bins, and park furniture. Added to the estimated $350 million in deferred-maintenance backlog, $100 million is needed for infrastructure improvements, such as repairing or building additional food and restroom facilities, and another $50 million for educational programming. In the summer of 2008, the Trust for the National Mall launched a new campaign, "Help Save America's Front Yard," in conjunction with the broader Park Service Centennial Challenge.[95] In 2011 the Trust launched its $350-million Mall campaign with former first lady Laura Bush serving as chair. Ultimately the Trust wants to raise a total of $700 million to cover all deferred maintenance as well as establish an endowment for future projects and needs. However, it remains to be seen how successful the Trust will be at securing funds for less than glamorous maintenance projects such as restroom repairs. As of 2014, the Trust had raised money to restore the Japanese Lantern on the Tidal Basin, rebuild the Lincoln Reflecting Pool, retrofit street lighting along some of the Mall with LED energy-saving bulbs, and, following a 2011 earthquake, restore the Washington Monument. Park Service Superintendent Robert Vogel said that "thanks to this support, the Washington Monument shines a little brighter, the newly restored grass lawn is staying a little greener, and the history of the World War II Memorial is reaching a little further. Our successful public-private partnership with the Trust for the National Mall shows how much can happen to help advance the parks' mission."[96]

The Trust for the National Mall is one of many recent examples in which public-private partnerships have been seen as a new model of governance for public space. The model was first tried in 1980 in the aftermath of the fiscal crisis in New York City, when the city Parks Department faced severely constricted funds. The deterioration of Central Park was attributed to both mismanagement and cutbacks in the maintenance budget; the conclusion was that municipal officials could not be trusted with public property of such an exemplary public space.[97] As a result, the Central Park Conservancy was created, a public-private partnership for the provision and management of what had been a public institution.[98] Since then, numerous other "park partnerships" (usually called trusts or conservancies) have been formed at many national parks, including the Yellowstone Foundation, the Yosemite Conservancy, the Grand Canyon Trust, and the Golden Gate National Parks Conservancy in San Francisco. These are considered non-profit partners but they represent the "private" side of the public-private partnership in that they raise money from private-partner contributions that are voluntary and discretionary. Critics of public-private partnership argue that this paradigm for administering local public spaces removes their governance from direct public accountability and their use from an open political process.[99]

While there is no doubt that the Trust for the National Mall will play an important role in assisting the Park Service, an underlying question remains: Why should a premier public space like the Mall require a private partner? Is it not the role of government to provide the necessary money in the first place? Are we letting Congress off the hook for its financial neglect by raising the money privately? Consider the next example.

Mallapalooza 2015: Déjà Vu All Over Again?

In September 2015 the Trust for the National Mall organized the Landmark Music Festival, also known as "Mallapalooza." The Trust called this event "a monumental two-day event to raise awareness for hundreds of millions of backlogged repairs needed for the historic site in the nation's capital." Forty bands performed on five stages over two days. The festival also included a food court, which featured D.C. favourites such as Ben's Chili Bowl, Shake Shack, and Old Ebbitt Grill as well as dishes prepared by celebrity chef José Andrés. More than fifty thousand people attended the event. The Trust for the National Mall stated that it intended to use the festival as a way of educating the Millennial generation about the history and significance of the Mall. To this end, the Trust had a tent where videos were shown highlighting the history of protests on the Mall and documenting how monuments had been built in the park over time. It also asked concert-goers to create their own virtual monument for a cause or person that inspired them. According to the Trust, more than $570,000 was raised for the Mall, some of which was to be devoted to deferred-maintenance issues.[100] How did it accomplish this? There was an admissions charge.

The price to attend for a single day was $105; a two-day pass cost $175. And for those who were wanted VIP passes, $900 would get access to air-conditioned restrooms and spa treatments. Clearly, tickets were not cheap. The decision to charge admission to the music festival troubled many who saw this as potentially setting a precedent about charging to attend events on the Mall, a place that is supposed to be free and open to the public. Certainly, the Mall needed the money. But this event, much like the 2003 NFL Extravaganza, raises questions about how to strike a balance between commercialism and privatizing the Mall, on the one hand, and appropriate use of the space and public access, on the other. How can one justify, for example, saying "no" to spectacles like the NFL Extravaganza but "yes" to the Landmark Music Festival? In the future, could there be other paid concerts or events elsewhere on the Mall? Robert Vogel, director of the National Capital Region of the Park Service, tried to reassure people that this was unlikely since the Park Service would permit only events that provide "a meaningful association between the park area and the event and that contribute to visitor understanding about the significance of the park area."[101]

The 2015 "Mallapalooza" sparked, yet again, another conversation about the appropriate use of the Mall, specifically, how decisions are made about use and access, and the tension between raising money for the Park Service while maintaining access in a park that does not typically close off areas to the public. It also underscored the "new normal": the Park Service and its partner, the Trust, are looking for ways to raise money for deferred maintenance because they know that Congress is unlikely to do the right thing any time soon by funding the parks appropriately.

The National Mall – Tragedy of the Commons?

The challenges to managing the National Mall are substantial. It is a place that is a victim of both its popularity and its status as a political orphan. The complexity of management and the layers of bureaucracy create tremendous political pressure along with competing objectives and practices. There is no single agency considering the needs of the Mall that treats the site as a unified whole. There is no comprehensive vision for the Mall's long-term future. The layers of bureaucracy and the strong federal presence have created their own version of a bureaucratic tragedy of the commons. This critique of fragmented management is not intended to be more "bureaucrat-bashing" or a validation of a grossly negative portrayal of government as a whole and bureaucracy by implication.[102] Rather, my objective is to underline the significant challenges in managing this very important public space.

Although there is no "one best way," there are approaches that can enhance and protect common space. One important trend has been increased public participation in public-space management. Scholars have noted that decentralization and increased participation are effective. According to political scientist Elinor Ostrom, when participants themselves have input into the governing structures of parks, the outcome is a better form of governance.[103] Poor management can result from a top-down approach such as that taken in the case of the Mall. Currently, public participation in the planning and development of the Mall seems an afterthought more than anything else.

I return briefly to the model of the tragedy of the commons. In the wake of Hardin's essay, others have discussed how to legislate appropriate use of the commons. In order to prevent tragedy, many models suggest that managing access should consider the exclusion of others from using the resource. Averting a tragedy involves restraining both consumption and access. However, the Mall is, by definition and function, a public space; restricting access is not feasible, nor is it the answer to poor management. Neither is more legislation. As this chapter has detailed, the outcome of poor Mall management stems not from fragmented management per se but from fragmented management that is often riddled with conflicting interests, incoherent policy, and, sometimes, outright disregard. The Mall is afflicted with *over*-governance and poor coordination, and without a clear single agency "in charge," each individual committee, agency, and commission follows its mandates to the exclusion of the collective good of this public space. At the same time, embracing the public-private partnership model may not be the best solution either. The stewards of the Mall – Congress and federal agencies – have not done a good enough job. We need to have a larger public discussion about the Mall and how it should be managed and developed. Other units in the national park system have acknowledged the need to define a more viable management structure in order to deal with the unique circumstances they face at the local and regional levels.[104] It is time for us to consider such changes.

PART II   USE AND DEVELOPMENT PRESSURES

The chapters in this section focus on public-space use and development pressures on the Mall. Public spaces can be used for many purposes: recreation and play, contemplation, celebration, protest, and commemoration. On the Mall, all of these uses co-exist. However, recent trends in use and development have begun to affect the Mall's aesthetics, symbolism, and access. This section considers two prominent use and development trends: commemoration and security.

Commemoration

Scholars argue that the last three decades have witnessed the emergence of a memorial culture. The impulse to commemorate is part of a broader social reconstruction of national identity in America. Cultural historian Erika Doss observes that "contemporary America is deeply engaged in 'memorial mania,' a national obsession with issues of memory and history and an urgent, excessive desire to secure those issues with various forms of public commemoration."[1] She notes that war memorials, especially, are flourishing. This current obsession follows a period when American culture was largely disinterested in memory. However, "with the construction of the Vietnam Veterans Memorial on the Mall in 1982, it seemed as if the mourning and memory that had been held in check were suddenly released in a national embrace of remembering."[2] On the Mall, the result has been numerous new memorials and museums.

Seen in a critical light, the impulse to commemorate has created "memorial fever" and a rush to commemorate events or people too quickly. Although federal laws stipulate that a memorial or monument may not be erected on federal public land until at least twenty-five years have passed since the event took place or the individual died, the "rush to commemorate" has not abated; instead, it has become a "right." For example, conservatives proposed a Ronald Reagan memorial while Reagan was still alive (an odd spin on "commemoration" since the word is defined as an act of honouring "the memory of someone or some event"). Commemoration is happening quickly these days. There was a rapid process of commemoration following the 1995 bombing of the Alfred P. Murrah Federal Building in Oklahoma City. The explosion, which destroyed the entire front of the building, killed 168 people, including 15 children who were in the daycare centre. Within days of the bombing, the mayor's office, the governor's office, non-profit agencies, and citizens of Oklahoma City began to receive suggestions, ideas, and offers of donations related to the creation of a memorial. Within a few months, Oklahoma City Mayor Ron Norick appointed a 350-member Memorial Task Force charged with developing an appropriate memorial to honour those touched by the event. Within five years, the memorial had been designed and dedicated. Similarly, before the dust and smoke cleared from the Lower Manhattan skyline after the terrorist attacks of 9/11, politicians, scholars, and newspaper editorialists talked about what kind of monument or memorial should be built at what has become known as "ground zero."[3] Marita Sturkin has argued that, in some cases, commemoration has been confused with healing a national trauma, and that the rush to commemorate has resulted in memorials that are more about tourism and consumerism (e.g., 9/11 teddy bears or key rings that can be bought at the memorial gift store) than remembering tragedies in a meaningful way.[4]

Today, the Mall is the preferred location for the expression of national memory and national identity, a site of national commemoration for individuals as well as events in U.S. history. Since the 1980s, seven new memorials have been constructed on the Mall, including the Vietnam Veterans Memorial, the Korean War Memorial, the Franklin Delano Roosevelt Memorial, the George Mason Memorial, the World War II Memorial, and the recently completed Martin Luther King, Jr Memorial. Two museums have been added: the Museum of the American Indian and the approved (and under construction) Museum of African American History and Culture. Two more memorials have been approved but not yet constructed: the National Liberty Memorial (also known as the Black Revolutionary War Patriots Memorial) and the John Adams Memorial. Yet there continues to be proposals for new memorials. Women, who still lack a presence on the Mall in the form of statuary, have made their presence known by marching in protest on several occasions, such as the march of the suffragist movement in the early twentieth century and more recently the Million Mom March; the gay community has been moving from the margins to the centre with protest marches and the AIDS Quilt display. Every year Congress reviews bills for new memorials in the Monumental Core. Indeed, even in the face of $350 million in deferred maintenance, it seems willing to approve new memorials, each of which will be inordinately expensive and, once completed, will add to the maintenance budget. Is our commemorative culture so politically powerful that Congress lacks the political will to deny memorials, or to create a budget that will support the maintenance needs of a Mall with more and more memorials?

The pressure for new memorials can reshape the use and symbolism of the Mall – what are some of the impacts, both positive and negative?

Chapter 4, which documents the building of the Martin Luther King, Jr Memorial, argues that this memorial is an indication that our commemorative culture has become more inclusive, making "space," both metaphorically and literally, for the commemoration of the civil rights movement in U.S. history and, by extension, the contributions of African Americans. This is a positive trend that expands the American story to include minorities and gives new voices a place on the Mall. At the same time, the MLK Memorial also underscores a more problematic trend: the escalating cost of memorials on the Mall. Memorials cost hundreds of millions of dollars, and this has shifted strategies around fund-raising: corporate sponsorship is now imperative. It is not clear if corporate sponsorship has influenced either memorial design or location, but we have yet to discuss this potential. Is such sponsorship in the nation's premier public space acceptable, particularly because this is a national park?

Chapter 5 considers the consequences of this new commemorative culture for public space. In particular, the chapter recounts the controversy and debate over the World War II Memorial, completed in 2004. The controversy was less about design and more about site location. The debate focused on the loss of open space and whether the location selected would interrupt the established narrative of the Mall. From the debate and surrounding discourse, it appears that there was not much value placed on the Mall's open space; nor do those seeking new memorials acknowledge that each new memorial will alter open space. I argue that the increasing value placed on commemoration as opposed to the Mall's other uses (such as recreation or protest) reflects how pressure for commemoration can significantly affect public space. In the case of the World War II Memorial, the trade-off was the loss of 7.4 acres of open space on the Mall. If the trend for commemoration continues, we need to ensure a more open and thoughtful discussion about what is gained and what is lost with the construction of new memorials. Given that the Mall is finite space, these are important considerations.

Security and Fortification

Chapter 6 considers another trend in the development and use of public space: security and fortification. Since 11 September 2001, security in the United States has pre-empted concerns about access to public space in many cities, despite growing debate on the issue. Military and geopolitical security has penetrated into the practices of governance, design, and planning.[5] Much of the debate on the fortification of "public space" has focused not on genuine public spaces but on space that acts as a conduit for expressions of social, economic, and political change and contestation – for example, shopping malls, urban gardens, or private space such as gated communities.[6] Unlike other public-space security plans, changes to the Mall can occur only with federal approval. This is one reason why an examination of the Mall's security plan is important: that plan sits within a wider context of national discourse on security and fortification.

In a post-September 11th world, there is the discursive paradox of both freedom and hyper-security reflected on the Mall. Fortification was a trend in Washington, D.C., before the events of 9/11, but, in the years afterwards, security and fortification took on heightened significance. The National Capital Planning Commission's comprehensive security plan coordinates security planning in monuments, memorials, and public space in the Monumental Core area. The plan is, however, a fundamental reorganization of physical and symbolic space. It provides a glimpse of the mindset of planners, architects, developers, and security personnel. Of particular note is the tendency to build counter-terrorism measures underground, such as the recently completed Capitol Visitors Center.

Federal agencies in charge of the Mall have not always encouraged thoughtful and genuine public debate before approving plans to make changes. Because the Mall represents the fundamental principles of democracy in both form (monuments and memorials) and function (public space), fortification and security is explicitly at odds with the Mall's symbolism. In theory and law, public access to the Mall should never be impeded; in reality, there are often pressures for change and adaptation. Debates about security connect to broader planning and management issues about how to balance the competing needs for security and public access in a public space that embodies the ideals of democracy, freedom, and openness.

CHAPTER 4

Making Space for the Dream

In late August 2011 the Mall's newest memorial, the Martin Luther King, Jr Memorial, was opened to the public.[1] Authorized in 1996, the commemoration process endured fourteen years of fund-raising challenges, artistic controversy, and federal bureaucratic squabbles. This chapter examines how the impulse to commemorate represents an extension of American history and identity by including previously marginalized or ignored groups. The civil rights commemoration movement and the MLK Memorial can also be situated within this broader set of trends in commemoration and national memory.

The story of the MLK Memorial builds on discussions about how commemoration in public space shapes new national narratives and are also shaped by wider issues present in national discourse. As our national discourse has embraced a more inclusive history, commemoration and expressions of national identity have also changed. This memorial represents a significant departure from other memorials on the Mall in that it was the first one to commemorate an African American and, by extension, to recognize and legitimize the modern civil rights movement. In so doing, it has expanded the role of the Mall to express national identity by recognizing the existence of a more racially and ethnically diverse society.

All civil rights memorials are a way to evaluate whether equality and justice have meaning, and to what degree society has fulfilled the civil rights movement's goals.[2] The MLK Memorial on the Mall confers a *national* legitimacy on the civil rights movement and its objectives. It boldly challenges the Mall's dominant narrative, which is devoted largely to national identity and national history as defined and embodied mostly by white men (the Washington, Lincoln, Jefferson, FDR, anf Grant memorials, for example). The creation of the MLK Memorial is a radical departure from the past because it commemorates not only Martin Luther King, Jr but also the struggle of African Americans for equality, justice, and freedom. It thus corrects the implicit bias on the Mall towards a narrow definition of national history and national memory that has ignored minorities (African Americans in particular but also Native Americans, Hispanics, and Asians).

Two important ideas emerge. Not only has the completion of the MLK Memorial expanded the narrative of this public space and signalled that the Mall is extending the American story to include those previously left out, but the increasing cost of building memorials on the Mall has shifted strategies around fund-raising and may be evidence of a new direction in commemoration: corporate sponsorship. What might the consequences be? We have made space for an expanded national narrative. But should we also be concerned about the need for corporate sponsorship to express this narrative?

The Civil Rights Commemoration Movement

Efforts to establish civil rights memorials around the United States gained momentum in the mid-1980s in part owing to the designation of Martin Luther King, Jr's birthday as a national holiday,[3] an act that conferred a sense of legitimacy on advocates of the civil rights commemoration movement. In many cities and towns across the United States (particularly in the South), local efforts have succeeded in renaming streets, schools, and other public venues after Martin Luther King, Jr, Malcolm X, Rosa Parks, and other movement leaders.[4] Other efforts to commemorate the civil rights movement have met with varying degrees of success and opposition. Many of the statues to movement leaders such as Rosa Parks or Thurgood Marshall have tended to be located in their hometowns or at specific sites of protest or resistance. Interestingly, many of the "sacred" sites of the movement are mundane, everyday places such as beauty salons, barbershops, community centres, and lunch counters – where the movement actually came together.[5] But, regardless of whether the site is a public square or a more "mundane" place, statues, plaques, and designated historic sites connected with the civil rights movement all stand as of evidence of the growing desire to make good on America's promise of equality and justice.

Scholarship has introduced important themes about the ways in which remembering the Civil War or the modern civil rights movement includes both obvious and convert discussions of race.[6] Efforts to commemorate the civil rights movement boldly challenge the representation of the past by including new Black heroes and experiences. For example, geographer Jonathan Leib's examination of the debate over a proposed statue to Arthur Ashe on Monument Avenue in Richmond, Virginia, reveals issues of race and power.[7] Monument Avenue in Richmond was dedicated to honouring Confederate leaders in the Civil War; when the proposal to place a statue to Arthur Ashe was introduced, it ignited a debate about the symbolism of Monument Avenue and whether Ashe's statue should "intrude" on the narrative. Similarly, geographer Owen Dwyer has commented on debates surrounding the placement civil rights memorials, noting that the location of these memorials can be highly contentious, particularly if they express ideas at odds with existing public spaces that glorify the heroes of the Civil War.[8] Another geographer, Derek Alderman, has noted that the act of renaming a street or school after a civil rights leader, even King, Jr, is not without controversy or compromise and that, in some cases, a subtle form of racism resists such efforts.[9] In their book, *Civil Rights Memorials and the Geography of Memory*, Owen Dwyer and Derek Alderman write that civil rights memorials simultaneously challenge and confirm the conventions that characterize commemoration in America and that the last twenty years of building such memorials around the United States offer insights into the movement's victories and shortcomings.[10] Civil rights memorials provide a glimpse of competing interpretations of memory, as well as the power relationships that can ultimately determine its realization.

Civil rights memorials are a litmus test for how far society has progressed towards racial equality and justice, that is, to what degree society has fulfilled the civil rights movement's goals.[11] As with many civil rights memorials, the MLK Memorial was the first on the Mall that was dedicated not to a president or war hero but rather to a man who fought to expand citizenship to those who had been denied it. The memorial was also the first, in a memorial landscape that has tended to focus on wars (the War of Independence, Civil War, Vietnam, Korean, and World War II), to speak to the fragile nature of peace and the power of non-violence.

The MLK Memorial thus corrects an implicit (or perhaps even explicit) bias on the Mall towards a definition of national history and national identity that has ignored the role and contribution of minorities. As one supporter noted, "When future generations visit Washington, they will see a Mall that more closely reflects the diversity of our great nation."[12] The MLK Memorial expresses the African American struggle for equality, justice, and democracy and expands the national discourse on the principles and realization of democracy.

The Martin Luther King, Jr Memorial

In 1968, after King's assassination, the Alpha Phi Alpha fraternity proposed to erect a monument to the leader of the civil rights movement. King was a member of this fraternity and had been initiated while he attended Boston University. Decades passed. In 1986, after King's birthday was designated a national holiday, the fraternity's efforts resumed and gained political momentum. In 1996 President Clinton signed congressional legislation proposing the establishment of a memorial in the District of Columbia to honour Dr King. The legislation also permitted Alpha Phi Alpha to establish a foundation and to raise the estimated $100 million needed. The process of designing, funding, and constructing the memorial was administered by a non-profit organization created in 1998, the Martin Luther King, Jr. National Memorial Project Foundation (hereafter the MLK Memorial Foundation). The realization of the memorial, as noted, was not easy or quick. Table 4.1 highlights the key milestones in its story.

The MLK Memorial is less about the man and more about the legacy of the movement he led and and the enduring idea he represented. This is true of many of the memorials on the Mall – the Lincoln Memorial is as much about the preservation of the Union as it is about Lincoln the president. In this respect, consider the guiding theme of the MLK Memorial design competition: "The Man, the Movement, the Message." The competition to design the MLK Memorial, then, sought to represent the larger civil rights movement. To be sure, that movement in fact consisted of many movements with many leaders, not solely Martin Luther King, Jr. However, King, the most widely recognized leader, has become the de facto representative of the movement, in part because the campaign to commemorate civil rights has tended to focus on key individuals and pivotal moments rather than the ongoing grass-roots struggle.[13]

Table 4.1 Milestones in the History of the MLK Memorial.

1984	Alpha Phi Alpha Fraternity proposes to build a national memorial to Dr King.
1996	President Clinton signs congressional legislation proposing the establishment of a memorial in the District of Columbia to honour Dr King.
1998	National Capital Memorial Commission votes to recommend Area I (central core of the National Mall); several months later, this is approved by both House and Senate resolutions.
1998	Charter for the Washington, D.C., Martin Luther King, Jr. National Memorial Project Foundation approved (this will be the fund-raising organization for the Memorial).
1999	Design contest is announced.
2000	900 entries from 52 countries submitted to the design competition.
2000	Entry submitted by ROMA Design Group of San Francisco selected as winning design.
2001	MLK Memorial Foundation launches fund-raising campaign.
2003	Public meeting convened to solicit comments and concerns about the proposed Memorial on 7 January.
2005	National Capital Planning Commission approves preliminary design.
2006	NCPC approves final design.
2006	Ceremonial groundbreaking on the National Mall.
2006	Design team tours granite quarries and fabrication sites in China.
2007	MLK Memorial Foundation announces that Lei Yixin will be the project sculptor, who will carve the image of Dr King into the "Stone of Hope."
2008	National Park Service asks design team to make the security features "more robust."
2008	Commission of Fine Arts criticizes the design on 18 September.
2009	Memorial's final design approved and building permit issued.
2009	Construction begins, December 2009.

Source: Washington D.C. Martin Luther King, Jr National Memorial Project Foundation, "History of the Memorial, 2009," http://www.mlkmemorial.org (accessed 20 April 2010).

Locating the Memorial

Often, a memorial is located where the event occurred or the person was born (or died). In the case of the Mall, however, there is only one memorial with a site-specific connection to the event and person commemorated: the MLK Memorial. Otherwise, the location of a Mall memorial can be arbitrary (i.e., an available area is selected) or it can be more purposeful and symbolic (the area selected reflects how the memorial will be interpreted within the broader iconography of the Mall – such as was the case with the World War II Memorial).

The MLK Memorial commemorates the 1963 March on Washington, where Dr King delivered his famous "I Have a Dream" speech from the steps of the Lincoln Memorial (see Figure 4.1). King and other march organizers had

Figure 4.1. The iconic image of Martin Luther King, Jr and the 1963 March on Washington. Courtesy of Library of Congress.

deliberately selected the Lincoln Memorial because of the symbolism of Lincoln as the Great Emancipator and also as tribute to the Marion Anderson concert that had occurred there on Easter Sunday, 1939. As an African American, Anderson had been previously denied the right to perform at Constitution Hall. First Lady Eleanor Roosevelt worked in tandem with the National Association for the Advancement of Colored People (NAACP) and other artistic and civil rights organizations to arrange and publicize the Lincoln Memorial concert. That the Lincoln Memorial was chosen for the 1963 march, therefore, deliberately reflects what geographer Ken Foote calls "symbolic accretion," defined as the strategy to enhance of the reputation of a cause via the proximity of an established memorial landscape.[14] These examples are powerful reminders that memorials can been seen (and used) differently; in the case of Marion Anderson and Martin Luther King, Jr, Lincoln was viewed as emancipator and humanitarian more than savior of the Union.[15] This story reminds us that the symbolic trajectory of any memorial is difficult to predict. Since 1963, the Lincoln Memorial and the "I Have a Dream" speech have become forever linked, and further sanctified by the pilgrimage of civil rights tourism to D.C. In 2003 an inscription in the granite steps of the Lincoln Memorial marks the location where King spoke to the crowd. During the summer months, at 1:00 p.m. and again at 2:00 p.m., a park ranger sets up a boom box on the steps of the Lincoln Memorial and plays the tape of the speech.

When the decision was made to construct a memorial to King, the enduring image of his speech on the steps of the Lincoln Memorial posed an interesting dilemma. Where would the MLK Memorial go? According to congressional law, each memorial is sacred and cannot be "overlapped" or encroached upon by another. The MLK Memorial could not, legally, be constructed on the Lincoln Memorial grounds; it would have to be placed elsewhere.

In 2003 Congress recognized the "commemorative pressure" on the Mall and declared it no longer available to new memorials; however, the MLK Memorial had been approved for the Mall prior to that date, so it was exempt from the new law (construction had not yet started because the project was still in the fund-raising phase). Whatever site was selected for the memorial would be of significance, not just unto itself, but also in relation to the narrative of the Mall. Legislation that approves most memorials on the Mall also provides a list of several sites from which to select. Congress then leaves it up to three federal agencies (the Park Service, the Commission of Fine Arts, and the National Capital Planning Commission) to approve both the design and the site selection of the memorial.

Congressional legislation initially listed several sites for consideration. Eventually, two sites remained in contention: the Tidal Basin and the Constitutional Gardens. The MLK Memorial Foundation preferred the Tidal Basin site, a four-acre crescent-shaped area bordering the basin's western area, and recommended against Constitutional Gardens. However, the NCPC initially voted for the east end of Constitutional Gardens. Its members felt that the Tidal Basin site might be too small and would face too much traffic and airplane noise and might require the relocation of roads. Constitution Gardens, in contrast, was a "dignified space with a strong sense of place that offered a worthy setting in which to honor a pivotal figure in American history."[16] The other two agencies, the Park Service and the Commission of Fine Arts, requested a re-evaluation of the Constitutional Gardens site, noting that they preferred the Tidal Basin. Finally, in 1999, after a year of negotiations, the Tidal Basin site was selected when the NCPC reversed its earlier decision. The location was considered a triumph; as Harry E. Johnson, Sr, president and CEO of the MLK Memorial Foundation, noted, "one of the most prestigious sites remaining on the Mall has been selected and approved for the

Table 4.2 Timeline of the MLK Memorial Site Selection

1998	National Capital Memorial Commission votes to recommend Area I (central core of the National Mall); several months later, this is approved by both House and Senate resolutions.
October 1998	NCMC approves Constitutional Gardens for the MLK Memorial.
March 1999	NCPC votes to approve the east end of Constitutional Gardens.
April 1999	CFA reviews request by MLK Memorial Foundation to locate the memorial at the Tidal Basin. CFA votes unanimously to reject the Constitution Gardens site and tells the Foundation to study two additional sites, one on the west end of Constitutional Gardens and another on the steps of the Lincoln Memorial.
December 1999	NCPC votes unanimously to rescind its 4 March 1999 action and instead approves a four-acre site adjacent to the Tidal Basin.
	Media coverage of site approval featured on CNN, NBC, ABC, COX, CBS. and NPR. More than seventy-eight articles are published in major newspapers.
December 2000	Marble and bronze plaque laid at site of memorial

Source: Washington, D.C. Martin Luther King, Jr National Memorial Project Foundation, "History of the Memorial, 2009," http://www.mlkmemorial.org (accessed 20 April 2010).

Memorial." (See Table 4.2 for a timeline of the legislative and procedural events that led to the Tidal Basin site being selected.)

The selection of the Tidal Basin was deliberate and symbolic. First, the cherry trees there bloom around the anniversary of Dr King's death, accentuating the memorial message. Secondly, the area chosen near the Tidal Basin was within the sightline of both the Lincoln and Jefferson memorials. (Figure 4.2 shows the location of the MLK Memorial relative to the Mall.) The Tidal Basin site was highly sought after because it creates a visual "line of leadership" from the Lincoln Memorial (site of the "I Have a Dream" speech) and across the Tidal Basin to the Jefferson Memorial. By being positioned to "look across" the Tidal Basin to the Jefferson Memorial, the memorial would thus symbolically juxtapose the democratic ideals of liberty, equality, and justice held by the founding fathers, as symbolized by the Jefferson Memorial, with the objectives of the civil rights movement. Through its placement, the MLK Memorial would reside with "fellow advocates of democratic ideals."[17] The location would also reflect King's reminder to his audience in his "I Have a Dream" speech: "When the architects of our republic wrote the magnificent words of the Constitution and the Declaration of Independence, they were signing a promissory note to which every American was to fall heir. This note was a promise that all men, yes black men as

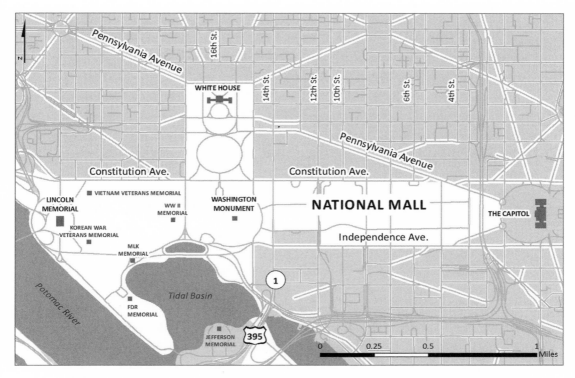

Figure 4.2. Map of the memorials on the Mall, including the MLK Memorial. Map by author.

well as white men, would be guaranteed the 'unalienable Rights of Life, Liberty and the pursuit of Happiness'... We refuse to believe that the bank of justice is bankrupt. We refuse to believe that there are insufficient funds in the great vaults of opportunity of this nation."

The symbolic connection between the MLK Memorial and the Jefferson Memorial is a powerful one, as was evident in much of the reaction once the site was selected. One commentator noted, "Having a memorial between two great presidents, President Lincoln and President Jefferson, is certainly very, very fitting as Dr. King did represent the ideals of freedom and democracy that are so important to our country."[18] Another observed that King's sculpture gazes "across the Tidal Basin at Thomas Jefferson, as if waiting for ripened promises to be harvested."[19] Interior Secretary Ken Salazar declared, "It is fitting and appropriate that we honor Dr. King's extraordinary life and legacy with a memorial here on the National Mall, alongside the timeless landmarks of American democracy and freedom."[20]

The Design

In addition to the location of the memorial, the memorial design is worthy of discussion because it shows the political process involved in the interpretation of both Dr King and the legacy of the civil rights movement. In 1999 the design competition elicited more than nine hundred ideas from around the world. Six finalists were chosen, and in September 2000 the winning entry was announced. According to the MLK Memorial Foundation, the memorial was intended to capture the essence of King's message of freedom, opportunity, justice, and human dignity.[21] Harry Johnson, Sr of the Foundation commented that the memorial "will serve as a stage to honor his national and international contributions to humankind … the Memorial will remind the world of his dedication to the idea of achieving human dignity through global relationships, and instill a sense of duty within each of us to be responsible citizens and conscientious stewards of freedom and democracy."[22]

Plate 1 and Figure 4.3 show the memorial's design elements. The memorial conveys the four fundamental themes that defined King's life: democracy, justice, hope, and love. Three of these – justice, democracy, and hope – are central to the design and are represented in three natural features within the memorial landscape: water, trees, and stone. Together, all three resemble a simulated stone mountain from which the centre has been carved out and placed by itself in the foreground. Water is used to recall the theme of justice and to build on the "crescendo effect" of King's sermons and speeches. It also references King's words "Let justice roll down like waters and righteousness like a mighty stream." Trees reinforce the "spatial integrity of the Memorial" and stand for seasonal change and annual growth. The trees are to unite the central themes of the memorial as they are placed around the memorial in clusters.[23] The most important natural element is stone. Stone is used throughout the memorial to "display the different ways King and other civil rights activist acted out their faith that the democratic ideals of the founding fathers can be realized through struggle and sacrifice."[24] Several stones stand at the entry portal; one is smooth and polished, the other rough. The rough stone, the "Mountain of Despair," is inscribed with the "Promissory Note." The centrepiece of the memorial is the "Stone of Hope," which depicts a 30-foot likeness of King in a business suit with his arms folded as if emerging from the stone. It references part of the text of King's "I Have a Dream" speech: "With this faith, we will be able to hew out of the mountain of despair a

Figure 4.3. The wall surrounding the Memorial is inscribed with quotes from King's sermons. Photo by author.

stone of hope." The sculpture is taller than the 19-foot statue of Jefferson and the 19.5-foot statue of Lincoln in the Lincoln Memorial and weighs thousands of tons.

In addition to the central element of the Stone of Hope, the memorial features more than a dozen niches along the upper walkway that commemorate the contribution of many individuals who gave their lives to the civil rights movement. A crescent-shaped stonewall is engraved with fourteen quotes from King's works, reflecting the themes of democracy, hope and justice.

Memorial Controversies

No memorial escapes controversy. Kirk Savage has shown this has been especially true for each and every memorial or monument on the Mall, including the first, the Washington Monument.[25] With the MLK Memorial, three controversies are worth discussing for they resonate with broader issues and debates in contemporary society.

The first is the bureaucratic challenge that occurred in 2008. The National Park Service, the CFA, and the NCPC disagreed about whether the security plan was adequate, thus delaying the project for nearly a year. Since 2001, new memorials must include security plans. The Park Service, concerned about car bombs, insisted that the MLK Memorial design team add more robust security and suggested a series of bollards or security pillars at the main entrances and other entry points to prevent any vehicle from crashing into the memorial area. However, the other two agencies, the CFA and NCPC, rejected these barriers as being overly restrictive and instead favoured subtler security that would honour King's philosophy of freedom and openness. It is worth noting that the CFA and NCPC sensitivity to more "subtle security" is highly ironic, since both agencies had approved other highly visible security barriers at the Washington Monument, the Lincoln Memorial, and the Jefferson Memorial several years earlier. While the agencies debated the style of security, the MLK Memorial Foundation felt stuck in a bureaucratic stalemate. "It appears to us that we're the one caught in the middle," said Ed Jackson, Jr, executive architect of the memorial.[26] The Foundation was frustrated with the delay primarily because it was not given specifics about what to include in the new security features, and it appealed to Congress for help. Finally, Interior Secretary Salazar interceded and in October 2009 a compromise was reached. The revised security plan featured a low-walled island of elm trees as the main vehicle barriers to the entrance and overall had less intrusive security barriers. This controversy highlights the highly political nature of commemoration on the Mall and the complex array of federal agencies that have oversight and approval authority for design and location. The bureaucracy has turned the approval of a new memorial into a time-consuming, often mysterious process. Indeed, bureaucratic tangles over security, design, and location are the rule rather than the exception.

The second controversy, in late 2007, concerned the design of the King sculpture for Stone Mountain. The rhetoric focused on two themes that related to the memorial's relationship with China: first, that "outsourcing" the sculpture to China was at odds with the U.S. commitment to human rights; and second, that the memorial ought to be sculpted by African American artists, who have "the right" to interpret this history.

Human rights activists criticized the selection of the sculpture's artist, Chinese national "master sculptor" Lei Yixin, because Lei had created several memorials to Mao Zedong, someone who had killed and imprisoned many of his own people.

Others echoed such sentiments. Perhaps the more significant critique of the selection of the Chinese sculptor reflects the ability to determine the memorial's interpretation. "It is an insult. This is America, and, believe me, there's enough talent in this country that we do not need to go out of the country to bring someone in to do the work," said Gwen Moore of the California chapter of the NAACP, which passed a resolution against the selection of Lei. Gilbert Young, an African American artist from Atlanta, led a protest against the hiring of Lei and launched the website *King Is Ours.*[27] The group aimed to "repatriate" the MLK Memorial. The *King Is Ours* petition declared: "We demand the right to interpret and present our own historic proclamation in this first ever national monument to an African American man." It went on: "The planned monument to our beloved Dr. Martin Luther King, Jr. has been awarded to an artist from a country with a reprehensible history of civil rights violations against its people."[28] Another commentator noted that, although it shouldn't really matter who created the art, the MLK Memorial was greatly symbolic of a country still struggling with racial divisions and therefore "it just seems viscerally wrong that somebody from within that community was not chosen to do this work."[29] The *King Is Ours* petition was supported by the Barre Granite Association (VT) and the Elberton Granite Association (GA) and the Monument Builders of North America, a trade association that represents retailers and manufacturers of monuments, grave markers, and memorials in the United States and Canada.[30] These groups protested the use of Chinese granite, while also decrying the human rights record of the Chinese government. The MLK Memorial Foundation responded that the quality of Chinese granite was far better than what could be found in the United States. It also insisted that there was no African American sculptor who could do a thirty-foot statue in granite. Although the *King Is Ours* petition never received more than a few thousand signatures, it reveals that memorials (particularly their construction and/or construction materials) are situated in a global political economy that can lead to controversy.

Beyond the issue of "outsourcing," debates about the interpretation of King as a civil rights leader continued in 2008 when a progress report showing the King sculpture in miniature was submitted to the federal agencies for review. After reviewing the photos of the sculpture to date, the CFA expressed concern that the artwork appeared to portray King as "confrontational." The Commission criticized the sculpture for resembling the Social Realist style (which is code for communism), noting that it "recalls a genre of political sculpture that has

Table 4.3. Responses to "Do you Believe the Memorial to the Icon of this Country's Civil Rights Movement should be Crafted by an American Artist and Created of American Stone?"

Unidentified Female: It should be done by an American artist with American stone in America.

Unidentified Male: Martin Luther King is American, so it should be here, not in China.

Unidentified Male: What he did helped the entire world, so it doesn't matter where it comes from.

Unidentified Female: Martin Luther King was here. He wasn't in China. It should be built here.

Unidentified Female: I'm all in favour of the statue of Martin Luther King, but I think it ought to be made by an American artist.

Unidentified Female: Martin Luther King did things here in America, but it's affected everyone worldwide. So if it's done in China, I don't think that's a problem.

Unidentified Male: It should be done by an American artist.

Unidentified Female: Importing something all the way from China for what it is an American monument just doesn't make any sense

---

Source: CNN Lou Dobbs Tonight, 3 May 2007. Transcript from http://edition.cnn.com/ TRANSCRIPTS/0705/03/ldt.01.html.

recently been pulled down in other countries."[31] Arguing that King's image was too grim and totalitarian, the CFA recommended that the sculpture be reworked. Lei was told to remove the furrows in King's brow and add a hint of a smile to soften his image and to portray him in a kinder and gentler way. African American sculptor Ed Dwight (who has created some fifty-plus memorials including many of African Americans) concurred, noting, "Dr. King never stood like that, nor wore clothes like that, no did he look like that ... the design looks like a very big Chinese black man."[32] CNN's Lou Dobbs highlighted the controversy on his show in May 2007, and polled several people on the street for their opinion on outsourcing the work to China (see Table 4.3 for their responses).

On the other hand, some commentators countered, "We should all be able to agree that the Rev. Martin Luther King, Jr. was confrontational," noting that confrontation was the whole point to demanding (not requesting) equal justice.[33] Eugene Robinson, columnist for the *Washington Post*, wondered if the CFA was "not comfortable with the image of a stern-faced, 28-foot-tall black man with his arms crossed," and remarked that it was difficult to make a righteously angry man look like Mister Rogers.[34] "Here's what is really going on," he continued, "It's clear that some people would prefer to remember King as some sort of paragon of forbearance, who through suffering and martyrdom, shamed the nation into doing the right thing. In truth, King was supremely impatient. He was a man of action who used pressure, not shame, to change the nation ... Given a choice between a Martin Luther King whose saintly martyrdom redeemed the soul of white America and a defiant Martin Luther King who changed the nation through the force of his indomitable will, I'll take the latter." The sculptor, Lei Yixin, reminded the Commission that he did not design the sculpture but was carrying out the concept, which the panel had already approved. Passionate discussion surrounding the design of the MLK Memorial reflects the different visions of what King meant to the world.

The controversy over how to interpret King's legacy is not unique to the MLK Memorial on the Mall, and it is consistent with contemporary debates that have occurred with many memorials to civil rights leaders. Other statues of King have generated similar debate. Erik Blome's statue of King in Rocky Mount, North Carolina, for example, received a litany of complaints that King had been depicted as "arrogant" or "too passive" or "angry."[35] The controversy diminished, but the criticism *this is American history that ought to be interpreted by African American*s is a familiar theme in the actual building of civil rights memorials. Dwyer and Alderman contend that sculptures of King around the United States have often met with mixed reactions, suggesting the complex and emotional politics surrounding the content of King's legacy and arguments over who should interpret it and how it should be represented.[36] As their work has shown, there is not one single, correct way to portray King and debates on the subject will likely continue.

Not long after it was completed, the memorial generated more controversy – this time over one of the inscriptions. There was heated criticism over a quotation on the Memorial that read, "I was a drum major for justice, peace and righteousness." The quote came from a King sermon in 1968 in which he actually said, "If you want to say that I was a drum major, say that I was a drum major for justice. Say that I was a drum major for peace. I was a drum major for righteousness. And all of the other shallow things will not matter." This was the quote that was originally intended for King's memorial statue. But in the construction process the decision was made to truncate the statement. The sculptor and the engraver felt strongly that, because of space limitations, fewer words should be used on the statue.[37]

Many complained that the truncated quotation changed the meaning. For instance, the poet Maya Angelou argued that the quotation was taken out of context when it was paraphrased and shortened. Angelou said it made King sound "like an arrogant twit."[38] "The 'if' clause that is left out is salient," Angelou added. "Leaving it out changes the meaning completely." Department of Interior Secretary Salazar concurred: "Dr. King's family all agreed: They didn't like the quote as it had been abbreviated. Members of the civil rights community and many others we consulted with were all in agreement that the quote had to be changed. So we're going to do it."

Lei Yixin was flown to Washington, D.C., in the summer of 2013 to remove the quotation. Over a few weeks, the inscription was removed with a grinder and the sculptor and his team carved horizontal groves in its place to resemble the striations, or "horizontal movement lines," that appear elsewhere on the memorial. The changes cost between $700,000 and $800,000, which came from the funds raised to build the memorial.

The High Cost of Memorials: The Big Business of Commemoration

It is worth discussing the challenge of raising money for the MLK Memorial in part because commemoration on the Mall is now big business. The costs of memorials have gone up astronomically – the Vietnam Veterans Memorial cost $9 million in 1982; two decades later, the World War II Memorial cost $197 million, the MLK Memorial $120 million, and the designed but not yet under-construction Eisenhower Memorial is projected to cost $142 million. There are numerous reasons for this. One is that there are no real standards in memorial design and development. There exist no standard square-foot costs for memorials such as there are for standard office buildings or apartment structures. Each is unique in original design, building materials, size, and site conditions.[39] Monument design requires specialized subcontractors, experienced sculptors, and subject advisers, all of which adds to the design fee. In addition, memorials in Washington, D.C., are more expensive than those in other cities owing to the review process involving multiple congressional and public agencies. Architects and construction experts, summoned before agencies and congressional committees, expect to be paid for their time. There are expenses for many of the preliminaries, including design development, engineering studies, environmental-impact statements for the EPA and other agencies, and materials and websites for public presentations. On top of that, memorials always take a long time to go through the planning process:

costs accumulate, and architects charge for their time to design, redesign, and redesign again to meet the requirements of the various federal agencies that oversee memorials. One Park Service superintendent admitted that "these memorial projects just go on way too long and just add up costs."[40] All of this means that memorials on the Mall cost a lot of money.

The process of memorial approval is ridiculously complex. The National Capital Memorial Commission has outlined the twenty-four-step process for erecting a memorial in Washington, D.C.[41] Notably, step 23 is the *beginning* of construction. The prior twenty-two steps involve site approval and design approval, processes that involve multiple steps and multiple-agency review. Site selection involves the memorial sponsor identifying several potential sites and preparing studies of alternative sites, along with a preliminary environmental-impact assessment. Site study and the EIA are submitted to the Park Service, which then consults with the NCMC, the NPCP, and the CFA. After site approval, the three-step design process begins. Usually the memorial sponsor holds a design competition. The design is considered an initial concept that is then submitted to the Park Service, which refines the design and then submits it to NCPC and CFA. All three agencies will provide comments. The memorial sponsor and the designer address the comments and work on refining the preliminary design. The preliminary plan is then reviewed again by the Park Service, and when and if it is approved, the Park Service next submits it to the NCPC and CFA. Based on yet more comments and review, the designer then submits final drawings and specifications. Meanwhile, the memorial sponsor, which has been fund-raising from the beginning of the process, submits final drawings and specification, cost estimates, and evidence of funds on hand; eventually, if everything goes well, the secretary of the interior issues a final approval along with a construction permit. No wonder this can take years, if not decades. Some memorials get stuck in the process of moving from preliminary plans to final designs and back again – particularly if something in the design is controversial.

This has happened to the Eisenhower Memorial. A preliminary design by architect Frank Gehry proved controversial. The design won approval by the CFA but not the NCPC. Today it is in memorial purgatory. The memorial sponsor has already paid out $60 million; the project has been redesigned several times. There is still no final approval for the memorial, and it may be a long way off. As a colleague mentioned, "given this process, thank God there is only one National Capital." Clearly, the process for commemoration does not function efficiently.

By law, Congress does not pay for memorials on the Mall. Instead, legislation authorizes a memorial foundation to be created and to assume responsibility for raising all the money needed for construction. This is an important point because it shifts responsibility for any memorial away from the federal government and to the citizen groups that have organized the memorial foundation. Fund-raising is one of the first tasks of a memorial foundation and it must have 110 per cent of the estimated costs in hand before construction begins. When faced with a memorial that is projected to cost hundreds of millions, fund-raising strategies must adapt.

The ability to raise money in part suggests a national legitimacy, a "buy in" to the memorial's purpose and message. Not coincidentally, the farther removed from more contemporary history, the more difficult raising the funds can be. One contemporary example is the National Liberty Memorial on the Mall. Originally approved in 2005, the memorial will be dedicated to the over five thousand enslaved Americans and free persons of African descent who volunteered to serve as soldiers and sailors during the American Revolution. Although the Liberty Memorial Foundation has appealed to all descendants of African slaves and free persons, it has faced major obstacles in raising the money needed to begin construction.

Initially, the MLK Memorial was estimated to cost $100 million. By 2008, the estimate was increased to $120 owing to a rise in construction costs – although ground had not yet been broken. Congressional law mandates that 110 per cent of estimated costs must be raised before construction begins. Therefore, there could be no groundbreaking until all of the money had been raised. So, as the delays continue and the cost estimates increase, the more the foundation in charge must raise more money so that the memorial can proceed. And yet, the more money needed, the longer it takes to raise it and the more the costs increase. As we have seen, it took fourteen years to raise the money for the MLK Memorial. It was financed almost entirely with private money, much of that from corporations not individuals. This may represent a new trend in commemoration – corporate sponsorship.

Historically, raising money for memorials focused on a getting a lot of people to make small donations, a type of public subscription campaign. This strategy both raised money and showed that the monument had significant popular support. As memorials have become more expensive, however, it has proven difficult to raise the necessary money through individual donations alone.

As a result, the trend has switched instead to soliciting large donations from corporate donors. This strategy was true of the World War II Memorial, where large corporation donations helped build momentum in the fund-raising campaign. Corporate sponsors included Federal Express (not coincidentally, the co-chair of the World War II Memorial Foundation was the CEO of FedEx), Wal-Mart, and Lily, which gave more than $2 million each; Anheuser-Busch, Exxon-Mobil, the Walt Disney Company, Boeing, and Kodak, each of which donated in the $1 million range; and some fifty other companies that gave in the range of $100,000–$1 million.[42] It has also become common for the corporate donors to be listed on a "major donors" wall or sign.

The magnitude of the MLK Memorial was a challenge to the commitment to fund-raise and, by extension, a measure of the commitment and importance of Dr King's legacy. Would it be possible to raise $120 million dollars? Would it be possible to do so within a reasonable amount of time (so as not to lose momentum)? Acknowledged Harry Johnson, Sr of the MLK Memorial Foundation, "We want to create a sense of urgency."[43]

The Foundation used traditional strategies for large-scale fund-raising, including "Dream Dinners" held in Atlanta, Miami, San Francisco, Los Angeles, New York, Houston, Philadelphia, Chicago, and other cities. Former president Clinton, long-time champion of issues important to the Black community, spoke at such events, and other celebrities attended as well. In 2002 the actor Morgan Freeman donated his time to create a series of Public Service Announcements (PSAs) to raise awareness for the memorial. In 2003 Halle Berry and Al Roker were featured in other PSAs. The MLK Memorial Foundation also helped organize "The Dream Concert" to raise money. Held at Radio City Music Hall in September 2007, the concert featured an "all star" line up including Stevie Wonder, Aretha Franklin, Carlos Santana, Garth Brooks, Shaquille O'Neal, Ben Affleck, and Queen Latifah.

In addition to the more traditional fund-raising appeals, the MLK Memorial Foundation took advantage of newer technologies including the Internet and social networking (it has a Facebook page). The Foundation's website, called "BuildtheDream.org," accepted online donations. Yet, despite the multifaceted fund-raising efforts, the Foundation was challenged to raise the $120 million needed. Because of slower than anticipated progress, in 2003 it requested and was granted a congressional extension to the deadline to raise the money. By 2008, the Foundation had raised nearly all of the money, and by 2009, pledges

Table 4.4. Timeline of Fund-Raising Efforts

2001	Foundation launches fund-raising campaign.
2003	Foundation raises $25 million of the $100 needed.
2003	1996 law gave the Foundation until November 2003 to raise $100 million. The Foundation falls short of the fund-raising goal, and Congress grants it an extension to raise the additional funds needed.
2003	Yahoo! puts the memorial on its home-page to help increase donations to the project on fortieth anniversary of the historic March on Washington.
2005	Foundation has raised $40 million of the $100 million needed.
August 2006	Foundation has raised $63 million of the $100 million needed.
Jan 2007	Foundation has raised $76 of the $120 million needed.
June 2008	Foundation has raised $95 million of the $120 million needed.
Dec 2008	Foundation had raised $108 million of $120 million needed.
2009	Foundation launches "Facebook" to assist with fund-raising efforts.
2009	Foundation implements "text messaging" as a fund-raising tool.

Source: Washington D.C. Martin Luther King, Jr National Memorial Project Foundation, "History of the Memorial," 2009, http://www.mlkmemorial.org (accessed 20 April 2010).

from corporations and private individuals had reached the target goal. In December 2009 construction began.

Table 4.4 shows a timeline of fund-raising efforts and Table 4.5 highlights some of the major corporate sponsors. Because of the large costs of memorials on the Mall, memorial foundations have increasingly relied on corporate sponsors. GM, for example, was the first corporate sponsor of the MLK Memorial and donated $10 million. The corporations shown in Table 4.5 all contributed at least $1.5 million. What are the motives for corporate giving? A senior vice-president at Wal-Mart, Esther Silver-Parker, provided one rationale: she noted that the Black community is an important customer base for the company and that Wal-Mart wanted to contribute on behalf of more than 250,000 Black employees among its U.S. workforce.[44] It is interesting to note that, increasingly, large multi-million-dollar memorials are being funded primarily by corporations rather than private individuals. This raises interesting questions about the commercialization of commemoration and to what degree this is the new reality of the memorial process on the Mall or anywhere where memorial costs may run into the millions. Commercial sponsorship of public space is a contradiction. The Park Service, strapped for cash, has turned to corporate sponsors for special projects at many of its parks, but there is something problematic about corporate sponsors of memorials in the heart of the nation's public space. What precedent might this set for the future? How far away is the time when a corporate name or

Table 4.5. Major Contributors to the Memorial

General Motors*	Tommy Hilfiger Corporate Foundation
Alpha Phi Alpha Fraternity	Bill and Melinda Gates Foundation
WK Kellogg Foundation	NBA
Walt Disney Company	Coca-Cola Foundation
Ford Motor Fund	MetLife Foundation
Toyota	Verizon Foundation
Travellers	GE
Credit Unions of the United States	AARP
AFLAC	Boeing
BP America	CIGNA
Cummins	Dupont
Exelon Foundation	ExxonMobil Foundation
Fannie Mae	FedEx
Wal-Mart	

*GM was first major sponsor.

Source: Washington D.C. Martin Luther King, Jr National Memorial Project Foundation, "Quick Facts about the Memorial," http://www.mlkmemorial.org (accessed 20 April 2010).

logo is draped across a memorial? I can see it now: a restored Washington Monument, brought to you by Viagra.

Trends in Commemoration

Now complete, the MLK Memorial is a permanent, physical reminder of Dr King's vision and the objectives of the civil rights movement. Like most memorials, it has not been without controversy and challenge: raising $120 million for the construction was no small task, and conflicting views of the way in which King is portrayed on the memorial reflects the more complicated issue of what his legacy means to different people.

Scholars have documented many contemporary struggles and contests over attempts to establish civil rights memorials across the United States. In many cases there has been active resistance to building civil rights memorials, or even renaming streets after various civil rights leaders. Many civil rights memorials in cities, towns, or villages have encountered vitriolic debate and politics, but this has not been true at the national scale, as exemplified in the MLK Memorial on the Mall. Although no memorial is free of politics (it did, after all, take several decades to approve legislation for the MLK Memorial) and no memorial

is without controversy over design and location, the MLK Memorial never generated heated or emotional resistance (at least publicly). There was little *explicit*
challenge to the concept of creating a memorial to Dr King on the Mall. Perhaps it
is at the scale of "national discourse" more so than at the local, urban, or regional
scale that American society is more easily able to embrace a more complex,
diverse understanding of U.S. history and accept a more diverse national narrative. In addition, the abstract nature of national identity on the Mall is less threat-
ening than memorials established in public spaces at the local level. Because the
national scale of commemoration is more abstract, and the location so public
(belonging to the nation, but really no one place), there may be less opportunity
or less motivation for opponents to oppose commemoration initiatives. At the
same time, it may be easier for diverse coalitions spread throughout the country
to raise money and political clout to pass federal legislation for memorials on
federal public spaces, such as the Mall. Because residents of Washington, D.C.,
have been historically excluded from decision making about federal space in the
city, the lack of a genuine "local" constituency makes organizing resistance to
any proposed memorial on the Mall more difficult. For these reasons, national-
scale commemoration may not meet the fierce resistance and resentment of civil
rights memorials that has been well documented at the local level.[45]

Importantly, the MLK Memorial offers us a way to evaluate whether equality
and justice have meaning and to what degree society has fulfilled the civil rights
movement's goals. And yet the MLK memorial also marks a new reality: memorials are big business and the high costs may require memorial foundations to
turn to corporate sponsorship. What might the repercussions of this be?

The Martin Luther King, Jr Memorial on the Mall reflects a new writing of
national identity and national discourse on race. Thus, the Mall has, both metaphorically and literally, "made space" for the commemoration of the civil rights
movement.

CHAPTER 5

The Brawl on the Mall

On 21 October 2002 I joined a group of about fifty citizens to march on the National Mall. We were there to protest the Mall's most recently approved memorial, the World War II Memorial (see Figure 5.1). The controversy did not revolve around the design of the memorial, or even whether such a memorial should be built. Rather, the protest that day focused on its selected location. Because the Mall is one of America's most symbolically charged public spaces, the location of the new memorial was perceived to change dramatically both the use and the meaning of the Mall's axes. Many were apprehensive that the massive seven-acre memorial would prevent the gatherings for celebration, recreation, and protest that historically occurred in this space. For the next two years, the memorial was hotly debated and lawsuits were filed, but in the end the memorial was built in the planned location and officially dedicated on Memorial Day in 2004. Although critics lamented its enormity and criticized both its design (it was too triumphal) and its location (inappropriate and disruptive), the memorial has become the Mall's most visited. The purpose of this chapter is to examine the legacy of the controversy about how to balance open space and memorial space, and how to confront continued pressures for new memorials in what is a finite amount of land.

Few would disagree with the statement that the Mall has become one of the most important national public spaces for protest and demonstration. It has also become *the* place for national commemoration. The plethora of memorials on the Mall is a visible expression of the right to freedom of speech: every memorial has a message and an intended audience.[1] The Mall's centrality to national

Figure 5.1. A citizen's group, the National Coalition to Save Our Mall, protested the location of the World War II memorial (October 2002). Photo by author.

identity and national memory means that groups hoping to build a memorial or museum view the Mall as a way to confer national legitimacy on the event or person commemorated.

Yet increasing demands for memorials and museums challenge us to understand the development of the Mall's Monumental Core. Recent memorial proposals also challenge us to scrutinize the process of commemoration and the ways in which any new memorial will alter the Mall's symbolism and use.

National Discourse and Commemoration

Memorials located in public space are informed by and situated at the intersection of such concepts as iconography, public memory, landscape representation, and national identity. Geographers and other scholars have made important contributions to the literature examining public statuary, memorials, and monuments and how these shape the historical and contemporary urban landscape.[2] Most scholars argue that memorials and monuments are not merely ornamental features in the urban landscape but highly symbolic signifiers that confer meaning on urban space and thus represent the politics of power.[3] Geographer Nuala Johnson, for example, maintains that the monument landscape in Ireland reflects the emergence of a particular articulation of nationalism.[4] Geographer Robert Osborne's work on monuments in Montreal illustrates that monuments can serve as symbolic device that encode particular histories and geographies in the landscape.[5] And in the United States, as we have seen, geographer Jonathan Leib's examination of the debate over a proposed statue to Arthur Ashe on Monument Avenue in Richmond, Virginia, reveals issues of race and power.[6]

Memorials are intended, if not explicitly then implicitly, to stimulate debate. The debate often revolves around the interpretation of history, the meaning of the event or person, and how this meaning should be conveyed in the built form.[7] Yet the location of memorials is equally politicized but less examined. While memory and identity are abstract concepts, there is a geography – a physical location – to memory and memorials. In the case of the Mall, none of the monuments or memorials are graves, or contain sacred relics, but they have nonetheless become sacred ground. Thus, the location of a memorial is dependent upon how it is interpreted within Mall's broader iconographic landscape. This too, can be highly politicized and contentious.

The role of monuments and memorials is intricately connected to more abstract concepts of heritage and memory. Geographers and historians who conduct research on historic preservation and heritage have convincingly argued that these concepts are socially constructed, even "invented."[8] That is, built heritage exists because a particular society says an object, event, person, or place is valuable enough to ensure that it is passed along to the next generation.[9] Memorials and other forms of heritage are created in a social/political context where culture, location, class, power, religion, gender, and even sexual orientation will influence what is considered to be worthy of preserving as heritage.[10] Since heritage, national identity, and memory are socially constructed, they are also inherently contested.[11] The literature has revealed that heritage and memory (and by extension a memorial) is potentially subject to controversy, contestation, and continued negotiation among interested parties.[12] Those with the power can shape the creation of heritage or the location of a memorial; shifts in power or ideology can introduce new criteria. Each memorial represents a moment in time when a particular vision has captured hegemonic status, albeit briefly.[13]

Debates surrounding the design, construction, and location of memorials are significant for "decoding" iconographic images within a larger complex of cultural, social, and political values.[14] While memory is individual, commemoration belongs to a community. The act of commemoration requires public action (legislative approval, usually) and physical space for its realization. An analysis of the location of memorials thus provides a glimpse of competing interpretations of memory, as well as the power relationships that can ultimately determine its realization. The overt politics of memory is the political planning process by which the design and location are selected, often a matter of public record. In the case of the Mall, this is a process that involves Congress and several federal agencies, and so reflects a national agenda. The covert politics involves the power of one particular interpretation to rise above the others (to capture hegemonic status). The addition of each new memorial on the Mall reflects the power of a particular group of people at a specific time to determine which interpretation of the person/event will be unveiled and to place that memorial in a space that resonates with its interpretation. This discussion may provide another angle from which to consider the politics of memory and commemoration in urban space since little has been documented about memorials on federal lands (the literature has tended to focus on private spaces or municipal public space).

Federal public spaces, like the National Mall, are inherently different – they are controlled not by municipal governments and planning departments but by Congress and federal agencies. Following the Civil War, Congress created a generalized procedure for the creation of public memorials.[15] The steps are: 1) a private group interested in sponsoring a memorial forms a committee that solicits members of Congress to sponsor a bill allowing the memorial to be installed on federal land; 2) as part of the bill, Congress forms a memorial commission, which is responsible for raising the funds for the memorial and installing it; 3) once the memorial commission is established, the memorial enters the twenty-four-step process discussed in the previous chapter. Every step is politicized and highly charged and memorials and monuments placed on federal public lands like the Mall encounter an unusual type of political process, one that may not be attuned to local or regional concerns but is more reflective of a national political agenda.

Commemoration Pressures on the Mall

By the mid-twentieth century, the Mall had become the focal point of new proposals for memorials.[16] This pressure to develop memorials on the Mall will not abate any time soon. Numerous bills already proposed in previous sessions are

Table 5.1. Is there room on the Mall for ...

- a Ronald Reagan Memorial;[17]
- a National Slave Memorial;
- a Cold War Memorial;
- a Pyramid of Remembrance (to victims of 9/11);
- a Memorial to Children of the American Revolution;
- a Memorial to Black Revolutionary War Patriots;
- a Memorial to Thomas Paine;
- a Tiananmen Square Memorial Park;
- a Hispanic Vietnam Veterans Memorial;
- a Memorial to Davy Crockett;
- an Armenian Genocide Memorial;
- a National Women's History Museum;
- a National Health Museum; and
- a Memorial to American Astronauts?

likely to be reintroduced in future congressional sessions in hopes they will pass and be signed into law (see Table 5.1).

Today, the Mall's importance in national commemoration should be seen against the backdrop of the explosion of American historiography. Our view of what constitutes history, citizenship, and culture has expanded. History has become popularized in movies, television, novels, and even "edutainment." The Mall has become the physical presentation of American history as an ideal. Most of the structures, statues, and even landscaping on the Mall carry this message. Seen in a positive light, as argued earlier, proposals for memorials represent an expansion of history and identity by including the previously marginalized or ignored. The newly completed Martin Luther King, Jr Memorial acknowledges the struggle for civil rights among African Americans; similarly, the newly completed National Museum of the American Indian reflects Native American experiences and history. The demand for new memorials is part of a larger politics of identity that seeks to make the Mall more reflective of a multicultural America both in history and today. The addition of more memorials could make the Mall more "public" through inclusion. But it also has generated tension between those who want to preserve the Mall's open space and those who advocate for the placement of a given memorial. The legacy of the World War II Memorial suggests that this debate has been tipped in favour of commemoration at the expense of other uses of the Mall, particularly if that use is open space or recreation space.

It might be useful to distinguish between "active" and "passive" citizenship in public space. Both occur on the Mall. The Mall provides space for active citizenship, which includes political protests, national celebrations, and public gatherings. Active participation seeks to include rather than exclude "undesirables" and often attempts to extend or reinforce notions of citizenship and democracy.[18] On the other hand, passive citizenship involves the consumption of public space. Passive consumption of public space on the Mall includes activities that are important but may not involve democratic values, such as picnics, jogging, or visiting memorials and monuments. Open space is often seen as encouraging passive use and is less important compared to active citizenship activities. But this is problematic and may reflect a society that has still not learned how to value open space.

The World War II Memorial

The World War II Memorial, dedicated in May 2004, generated intense controversy over its design and selected location. Debates about the location focused on how the memorial would change the use and symbolic meaning of the Mall. The "brawl over the Mall" reveals an increasingly pressing tension: Should the Mall be developed to value memorials and commemoration over all else, or is it important (and valued) primarily as an actively used public forum and open space?

The location of any memorial alters the meaning of the Mall by adding new interpretations of history, meaning, and national identity. A change to the axial relations, in particular, such as a new memorial in between established points, changes this meaning more significantly than a memorial placed off to the side of the Mall. The Mall's text is widely recognized by Congress as well as the federal agencies that have jurisdiction over the Mall (the Park Service, the National Capital Planning Commission, etc.). This means that key decision makers with the authority to approve both the design and the location of memorials understand the Mall's symbolism. The location of any memorial would not be an accidental intrusion into the existing text: it would be intentional.

The move to create a World War II Memorial was part of a general trend to revisit the war and its meaning in literature – for example, Stephen Ambrose's *Citizen Soldiers*, Tom Brokaw's *The Greatest Generation*, and James Bradley's

Flags of Our Fathers – and movies, such as Stephen Spielberg's *Saving Private Ryan*. There was also a sense of urgency to honour those who served; of the sixteen million who served in uniform in World War II, fewer than four million were alive in 2000. Although there are many WWII memorials – in state capitals, town squares, cemeteries, and even in D.C. – most celebrate various branches and units of the military (the Iwo Jima memorial, for example, is dedicated to the Marine Corps). Before 2004, there was no memorial in D.C. that honoured everyone who served. The political pressure to acknowledge a generation quickly disappearing captured sufficient political power to generate majority support in Congress and the White House (which could have vetoed the bill) to make this memorial a reality.

While new memorials have the power to enrich national memory and national history, there is simultaneously tension over how to integrate the new and old national-identity narratives.[19] And, while more memorials could enhance the meaning of the Mall for those who have been marginalized, they will also shrink the Mall's open space. This is because the geography of the Mall is limited and therefore each memorial not only transforms the Mall's meaning and function but also converts open space/green space to commemorative space. Though this is not necessarily negative, what is disturbing is that this trade-off is not acknowledged by the groups seeking new memorials. There has been a lack of public discussion about these consequences. In other case studies examining changes to or restrictions on public space, conflict often occurs around two opposed ideals about public space: leisure and recreation versus political protest, or perhaps more accurately, public space as exclusive versus inclusive.[20] Yet the Mall is different. Historically, the Mall's role in providing open space for leisure and recreation has gone hand in hand with it role as a centre stage for political protest. These two uses are not diametrically opposed. Rather, the struggle for the Mall revolves around open space and political discourse (active citizenship), on the one hand, and national commemoration, on the other (not inherently passive citizenship, but increasingly so). This unusual struggle reflects the fact that few urban public spaces are asked to serve as open space, protest space, and commemorative space simultaneously.

In addition to the larger politics involved in revisiting issues of national memory, history, and identity, there exists the explicit or overt politics of the memorial-realization process itself. Memorials and monuments on the Mall must be designated through federal legislation; so the initial politics of public memory on the Mall takes place in Congress, which is itself often responding to broader social/political pressures to reconsider national identity. Congress can alter the meaning of the Mall by approving or killing bills proposing a memorial, but it can also subtly rewrite the Mall's iconography by including in the legislation the designation of a specific location for that memorial. Once a memorial has been approved through public law, its design and location (if not already specified) will be determined by multiple federal agencies and commissions. Federal law, as already explained, requires each new memorial to be funded completely through private sources. I suggest that this makes any proposed memorial *more* likely to be approved since Congress only needs to agree that the memorial has merit; it does not have to wrestle with the more politically charged issue of how to pay for it, what it should look like, and where to site it. A bill for a memorial before Congress is more likely to gain majority support when public monies are not expended.

The National Park Service, the Commission of Fine Arts, the National Capital Planning Commission, the Army Corps of Engineers, the American Battle Monuments Commission (ABMC) (if it is a war memorial), and the D.C. Office of Historic Preservation (the sole representative from the city) are all part of a complicated memorial-approval process. These federal agencies answer primarily to Congress and the Executive Branch and not necessarily to a local constituency. Prior to the public controversy over the World War II Memorial, these federal agencies made decisions with little, if any, genuine public participation in commemoration planning.

Interestingly, the city has had little input on the commemoration planning on the Mall. Although the Mall and the city share a common master plan, early history, and evolution, they are also distinct spaces. But because the Mall is federal space, the city lacks authority over how it is used and developed. With regard to the WWII Memorial's location, nearly every D.C. political elite expressed opposition (including the mayor and the D.C. congressional delegate). They had little power to reverse the site selection. The Mall is deeply embedded in national politics and thus subject to broader debates about what people and events should be remembered, and what should not. Thus, commemoration on the Mall can be seen as associated with and part of a broader national discourse on memory and national identity.

What makes the World War II Memorial worthy of closer scrutiny is that key decision makers involved with the memorial, mostly at the federal level, controlled the vision of how it would convey history and national identity. There was little public discussion or public input in the commemoration process, even though this is a premier public space. It is possible that the decision makers advanced a broader social agenda that sought to rewrite the text of the Mall by including their vision of history and national identity. Since the Mall's text or iconography is generally understood, these individuals understood exactly how the memorial would affect the meaning of the Mall and intended to alter it. In addition, whether or not they realized it, their decision to locate the memorial in a prominent location that had traditionally been used as a public forum or recreational space reflects the increasing value placed on commemoration vis-à-vis the Mall's other uses. In this respect, the story of the WWII Memorial not only shaped how the public views and values the past, it also reveals a great deal about the interests, concerns, and choices of those in the present.[21]

While controversies have followed each and every memorial in Washington, D.C. (starting with the Washington Monument), the controversy over the WWII Memorial reflects broader contemporary issues about the accelerated loss of open space on the National Mall, threats to access in public space, how the memorial changes the meaning of the Mall, and how public space should convey memory.[22]

The WWII Memorial Design

In 1993 Public Law 103-32 authorized the creation of the National World War II Memorial in Washington, D.C. The law designated the American Battle Monuments Commission as sponsor of the memorial and the party responsible for raising the $100 million from private sources for its construction. It also detailed design criteria. First, the memorial must "convey, through a variety of means and art forms, the meaning of WWII to America and the world." It should remember all who served, both in the military and at home, on land, at sea, in the air, in barracks and battlefield, in factories and on farms. It should also "celebrate patriotism, valor, sacrifice, and national unity." It was to be a memorial not only to those who fought but also for the entire war effort – all in one memorial. In addition, the law mandated that "the resulting work must be respectful of and compatible in configuration and quality with its historic surroundings."[23] Because this memorial would be built on the Mall, the process of selecting both the design and the location was more politically convoluted than for memorials built in private space or on other publicly owned land where the jurisdiction over space is not so fragmented. At the same time, since this is national public space, the law mandates that the process should involve public participation.

The selected design was a memorial plaza conceived by Friedrich St Florian, former dean of Rhode Island School of Design and practising architect. After several revisions, his design called for a sunken granite-stone plaza, stretching more than 400 feet across the central panel of the Mall. The plaza would be framed at the north and south by two forty-one-foot-high triumphal arches and ringed with fifty-six seventeen-foot-tall pillars, each one hung with a bronze wreath. Four sculpted eagles holding victory laurels in their beaks would sit atop the arches. In the centre of the memorial would be two waterfalls. A Freedom Wall, which featured 4,000 gold stars (one for every 100 Americans killed in the war), would anchor the western part of the memorial. In total, it would cover 7.4 acres at the selected site (see Figures 5.2 and 5.3).

Earlier in the design-review process, the CFA felt that St Florian's initial design was "too overwhelming" and "too destructive of the Mall" and instructed him to revise it. The new design corrected the problem of being "too overwhelming" by sinking much of the memorial below street level. In addition, the tall vertical elements – the pillars – were lowered, to lessen the intrusion on the site. St Florian also added additional waterfalls and restored areas of grass (which he had initially envisioned to be paved in granite) to meet the CFA's request for more sensitivity to the water features and open elements of the Mall. In July 2000 the CFA voted unanimously to accept the revised memorial design; the Department of Interior, the Park Service, and the NCPC approved it in September. The design was now approved; only an act of Congress could overturn the design and site selected.

Debate over the Design

When St Florian's design was presented to the public through the media around the country, it set off a storm of controversy. Architects, architectural critics, and art historians led the debate over the design, primarily in outlets such as television, newspapers, editorials, and trade journals. They criticized many elements about the design.

Neo-classical antecedents are prevalent in St Florian's design. While neo-classical style is familiar to D.C., some critics believed that the scale and enormity of the design was too grandiose and out of place. As one art historian noted, "it is clearly good classicism. But is it a good monument?"[24] The *Washington Post* called it "a granite atrocity" and a "massive mausoleum."[25] "This just seems so

Figure 5.2. The World War II Memorial with the Lincoln Memorial to the west. Photo by author.

Figure 5.3. The Atlantic Arches at the World War II Memorial surrounded by pillars representing each of the states and U.S. territories. Photo by author.

uninspired," said Yale architecture scholar Vincent Scully.[26] The *Los Angeles Times* called the design sterile and lacking a sense of the personal heroism and sacrifice that epitomized this conflict.[27] The editorial also noted that the classical elements seemed remote, in contrast to the way visitors to the Vietnam Veterans Memorial reach out to touch names etched into the black granite. Another editorial claimed that the design was "simultaneously busy and gloomy, not sublime and inspiring."[28] Richard Longstreth, then vice-president of the Society of Architectural Historians, called the memorial "among the very worst proposals ever made."[29]

Some critics felt that it was "a cluttered design."[30] It was certainly busy: in the centre was a sculpture titled "The Light of Freedom." Around this unifying sculpture were fifty-six pillars, two triumphal arches, a gold-star memorial wall, two waterfalls, four pools, eight monumental bronze eagles, fifty-eight bronze wreaths, and twenty-four panels featuring images of the war. All that is missing, quipped one critic, is a partridge in a pear tree. As Marc Fisher, art critic, said, "we have a memorial that tries to compensate for its lack of boldness and purpose with an excessively busy design that includes arches, pillars, ramps, wreaths, bronze columns, hanging sculptures, wall sculptures, even a sculpture in water, tall fountains, arcing fountains, a field of stars, light shows, ceremonial walkways – all smack in the center of the Mall."[31] Some criticized the memorial for not being emotionally engaging and that it relied too much on elements and symbols without meaning.

Opponents said that the triumphal arches and pillars were inappropriate (at one point, the design also included a sarcophagus-like feature, which also drew criticism and which St Florian removed in the revised version).[32] Architectural critics criticized the arches because they represent the iconography of imperial authority, noting that, in this instance, the neo-classical elements resembled the work of the Nazi architect Albert Speer. Supporters of the design countered that the term "imperial" was off the mark. Certainly, St Florian did not intend his design to be associated with imperial authority, and J. Carter Brown, then CFA chairman, lamented the "Speer Smear" as inaccurate and mean.[33] Brown also noted that the design's vertical dimensions were modest in relation to the principal visual features of the Mall. He reminded critics that the Lincoln Memorial is based on a temple form inherited from the Roman Empire, and that the Washington Monument is an obelisk of the type used by autocratic pharaohs and oligarchic priests; yet neither monument is criticized for its appropriation of these visual traditions.[34]

Still other critics, including those with academic credentials, have explored the WWII Memorial as it relates to general trends in building memorials in contemporary society. In this respect, the debate about the design marks a key moment in the production of the memorial and illuminates its connection to national history and identity. The objectives as mandated by the legislation made it difficult for the memorial to be uncontroversial. The fear of leaving something out might account for its clutter. But, as a result, some complained that the memorial "fails to speak." Historian John Bodnar called St Florian's design "bland and innocuous, neither on the side of victory nor on the side of the tragic dimensions of war."[35] George Mosse, author of *Fallen Soldiers: Reshaping the Memory of the World Wars*, sees the triumphal posturing as only a *partial story of war*; a good memorial should also contain a warning against war.[36] The editor of *Architecture* magazine felt that the WWII Memorial was "a museum masquerading as a memorial."[37] These comments resonate with recent literature that critically examines the production and design of memorials.

Debates over memorials are really debates about national identity, the national story, and about how to interpret history and memory. However, there was actually little debate about what the memorial should be about *before* the design contest, a missed opportunity to engage in a more reflective discussion on the meaning of the war and national memory. Historian Kristin Haas has alleged that the WWII Memorial is a memorial that "doesn't dare to know," a shrine to sentiment, to an idealized, generic vision of the "good war."[38] She notes that World War II, unlike the Vietnam War, has been uncritically accepted, made sacred, and so there has been tremendous silence on its meaning. "This memorial seems only an exercise in nostalgia that proclaims 'Hooray for us,' and does not engage in any debate," observed another critic.[39] The World War II Memorial, like most memorials, is only a selective aid to memory.[40] Critics contend the memorial focuses only on the triumph, dismissing the dark and painful side of the war. These more theoretical and complex critiques have also been part of the debate about the memorial, but not to the extent that many feel they should be.

While the WWII Memorial design controversy offers fascinating and important links to broader debates about memory and commemoration, I want to shift to the equally compelling debate about the memorial's location, an element of the controversy that will have a lasting impact on the Mall. The location of the memorial is one of the most conspicuous and central places on the Mall, the Rainbow Pool, a site acknowledged to be on the core axis. The debate over the memorial's location, then, exposes not just the politics of memory but the politics of *locating* memory in public space.[41] It also unveils an enduring and unresolved tension: how to balance our need to commemorate with other public-spaces uses such as recreation, open space, and protest.

Selecting the Site

There were originally six sites considered for the World War II Memorial: the Tidal Basin, West Potomac Park, Constitution Gardens, Freedom Plaza, the Capitol Reflecting Pool, and the Washington Monument grounds (Figure 5.4 shows all six). These six sites are off to the side of the central axis of the Mall. Initially, the American Battle Monuments Commission and the Memorial Advisory Board requested the Constitution Gardens. The site needed to be approved by the Park Service, the NCPC, and the CFA. In July 1995, prior to the design contest, the NCPC agreed that Constitution Gardens was the preferred site. Then confusing events transpired. According to one report, J. Carter Brown, chairman of the CFA, said that the Constitution Gardens did not convey the historical significance of WWII, and that the CFA would be open to suggestions from the ABMC. Brown was one of the key decision makers and some see his role in this memorial as more influential than that of any other.[42] Some have suggested that the Constitution Gardens site was reconsidered because of the objections of architect David Childs (of the New York firm of Skidmore, Owings and Merrill), who was chairman of the NCPC from 1975 to 1981. He also had designed the Constitution Gardens in the early 1970s for the nation's bicentennial in 1976. According to sources, he wrote a letter to Brown vigorously objecting to the Constitution Gardens because, he argued, these were not intended to be a memorial garden. One critic suggested that Brown protected his friend's (Childs's) project by relocating the memorial elsewhere.[43] (On a side note, David Childs was chair of the CFA from 2002 to 2005, taking over after Brown died in 2002.) What does appear clear is that Brown closed down debate when he ignored the recommendations made by the numerous organizations that were authorized to select the site. According to Elizabeth Meyer, a landscape architectural theorist, Brown selected a "site far more prominent than the sites of two recently completed memorials to two 'lesser' wars, the Vietnam and Korean; the perceived hierarchy of wars trumped the spatial hierarchy of the city's urban form."[44]

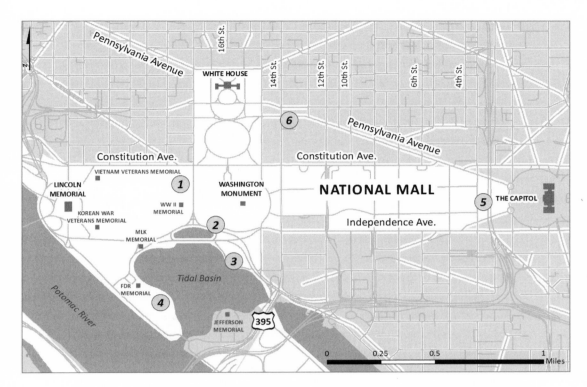

Figure 5.4. A map of the six sites originally considered. The final location is highlighted. Map by author.

A few weeks after Brown suggested that a new location be considered, the ABMC began to lobby instead for the Rainbow Pool, *not* one of the six original sites proposed. The Rainbow Pool sits at the end of the long, rectangular Reflecting Pool in front of the Lincoln Memorial. Who first suggested to the ABMC that this site would even be considered appropriate is still unclear. Six weeks later, the CFA voted to locate the memorial at the Rainbow Pool; two weeks following that, the NCPC changed its mind and approved the Rainbow Pool site. The Park Service quickly followed. Within a month, on Veterans Day 1995, President Clinton dedicated the Rainbow Pool as the WWII Memorial site.

Confidence in the site-selection process was challenged when Haydn Williams, chairman of the ABMC, was quoted as saying, "We got the site before they [the public] knew what hit them."[45] J. Carter Brown defended the decision to select the Rainbow Pool, noting that to have located the memorial in the Constitution

Gardens would have been to relegate it inappropriately as a "footnote to the Vietnam Veterans Memorial."[46] Brown's power was well known and respected; he had been called "Washington's Grand Vizier of Taste" and, as chairman of the committee that awards the prestigious Pritzker Prize for architecture, he probably had little trouble influencing architects who might object to his dictates.[47] One critic of the location process contended: "Attempts to assure a memorial that properly honors World War II while also respecting the Mall have been abandoned. Once the CFA proposed and then approved the Rainbow Pool site ... one agency after another eventually fell into line. The result in this case is a memorial that is a marriage of poor design, expediency, and neglect ... A public process has been stymied. Historic preservation has been ignored. The process speaks loudly of a concentrated effort to keep the public in the dark while creating the appearance of unstoppable momentum in the face of an upcoming groundbreaking."[48]

At the least, the selected site was the outcome of some interesting behind-the-scenes manoeuvring, leaving one observer to comment, "The site selection for the World War II Memorial has more subplots than an episode of 'Survivor.'"[49] Although the site received approval of all the necessary federal commissions as early as 1995, the reality of it was not appreciated until 2000, when St Florian's design was revealed. The power of the design to resonate with the location was explicit and intentional, not accidental. It reflected the power of key individuals (such as J. Carter Brown) to control and determine the process of site selection, which would advance their interpretation of the meaning of the memorial and its relationship to the overall iconography of the Mall. However, the site selection must have been supported by other members of the political elite – the president, key members in Congress – or, otherwise, ranking committee and subcommittee members of Congress could have called an oversight hearing to discuss the location. The selection of the location for the WWII Memorial therefore illustrates the complex politics of commemoration at the national scale.

Debate over Location

Concerns about the location have been as, if not more, prominent than those about the design. One commentator for the *Wall Street Journal* likened the memorial's location to "Mauling the Mall."[50] An editorial in *USA Today* ran the caption "WWII Memorial Misplaced" and noted, "There's nothing wrong with the proposed National World War II Memorial that a change of location couldn't fix."[51] The *New York Times* argued, "Don't Mar the Mall," while the *Los Angeles Times*, in an editorial tersely titled "Wrong Thing. Wrong Place," not only criticized the design but also stated: "Even more troublesome is the memorial's proposed site, between the Lincoln Memorial and the Washington Monument. The Mall's long expanse of lawn is hallowed political ground ... [and the memorial] would probably truncate and disfigure this important space."[52] The *Washington Post* saw the memorial as "Inadequate and out of Place." Criticism of the memorial's location was found in newspapers and magazines around the country.

Concerns were raised that the design would block the famous vista of the Mall, and belatedly, critics came forth to condemn the site as inappropriate for any memorial.[53] *Los Angeles Times* writer Christopher Knight, one of the more persistent and eloquent critics, said: "In many respects, this memorial merits approval. Except for one thing: It's in the wrong place. Despoiling one of the most powerful public spaces in America to build it will disfigure the memory of the war in ways those veterans surely don't deserve."[54] Roger Lewis, architect and architectural historian, summed up the controversial relationship between memorial design and location: the "Memorial is envisioned as a space rather than an object, a place to be rather than an object in a place."[55]

Some politicians reacted negatively to the selected location, but most were Democrats in a Republican-controlled House and Senate. Senator J. Robert Kerrey (D-Nebraska) asserted that the memorial "will change the entire nature" of the Mall.[56] He voiced strong disapproval, writing to the ABMC, "Just like Cinderella's stepsisters whose feet were too big for the glass slipper, the World War II memorial is simply too big for this site." He worried that the National Mall "will become a World War II mall with the Lincoln and Washington at either end."[57]

One of the more vocal opponents to both the design and the location was a local grass-roots organization, the National Coalition to Save Our Mall, the organization behind the October 2002 protest I attended. The Coalition was founded in 2000 by WWII veterans, planners, architects, and other Washington-area citizens. They were emphatically opposed to the location of the WWII Memorial. Coalition members, feeling that they were fulfilling a much needed role by championing the Mall, called the design "an intrusion" which detracted from other monuments. They noted that the memorial's sheer size would change the Mall forever, argued that it should not be located in the "sacred center" of the

Mall, and voiced the suspicion that the decision to select the Rainbow Pool site had been the product of "behind the doors" politics. The Coalition held several protests near the site, appealed for public pressure, and filed a number of lawsuits to prevent the memorial's construction from starting. It based its lawsuits on three legal issues. First, the EPA requires that the Park Service prepare an environmental-impact assessment on the project. By 2000, no EIA had been completed, but the Park Service waived the requirement. Secondly, the Historical Preservation Act of 1964, section 106, requires that meetings be open to the public. The Coalition argued that the public had been shut out of the process. Thirdly, the Coalition tried to fight the WWII Memorial location as a violation of the 1986 Commemorative Works Act. Among the procedures established, this law stated that no new commemorative work should interfere or encroach upon any existing commemorative work. The Coalition argued that the Rainbow Pool was an intrinsic part of the Lincoln Memorial and that building the WWII Memorial there violated the law by encroaching on the Lincoln Memorial grounds. In March 2001 the Justice Department issued a temporary restraining order to prevent the Park Service from beginning construction on the memorial. Two weeks later, Senator Tim Hutchinson (R-Ark) took drastic action, filing a bill to eliminate the lawsuit. The bill passed and the lawsuit was dismissed. In the end, the argument of memorial supporters that the delay affected aging veterans proved persuasive.

Ultimately, the Coalition lawsuit was more of a nuisance than a genuine threat to overturn the site selection, since key decision makers had the power to shut down public debate.[58] However, the emergence of a citizen's advocacy group is an interesting political development that suggests a shift, however small, in the power relationships between the public and the federal agencies in charge of the Mall: never before had these federal agencies faced public dissension and legal action from citizen's groups like the Coalition. Today, the Park Service, the CFA, and the NCPC must deal with the ongoing advocacy and lawsuits of the Coalition, a shift in the balance of power to some degree.

Despite the fact that there was growing public criticism of the location, the federal agencies involved resisted any serious discussion to reconsider the location. The power to locate the memorial played a central role in not only the memorial's design but also in a rewriting of the Mall that places great emphasis on World War II as a triumphant contribution to national identity and the defining memory of the twentieth century.

NTAIN OF DESPAIR,

OF HOPE

Plate 1. The Martin Luther King, Jr Memorial. Photo by author.

Plate 2. Robert Mills's 1845 sketch of the Washington National Monument. Courtesy of Library of Congress, Prints and Photographs Division, http://www.loc.gov/pictures/item/2002723506/.

Plate 3. A view of the Washington Monument Grounds in a proposal for the 1892 World's Fair competition. Courtesy of the George Washington University Museum, Washington, DC. AS 268 The Albert Small Washingtoniana Collection.

Plate 4. "Monument of Unity" reinforces the circle of the Washington Monument as the symbol of the U.S. as one nation. The design includes a museum and the glass roof casts both direct and indirect light. Design by Jacques Prins, Kevin Battarbee, and Egidijus Kasaka-tis (Netherlands). Courtesy of National Coalition to Save Our Mall.

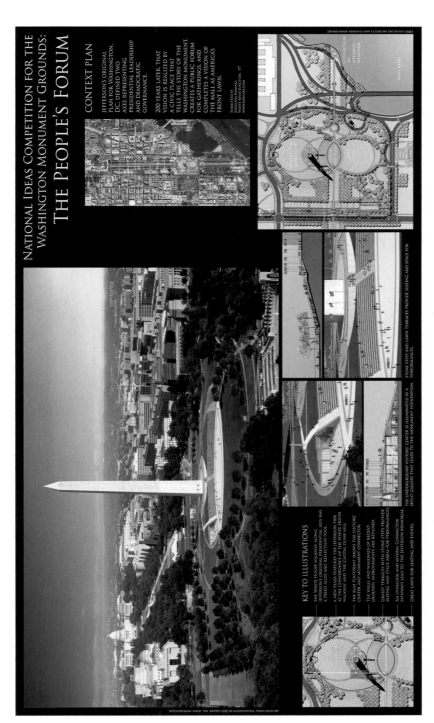

Plate 5. "The People's Forum" expands on the idea of the Washington Monument Grounds as a gathering space. The design includes a new 3,000-seat amphitheatre that encircles the monument's base and recalls the amphitheatres of Rome and Greece. Design by Karolina Kawaika (USA). Courtesy of National Coalition to Save Our Mall.

Plate 6. "An Inclined Plane" extends the Mall over the two streets so that people can walk to the monument without having to cross traffic. The designers also create a platform for viewing historic events. Fountains hearken back to the McMillan Plan water features. Design by Julian Hunt, Lucrecia Laudi, Monling Lee, and Miguel Angel Maldonado. Courtesy of National Coalition to Save Our Mall.

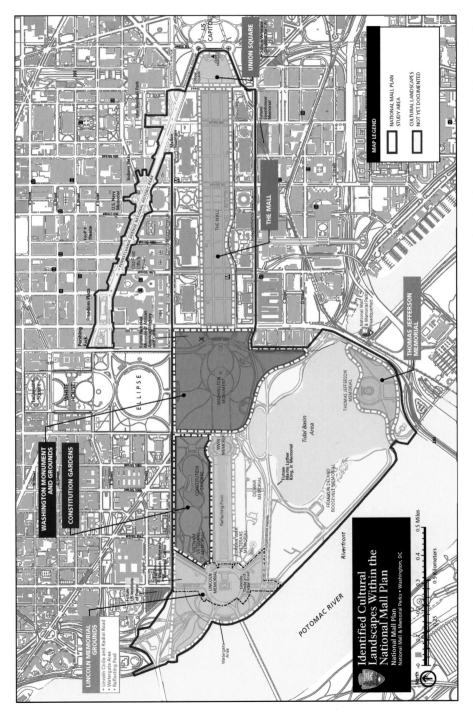

Plate 7. The National Park Service divided up the Mall into different cultural landscapes for the planning process. Is this yet another example of continued fragmented planning? Note that the Smithsonian and White House/Ellipse Areas were not part of the plan's study area. Courtesy of National Park Service, National Mall Plan.

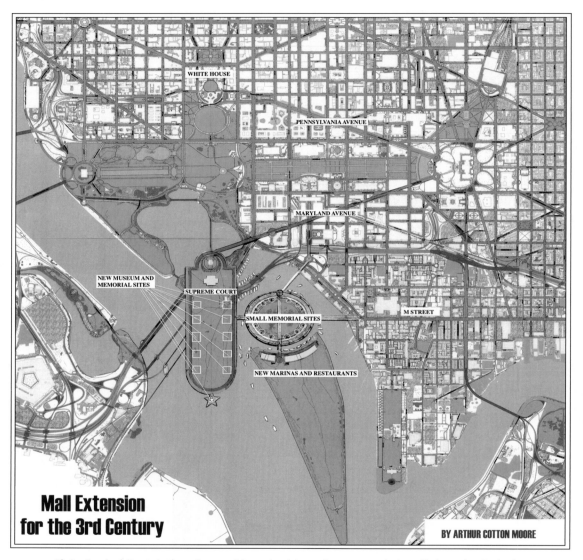

Plate 8. Architect Arthur Cotton Moore's vision of an expanded Mall that also includes East Potomac Park. Courtesy of National Coalition to Save Our Mall and Arthur Cotton Moore.

Memorials, Monuments, and the Meaning of the Mall

The selection of the Rainbow Pool became controversial because this north-south/east-west axis of the Mall had over the course of the twentieth century become defined through practice as informal open space. The grounds around the Washington Monument are used for kite flying, Frisbee, softball, and various gatherings – rallies, protests, family reunions – too numerous and diverse to catalogue. The trails on either side of the Mall are used for jogging, bicycling, and dog walking. These uses are fairly recent and while not as well documented as political protests are nonetheless forms of active engagement with public space and community. Opponents believed that this two-mile vista was threatened by the WWII Memorial's "intrusion." As one commentator lamented, "L'Enfant didn't figure on the fact that if he gave the nation a front yard someone would eventually want to take over the center of it."[59]

Opponents contended that the memorial would ruin the spacious layout that symbolizes the country's philosophy of openness and freedom. The World War II Memorial "will mar forever one of the most glorious spaces of any capital on the planet, a vast bucolic promenade stretching two miles from shrine to shrine," noted the conservative critic Charles Krauthammer.[60] Coalition Chair and President Judy Scott Feldman argued, "This memorial design goes against the qualities of openness and natural beauty that make the Mall a national treasure."[61] "Obstructing a great American vista meant to clear the mind and evoke our oldest traditions tramples on our heritage, casts doubt on our understanding of the link between the past and the future, and makes a mockery of our guardianship of the nation's priceless treasures," said D.C. Delegate Eleanor Holmes Norton. [62] WWII veteran Charles Cassell, a prominent Washington architect, wanted the Mall to remain "what it was supposed to be – one large, open, beautiful green concourse, an expanse which people use and admire."[63] Its beautiful green expanse is "one of the nation's major artistic monuments in itself and should not be intruded upon by a structure with focus on military conquest."[64] Those who were concerned about loss of open space acknowledge that there are many stresses on the Mall – it is not a pristine swathe of green.

In addition to concerns about the loss of recreation and open space, some worried that the WWII Memorial would break up the country's most important site for protest demonstrations. The area in between the Washington Monument and the Lincoln Memorial is a public space where people congregate and express ideas. The Rainbow Pool area has served as an open, spatially continuous gathering place for demonstration, celebration, and contemplation. Historian Lucy Barber has documented the emergence of the Mall as a focal point for public protest.[65] She notes that "marching on Washington" has contributed to the development of a broader and more inclusive view of American citizenship and has transformed the capital (and the Mall) from the exclusive domain of politicians into a national stage for Americans to participate directly. Opponents felt the WWII Memorial threatened the viability of this "stage of democracy." "Public space for public use – where Americans can gather by the hundreds of thousands to address their government – is precisely what this monstrosity will destroy," noted the *Hartford Courant*.[66] "The Mall is about to become a gated community," said architect Robert Miller.[67] The Coalition charged: "This is not about honoring veterans; this is about ruining the nation's most important gathering spot by putting up a monstrosity that will block the unimpeded walkway and the open vista that now exists."[68] Another powerful citizen's planning group, the Committee of 100 for the Federal City, echoed that the Mall axis should remain an open and unobstructed "forum of democracy."[69] But J. Carter Brown of the CFA labelled many of the WWII Memorial opponents "Mall purists" and remarked, "Washington shouldn't be allowed to be a nostalgia bath for the 19th century."[70] Brown's comment reveals an agenda to rewrite the meaning of the Mall through the site selection for the WWII Memorial.

The addition of a new memorial does not inherently impede public space on the Mall. Memorials can play a radical political role in and of themselves and hence can be part of the use of public space for protest. For example, the Vietnam Veterans Memorial speaks about the war in a critical way. Others believe that the Martin Luther King, Jr Memorial is a conduit for Black America to challenge the hegemony of White memory on the Mall and in national history. At the same time, however, more and more memorials may physically prevent the sort of political gatherings that characterize the Mall as a "public forum." This remains to be seen – there has been no significant impediment to any protests or marches since the memorial was completed, yet there have been few large-scale protests since then anyway. But it is also now a fact that the area south of the Washington Monument, where the WWII Memorial is located, is no longer available for protest space. While it is unclear whether the WWII Memorial will physically impede the Mall as a stage for public demonstrations, it has *visually and symbolically* interrupted a space that had historically been used as a gathering space during political protests.

In addition to concern about diminished open space and protest space, another aspect of the debate has focused on the rising demands for memorials, what opponents called the "cluttering" of the Mall. NBC Nightly News ran a story titled "How Many Memorials Are Enough?"[71] D.C. Delegate Eleanor Holmes Norton argued that "our generation will be blamed not only for obstructing the Mall, but for defacing it in the large chunks that would have to be carved out to make this space approachable ... We must not allow a unique space, embroidered with such special meaning, to send mixed messages."[72]

Because of increased demands for memorials, the location of the WWII Memorial at the Rainbow Pool came to embody growing opposition to the continued building frenzy on the Mall. The balance between the Mall's openness and the monuments is an important feature worth keeping. "What makes DC remarkable isn't just L'Enfant's plan. It's the counterpoint between vast, formal spaces and the monuments ... Monuments – especially ones with a high emotional quotient – don't do well cheek by jowl. They aren't stores in a shopping mall. The Mall is not a mall. Spacing the monuments out enhances their impact."[73] This idea of "spacing" monuments is also part of a wider aesthetic debate: the Mall provides the proper balance to a city populated with memorials; it heightens the visceral impact and importance of each monument while drawing them together.[74] The completion of the WWII Memorial signalled a new reality for the Mall: a tension between wanting to expand the American story through commemoration and concerns about memorial clutter and the loss of open space.

Rewriting the Mall?

If the Mall is a text, the WWII Memorial alters that text. Part of the controversy, therefore, has also revolved around how the memorial would rewrite that text and whether it was an appropriate alteration to the meaning of the Mall.

Opponents claimed the WWII Memorial represents only a special moment in our national history, not the founding ideals. Some contended that the memorial doesn't carry the same symbolic significance as the Mall's other axial components; it belongs on the Mall, but not on the sacred axis. Despite the many interpretations of what the Mall and the axis of the core area represent, opponents share the view that the WWII Memorial will "interrupt and actually break the continuity of that story."[75] Memorial supporters counter that war is intrinsically part of national identity as formulated in the twentieth century; therefore, its insertion between the Washington Monument and the Lincoln Memorial legitimizes the war's importance.

The location of the memorial between two of America's best-recognized structures is, for some, problematic: "To intrude upon that space, even to memorialize American heroes of the world's fiercest war, is to separate the Mall's aesthetic wholeness and interpose the 20th century between symbols of the 18th (George Washington) and 19th (Abraham Lincoln)."[76] Another stated that "since there is no monument to any war in the heart of the Mall, why should any other war now be granted so singular an honor? This question, so at least it seems to me, has not been satisfactorily answered by any proponents of the Rainbow Pool location."[77] Yet another contended that "the site symbolically establishes World War II as one of the three pivotal events in American history."[78] And another claimed, "A monument focusing on militaristic values of victory and sacrifice should not be interjected into such prominent juxtaposition with memorials that stand for the more universal American ideals of freed and idealism."[79]

However, others countered that World War II is intimately linked with our national ideals and democratic principles, which were upheld by others already commemorated on the Mall, since it was fought in defence of those very ideals and principles.[80] Memorial supporters contended that WWII was *the* defining experience of the twentieth century; the axial location would reinforce this interpretation. Supporters were also wary of putting the Mall "off limits," noting that the Mall's commemoration of American history should not be confined to the eighteenth and nineteenth centuries.[81] Congresswoman Marcy Kaptur, Ohio Democrat (and sponsor of the original WWII Memorial legislation), stated, "This will serve as an important reminder of the single most important event that shaped the 20th century."[82] Supporters of the memorial argued that only "a central location on the Mall's axis can do World War II justice and give it the hierarchical recognition it deserves."[83] The Park Service guide to the WWII Memorial comments that "placing the memorial between the Washington Monument and Lincoln Memorial reflects the importance of World War II in preserving and internationalizing democratic ideas won under George Washington and defended under Abraham Lincoln."[84] J. Carter Brown thought the Mall should be more than a recreational space. He claimed that the idea of the Mall as "sacred precinct" is consonant with the gravitas and significance of the WWII Memorial, which will actually "help define the space and *differentiate it from the recreational areas where people throw Frisbees and jog.*"[85] His comment was a not-so-subtle criticism of those who had "nostalgia for the status quo" of the Mall; it also reinforces my previous point about how key decision makers placed little value on the Mall's function as an open/recreation space. In essence, the issue behind the controversy is this: Will commemoration be more highly valued than other uses on the Mall? If we cannot strike the right balance, will this affect development and use pressures in other public spaces in other cities?

Ultimately, the memorial's axial location and the shift in its symbolism was acknowledged and directly worked into the final design. At the entrance to the memorial, on a large granite tableau about four feet in dimension, are carved these words of introduction: "Here in the presence of Washington and Lincoln, one the eighteenth century father and the other the nineteenth century preserver of our nation, we honor those twentieth century Americans who took up the struggle during the Second World War and made the sacrifices to perpetuate the gift our forefathers entrusted to us: a nation conceived in liberty and justice."

Reacting to Commemoration Pressure:
The Mall Is Now Closed (Maybe)

Prior to the WWII Memorial controversy, the Department of the Interior, in conjunction with the Park Service, had actually recognized the threat of continued pressure to add new monuments and memorials. Back in 1998 the Park Service declared a "moratorium" on the Mall and designated a T-shaped area called "The Reserve" as off-limits to future monuments (Figure 5.5). No more statues, walls, busts, or complexes would be erected. "The aim is to preserve its sweeping vistas and reciprocal views." The moratorium on new memorials on the Mall can be seen as a political act of open space/public space preservation, and clearly reflected increased concern about political pressures to locate memorials on the Mall's limited space. It might also be seen as a reaction against the discomfort caused by attempting to balance old history/identity with new history/identity. The 1998 decision, however, came after Congress had passed the legislation for the WWII Memorial, which effectively exempted the memorial from the moratorium. Furthermore, while advocates for the protection of open space and public space see the moratorium as a useful legal tool to oppose future Mall projects,[86] the authorizing legislation for many of the memorials currently pending

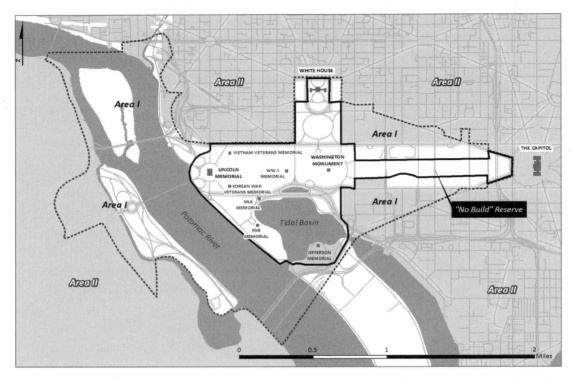

Figure 5.5. In 2003 Congress reaffirmed that the Mall is "complete" and created the area of the "No Build Reserve." Area I, however, remains open to future memorials. Map by author.

in Congress include the specific provision that the memorial be located on the National Mall. This highlights how the Mall is often subject to the whims of political elites searching for creative ways to circumvent the moratorium, and it underscores just how easily Congress can undo attempts to preserve and protect the Mall's open space, even when there is existing federal law to the contrary. There will be future legislation proposed for new memorials, and many more attempts to locate these new memorials on the Mall's "No Build Reserve." Will Congress have the political will to say no?

The WWII Memorial is now completed. The debate is over. On Memorial Day in May 2004, the Memorial was dedicated. Hundreds of thousands of people from all over the United States made the journey to celebrate its opening. Ironically, the eleven-year process of legislating, fund-raising, and then constructing the memorial lasted longer than it took to fight the war. The dedication was featured on television, in newspapers and magazines, and on websites around the country. The initial critics of the design and location were not assuaged by the celebratory atmosphere of the dedication, and remained stalwart in their disapproval of the finished product. *Time* magazine called it "A Monument to Blah," the *Los Angeles Times* said that it was "A Memorial to Forget" that "interrupts and permanently scars the most powerful symbolic narrative" of the Mall, and, in the *New Yorker*, Paul Goldberger assessed it as "a memorial that doesn't rise to the occasion."[87]

The controversy over the WWII Memorial may be over, but the issues raised continue to be debated. And they should. Commemoration of the Mall is a complex and controversial issue. On the one hand, society gains an appreciation for an event or person that is integral to American identity. On the other hand, space is transformed – open space may be sacrificed for memorial space.

Exploring the controversy over the World War II Memorial and the ways in which it has physically and symbolically changed the Mall reveals that these debates are increasingly important. The sheer size of the memorial may signal problems with future memorials as well. Green space and trees covering 7.5 acres were replaced by granite and more granite. The recently completed MLK Memorial consumed four acres of green space. Commemoration on the Mall now comes at the expense of open space, and yet there is little debate and discussion about the trade-offs involved.

CHAPTER 6

Securing the Mall

We look like a nation in fear.

> – *Washington Post* editorial, 2002

Can I take a picture of your gun?

> – A Grade 8 student from Indiana to a U.S. Capitol Police officer
> with an assault rifle strapped to his chests, *Washington Post*, 2005

On 20 January 2005, at his second inauguration, President George W. Bush took the oath of office and delivered a speech forcefully enunciating America's mission to spread the principles of democracy, freedom, and liberty throughout the world. This event took place amidst bollards, barriers, sentry boxes, more than thirteen thousand soldiers and police officers, and miles of security fences.[1] "Washington, D.C.," observed conservative commentator George Will, resembled a "banana republic."[2]

Responses to the potential of terrorism, whether domestic or international, have had a profound impact on the city, and the Mall. Intense surveillance and security have changed not only the physical landscape of the city but the symbolic landscape as well. Public spaces where the public might interact with the government and with each other are becoming more controlled and contrived. Or closed altogether. "In a city that symbolizes freedom, barriers abound," said Washington newspaper columnist Jan Cienski.[3] Another commented that it is the terrorists, perversely, who are memorialized in what has been taken away: the curtailed candlelight tours of the White House, and the now restricted West Steps of the Capitol, which once provided the best panoramic view of the Mall.[4] Barricades and bollards have become the newest accessory on the country's psychic frontier. Fortifications to the Mall, and to the memorials and monuments located there, change public access and its symbolic message. Is this an acceptable trade-off to make? Has it been made in a process that encourages public input and discussion?

Fear and Fortressing Urban Space

Fortification of urban space is not merely a recent phenomenon. Washington, D.C., for example, has been affected by several periods of heightened security and fortification, including the War of 1812, the Civil War, and World War II. To prepare for the British invasion of 1812, fortifications were constructed around the District perimeter (which proved ineffective as British troops burned the Capitol and the White House to the ground without encountering any resistance). In a scene eerily reminiscent of the 2005 presidential inauguration, the 1860 inauguration of Lincoln took place in a capital city bristling with bayonets for his protection. The summits of the city hills were transformed into a ring of forts – Fort Reno, Fort Totten, Fort Lincoln – that remain today (these are now part of the national parks of the Capital Region). Subsequently, the Civil War transformed the Mall (albeit temporarily) into grounds used for horse stables, cattle pens, corn houses, hay sheds, and quarters for officers and men.

Yet, despite a history of fortifications during wartime, nothing could compare to the permanent, long-lasting changes instituted by the recent security plan. This is because the new fortifications, while articulated as a response to the War on Terror, are unlikely to be dismantled should the war ever end; many of the proposed visible and invisible forms of fortification and surveillance have geographic and political implications that resonate beyond the short term.

Contemporary U.S. society continues to debate how to reconcile the need for anti-terrorist measures and increased fortification with democracy, liberty, and freedom. With regard to public spaces like the Mall, this debate centres on how to balance the physical alterations of enhanced security with the openness and accessibility inherently important in this symbolic space. The rise of security policing, new forms of surveillance, and control of urban spaces are subjects that scholars have explored for some time.[5] Long before the events of 9/11, urban scholar Mike Davis diagnosed what he called "fortress cities" as a response to perceived urban disorder and decay, primarily from domestic sources. He presciently noted that the car bomb could well become the ultimate weapon of crime and terror. Other scholars also predicted that urban authorities might create fortress-style rings of steel as a response to terrorism.[6]

The fortress metaphor describes a landscape that is demarcated by physical borders such as gates and walls and by invisible surveillance devices such as closed-circuit television that watch city streets, parks, and gated communities.[7] This is a vision of a city that can be controlled. Some see the vision as dystopian; others see it as empowering.

The global war on terrorism has altered security and fortifications of both private and public space in cities around the United States. Many accounts present bleak portrayals of future urbanism and design since the invocation of "national security" may trump issues of public access and public space.[8] It remains unclear how the need for improving security translates into acceptable levels of fortification and loss of public access to public space.

Commentators have discussed the costs and benefits of adopting counter-terrorism measures in the face of real or perceived terrorist threats.[9] Until the early 1990s, many U.S. cities had no comprehensive security and defensive strategy; attempts to protect against terrorism occurred specific target by specific target and often after an event raised the issue or pointed to vulnerability, or a direct threat was made.[10] Then, as perceptions of terrorism changed, new, more far-reaching responses emerged. Because terrorists prefer to target global cities to attract global media publicity and because most of the attacks until recently focused on economic infrastructure and financial zones, so did many counter-terrorism measures.[11] In the aftermath of 9/11, however, another shift occurred. Symbolic targets – such as monuments, memorials, landmark buildings, and other important public spaces – are now also at risk, leading to highly visible counter-terrorist measures.

A National Discourse of Hypersecurity

The impulse to hastily implement intrusive or highly visible security measures may be described as "hypersecurity." This term suggests that anything designed to protect people and buildings has been given instant legitimacy when associated with the phrases "national security" or the War on Terror. Hypersecurity measures are quickly approved but do not often involve substantial debate or public discussion and are not necessarily effective. For example, the Department of Homeland Security's advisory system of colour-coded threat levels has been at best an enigmatic disappointment that implies an impending terrorist strike but provides little in the way of steps to protect oneself. Washington, D.C., is frequently under "Code Orange" (a high risk of attack), although most of the public has little understanding of what this means or what to do about it (indeed, for the average person there is nothing to do). In some instances, the code system seems counter-productive, increasing confusion and ratcheting up the population's free-floating paranoia (recall the now infamous run on duct tape and plastic liners at hardware stores around the D.C. region, instigated by a well-meaning but panic-causing suggestion made by the Federal Emergency Management Agency [FEMA] of the Department of Homeland Security).

Yet in many areas counter-terrorism measures amount to little more than extensions of ongoing trends and plans.[12] This is important to keep in mind. September 11th has created a discourse of urgency that legitimizes the fortressing of "at risk" sites; the Mall is but one example. Some of these fortress measures on the Mall are visible (barricades around monuments and memorials); some are invisible (CCTV, for example). What is often overlooked, and more troubling, is that security efforts and the trend towards a fortress mentality on the Mall pre-date 9/11.

Security Pre-2001

As far back as the mid-1990s, there had been an "alarming proliferation of unsightly and makeshift security measures" in and around the Mall.[13] Many of these barriers were hastily erected as "temporary" anti-terrorists measures after the 1995 bombing of the Alfred P. Murrah Federal Building in Oklahoma City, when officials realized that small trucks could be used as high-explosive car bombs. More barriers were added after the 1998 car bombings of the U.S, embassies in Kenya and Tanzania. Most of the fortification was done piecemeal by different federal agencies for different purposes and was scattered throughout the city. One of the more visible measures, shortly after the 1995 Oklahoma City bombing, was the closure of Pennsylvania Avenue between 15th and 17th streets (immediately north of the White House) to all vehicular traffic. The closing of such a major thoroughfare in the city involved rerouting more than thirty-five bus lines and moving more than seventy-five thousand automobiles a day onto side streets. Locals still complain bitterly, but tourists have enjoyed a more pedestrian-friendly area in back of the White House.

The most ubiquitous form of security is the Jersey barrier, a mass-produced large block of concrete roughly ten feet long by three feet high. It is inexpensive (each barrier costs approximately $500) and portable (it can be picked up and placed where needed by a small tractor or forklift). The proliferation of Jersey barriers has drawn scorn from tourists, residents, and federal planners. Many of the security measures installed around the city, notably the Jersey barriers and chain-link fences, are more suitable for a highway-construction site than for the sensitive historic areas of the capital. But for many years officials were unable to agree on an alternative that would provide adequate security without intruding on the city's historic landscape.[14]

These so-called interim security measures threatened to become permanent fixtures in the city's landscape, in part because there was no money for anything nicer, and also because there has been a lack of coordination in planning new security. The *Washington Post* noted, "In Washington, D.C. so-called temporary buildings and structures have a history of lasting a long time." (Examples are the numerous "tempos" built during World War I and World War II that were on the Mall for more than fifty years.) Another editorial deplored "the ugly new look of the Capitol, which resembles nothing so much as a communist-era border strewn with ad hoc fencing, upended sewer drains and bored officers sitting in late-model cars with the engines running."[15] Yet another declared: "Real or imagined, you miss that old Washington ... we've surrounded it in barricades of worry. There are security lines and checkpoints and fences and Jersey barriers and rules, so many rules. It starts to feel like an insult."[16] Long before the events of September 11th, the nation's capital had become a fortress city peppered with bollards, bunkers, and barriers. This was particularly true of the Washington Monument.

A Tawdry Concrete Necklace

Memorials and monuments on the Mall have also been fortified significantly since the mid-1990s. Prior to September 11th, two highly visible temporary security measures at the Washington Monument included a ring of Jersey barriers and a visitors-screening facility attached to the monument entrance (see Figure 6.1).

Figure 6.1. The Washington Monument ringed by Jersey barriers prior to the implementation of the security plan. Photo by author.

Figure 6.2. Signs announcing that the Jefferson Memorial is open. So confused were tourists by the fortressing of the Jefferson Memorial that the Park Service responded by clarifying that the memorial was in fact, open, despite the intimidating ring of Jersey barriers, snow fences, and chain links fences surrounding it. Photo by author.

The long-standing "temporary" security measures at the monument have been the subject of ongoing criticism. *Washington Post* columnist Benjamin Forgey called the Jersey barriers "a tawdry concrete necklace" and said they were a "disfigurement" of an important public space.[17] The ring of Jersey barriers was an emergency measure, albeit one without any aesthetic quality.[18] Critics contended that these temporary security measures created a visual paradox: the Washington Monument's size, simple geometry, and soaring symbolism honouring not simply a president but the historic moment of the nation's founding have been contrasted with the out-of-scale attempt to protect the monument.

The Jefferson Memorial and the Lincoln Memorial were similarly fortified. The unsightly hodge-podge of Jersey barriers, planters, snow fencing, and flimsy barricades presents a vast contrast to what these memorials symbolize. The posting of a sign to clarify that the Jefferson Memorial is, in fact open, underscores how confusing and intimidating it can be to fortify memorials (see Figure 6.2).

In 2000, in response to unsightly security measures and the message of vulnerability that these measures communicated through their haphazard appearance, Congress charged the NCPC to work with other federal agencies and the private sector to create a comprehensive urban design that would provide security while maintaining the "unique character of the Nation's Capital."[19] Although the security plan was developed prior to 2001, the events of September 11th increased the sense of urgency to implement the plan and also shifted the discourse of national security in a way that has precluded an honest debate about the effects of fortification on the Mall.

Hypersecurity Post-9/11

Security became even more significant and highly visible following the September 11th attacks. Some of the visible changes included additional bollards and barriers around memorials and an increased number of Park Police cars parked in strategic places on the Mall and around the memorials. For nearly a year after September 11th, two Park Service Police cruisers were parked near the Washington Monument, just outside the ring of Jersey barriers. Other changes affected only specific events (such as the July 4th celebrations); still other changes were invisible, such as the installation of surveillance cameras on the Mall. The urgency and immediacy of security changes indicates that a hypersecurity mentality has resulted in little if any thoughtful discussion about how such changes would change public access to and the experience of the Mall.

One of the main narratives in this book is that permanent changes to federal public space such as the Mall should involve significant public input through an open, transparent planning process. The comprehensive security plan for the Mall, however, was not open; rather, it was fast-tracked as a response to what were seen as imminent threats to "national security." Such fortressing and restrictions to this public space may result in the erosion of civil liberties, although it is too soon to tell. Security changes may also rewrite the meaning of the Mall and how its open spaces are used. Concerns about the loss of civil liberties, restrictions on public access to public space, and the implied message of a new hypersecurity-oriented Mall underline the consequences of fortification. The Mall is an expression of democracy and freedom, and so fortifications to and restrictions on this public space are antithetical to its symbolic role in our national discourse.

Fencing in Independence Day

Since 2002, the Fourth of July on the National Mall means a double line of fences, closed Metro stations, blocked roads, checkpoints for searches of bags and parcels as well as "pat-downs" and possible screenings by metal detectors, and more than fifteen hundred police officers patrolling the Mall (on foot, on horseback, on Segways, and on motorcycles). The annual ritual of fireworks and concerts and picnics that draws hundreds of thousands of visitors has been altered by a massive security presence that casts a pall over the celebration.[20]

Of these new security changes, one editorial lamented: "Gone are the Fourths on the Mall when celebrants of freedom could roam without showing up on a government video tape."[21] The War on Terror and the increased security has changed one of the most popular annual events, affecting how hundreds of thousands of people experience the Mall on this day. Each July 4th, the Mall is now fenced, barricaded, and fortified; its openness is severely restricted, with public access altered in a highly visible way (see Figures 6.3 and 6.4). Sadly, this fortification of our celebration of independence has become so normalized that few protest the security measures. Indeed, it has become so routine that each year the *Washington Post* publishes a map showing visitors the security checkpoints without a hint of irony. July 4th security has never been seriously challenged or overtly resisted.

Watching Over the Mall

In March 2002 the Park Service announced that it would begin round-the-clock video surveillance at all major monuments on the Mall. Closed-circuit television cameras were installed for the first time to monitor public areas in and around the Washington Monument, the Jefferson Memorial, the Lincoln Memorial, the FDR Memorial, the Vietnam Veterans Memorial, and the Korean War Memorial (see Figure 6.5). Before approving the funds for the project, Congress held a hearing. John Parsons, then associate regional director for the Park Service's National Capital Region, testified that the $3-million program was justified because "these icons of democracy are high targets of terrorist activity. That is the camera's sole purpose."[22] He also noted that Park Police would use cameras "only in public areas where there is no expectation of privacy."[23] What is especially interesting is that Park Service officials acknowledged that, "although the process of planning

Figure 6.3. July 4th security includes numerous fences that cross the Mall, funnelling visitors to security checkpoints. Photo by author.

Figure 6.4. A very visible police panopticon closely monitors crowds at major events such as July 4th. Photo by author.

the CCTV system and obtaining funding for it had begun prior to September 11th, the installation of this technology became a higher priority after the tragic events of that date."[24] Other than this hearing, the decision to install surveillance occurred with little public input or discussion.

Reactions were mixed. Proponents of video surveillance and CCTV say that this technology makes it possible to cover larger spaces with the same amount of personnel. A nation-wide Zogby poll that reported 80 per cent of those surveyed favoured video surveillance in public areas.[25] But opponents are concerned about monitoring the Mall and the memorials, pointing out that there is a politics of seeing and of being seen.[26] One D.C. Council member commented, "At first, I thought Washington, because it's prone to more terrorist attacks, would be a place where visitors would want cameras, but I agree now with my colleagues who say Washington should be a beacon of freedom."[27] Another Council member noted that "these cameras have been set up to deal with demonstrations and dissent. This will have a chilling effect and discourage citizens from demonstrating openly here in the capital."[28]

Civil-libertarian groups expressed concern that video monitoring might discourage demonstrators, especially those who protest government policy. Even the conservative *Washington Times*, in an editorial entitled "Big Brother and the

Figure 6.5. A CCTV camera atop the Lincoln Memorial. CCTV cameras are also at the Jefferson Memorial and the Washington Monument. Photo by author.

Park Service," argued that taking steps to pre-empt terrorism is a good thing but pervasive monitoring is not the hallmark of a free and open society – accordingly, "such an invasion of public spaces must be condemned."[29] National Coalition to Save Our Mall Chair and President Judy Scott Feldman stated: "If we have to destroy our freedom in order to save it, let's at least take a little time to think it through. There's absolutely no assurance that cameras are the answer to protecting our monuments."[30] People should feel entitled to move about the capital freely, but fortifications and video surveillance communicate fear and retrenchment and undermine the basic premises of an open and democratic society. As the discourse of security and national security intensifies (or becomes entrenched), civil liberties may be sacrificed on the altar of safety: public access to public space may be curtailed in the name of protecting buildings and other national treasures.

Because of concerns publicized in newspaper editorials and articles, Congress held a second hearing on the use of cameras on the Mall. Maryland Congresswoman Connie Morella got to the heart of the issue by asking the Park Service, "Does the prevalence of cameras inhibit our privacy? Are these cameras effective in deterring or solving crimes? Who controls the cameras? Who has access to the recorded images? How long are these images retained, and for what purposes?"[31] John Parsons of the Park Service could not provide answers to these questions and admitted, "This hearing has brought us to an awareness that we need standards and policies."[32] His reply is telling: the Park Service had no written policies to cover video surveillance, yet the system was in place and functioning.

In addition to the installation of surveillance cameras and significant restrictions on access to the Mall for special events, there have been other more visibly intrusive and permanent security changes to the Mall.

The Security Plan for the Mall

Although work on the NCPC security plan began prior to September 11th, it was completed and approved in 2002. The plan aimed to balance the need for perimeter security in key federal zones in the city with the need to maintain the vitality of the public realm. It openly acknowledged that it focused security solutions on only *one* type of security threat: unauthorized vehicles approaching or entering sensitive buildings or monuments.[33] The plan did not address bombs carried by pedestrians, air attacks, or chemical and biological weapons. This is noteworthy, since implementing the costly security plan fully would not provide security against any and all potential threats.

As a way to mitigate the impact of an explosion originating from a vehicle parked or in motion, the NCPC recommend establishing a "Standoff Distance" of 100 feet for federal buildings and public spaces.[34] If a car bomb exploded outside of the 100-foot stand-off zone, experts agreed that there would be minimal damage to the building (and people inside). The stand-off zone allows for pedestrian traffic but not vehicles. It provides the space for security barriers as well as checkpoints to screen individuals, property, and vehicles. To secure this stand-off zone, the NCPC recommended that a variety of streetscape security elements be incorporated into security components in perimeter areas. These included hardened street furniture, bollards that impede vehicles, reinforced fences that incorporate greater architectural and historical sensitivity compared to Jersey barriers, and plinth walls that also double as planter beds and bollards.

The NCPC's security plan for the Mall was to be "functional, attractive, cost effective and *reflective of democratic values*."[35] This last statement is significant because it highlights that planners realized the need to balance security with the symbolic space of the Mall. Some aspects of the plan are more successful at balancing security and public access than others.

Since the Lincoln and Jefferson memorials are surrounded by generous expanses of open space, far exceeding the minimum 100-foot stand-off distances, the Security Plan called for security elements on the perimeter of the memorials. Plans to improve and coordinate security for these two memorials entailed removing the existing Jersey barriers and replacing them with large granite planters and retractable bollards around the perimeter of the memorials (granite is historically consistent with the materials used in the memorials). Each memorial was to be encircled by a granite plinth wall and planters that would more effectively create a permanent and landscaped pedestrian zone. In 2009 most of the security measures were completed at the Lincoln Memorial. However, as of 2016, some fourteen years after the plan was adopted, permanent security changes at the Jefferson Memorial have not been completely installed and the Jersey barriers remain in place.

The proposed security changes to the Lincoln and Jefferson memorials did not generate much public controversy, primarily because there were no obvious fundamental changes to public access to these memorials and because the visible changes are located at the memorials' perimeter. Still, it should also be noted that even these minor security measures will subtly change how people *approach and experience* the memorials.

Unlike the Lincoln and Jefferson memorials, the specific plan for the most visible and most cherished of monuments, the Washington Monument, generated intense public debate. Plans for the Washington Monument differed in both scale and function from the proposed plans for the other prominent memorials on the Mall. Many believed that the Washington Monument security plan would compromise both public access to and the symbolic character of the Monument. The Washington Monument grounds have historically served as the epicentre of public protests and demonstrations; they are a gathering place where protests often culminate in marches that encircle the monument and expand outward, filling the grounds. The security plan does fundamentally change how visitors approach and tour the monument.

Plans to change public access to the monument stretch as far back as 1973, when the Park Service first proposed to construct an underground visitor centre, connected by a tunnel to the monument. Owing to a lack of funding at the time, the proposal was never realized. But, like a phoenix, it has risen several times since. In 1993 the Park Service again pursued the idea of the underground visitor centre but dropped it when Congress rejected the high cost of the project.

In 2000 the Park Service conducted a preliminary planning study of a revised underground centre. The study was completed just prior to the fall of 2001. Following the attacks of 9/11, the Park Service joined the hypersecurity campaign, surrounding the monuments with additional Jersey barriers, stationing police cars around their grounds, and installing surveillance cameras on each of the memorials.[36] A month after the September 11th attacks, several Park Service officials testified to the NCPC and to Congress that the Washington Monument in particular was at an increased risk for terrorist activities, and that a threat to the monument was "a threat to *national security*" (my emphasis). The Park Service requested authority and funds to construct the underground visitor centre and tunnel as quickly as possible.

In the late fall of 2001, the Park Service held a private, invitation-only design competition for "Security Improvements" to the monument. It completed the new plan for security in December 2001. Installing permanent security measures on the Mall, and particularly at the Washington Monument, became a high priority for Congress and the Department of Interior, which responded by allo-cating $20 million for the implementation of the new security plan.

Three elements comprised the security plan: first, removal of the Jersey barri-ers and their replacement with a security element to protect the perimeter; sec-ond, construction of the underground visitor centre; third, the building of an underground tunnel to connect the centre to the monument. The Jersey barriers – the monument's tawdry concrete necklace – would be replaced with sunken walkways that were to be configured as a series of ovals extending east and west from the monument plaza. The twelve-foot-wide walkways would be located some four hundred feet from the monument, sunken into the ground three to four feet, and would serve as the vehicular barrier.[37] Apparently the planning team did not consider (or were not encouraged to consider) building a boundary wall at the street perimeter, as was the case with the Lincoln and Jefferson memo-rials; rather, the walkways were to be built in the middle of the swathe of green that surrounds the monument.

The underground visitor centre was to be approximately twenty thousand square feet and would house displays, restrooms, and a ticket booth. It would have skylights flush with the ground to provide views of the monuments and to let in natural light. After being screened by Park Service Police, visitors would then travel through a four-hundred-foot-long tunnel to enter the elevator at the base of the monument.

The original concept for the visitor centre and tunnel was not part of a security plan but rather was presented as a *visitor's enhancement plan*. In the post-September 11th world, however, the centre and tunnel became integral to "security," leading some to charge that the Park Service had seized on the climate of fear to push through its long-desired underground visitor centre and tunnel on the pretense of national security. As one commentator observed, "the bad idea of digging up the Mall suddenly gained prestige when it could be presented as part of a ter-rorism prevention package."[38] *Washington Post* columnist Jonathan Yardley con-curred, noting that "improved security is one thing and a construction binge of exceedingly doubtful efficacy is quite another … under the pretext of protect-ing the Monument against truck bombs and other forms of vehicular assault (jet airplanes don't seem to have crossed its radar screen), the Park Service has come up with a bizarre plan."[39] One criticism of the NCPC security plan is the lack of any participatory involvement in the plan on the part of local com-munities, the American public, or tourists, all of whom presumably frequent the

Washington, D.C., area and whom the plan purportedly is designed to protect. It is difficult for genuine discussion and debate when the "public" is largely ignored in the planning process.

Reactions to the Security Plan for the Washington Monument

The debate over the plan for the Washington Monument shows that it is difficult to keep a balance between the legitimate concern to keep the nation's monuments secure and implementing measures that ultimately reduce public access, a self-defeating outcome. The debate also reveals conflicting interpretations of security strategy, of aesthetics, and of how the plan would transform the meaning of the monument and its grounds.

Supporters of the security plan felt that the design was unobtrusive and that the pathways were graceful.[40] They considered an underground solution the safest and most efficient way to move visitors to the monument; adding interpretative exhibits and a bookstore was an efficient use of that space. Most of the supporters for the plan came from the federal agencies that worked with the NCPC to formulate it.

Public reaction in newspapers and on television was more critical. Opponents of the plan felt that these changes would impair public access and the character of this public space, noting the paradox of approaching a soaring obelisk connoting freedom and openness in a manner that resembled a burrowing, frightened animal. "There is something terribly wrong with getting in to the Monument via an underground passage – sneaking into monuments – would be wrong physically and symbolically."[41] Harry G. Robinson, III, then acting chairman of the CFA, declared, "Maybe the best tourist experience of the Washington Monument is not by walking through a tunnel into it"; and then CFA Secretary Charles Atherton agreed, stating that "nobody is happy to see people approach the Washington Monument in a tunnel."[42] Atherton went on, "The essence of the Mall is freedom of access. And as soon as you embark on creating such a space of freedom, you're bound to always invite the abuse of that freedom. I don't see how we can ever preserve that freedom and protect the park from the kind of attack that it's been subjected to."[43]

The National Coalition to Save Our Mall criticized the Park Service for "refusing to examine viable alternatives to its wasteful and destructive plan that will deface rather than enhance the Monument."[44] Coalition members argued that a simple perimeter retaining wall or a combination of walls and bollards bordering the streets around the monument would preserve the historic open spaces and be much less visually intrusive. They pointed out that this had been done for the Lincoln and Jefferson memorials and wondered why it had not been considered for the Washington Monument. Members speculated that the Park Service may have pushed for the sunken walkways to ensure that the underground centre would be built as well since both would involve considerable construction in the same general location.[45] The Committee of 100 on the Federal City asked the NCPC why there were not simpler solutions, noting, "These extremes measures can not be justified on paper or to the public."[46]

Construction of the sunken walkways began in 2004 and was completed in the summer of 2005. They alter but do not completely prevent the type of public protests and gatherings that occur on the monument grounds (see Figures 6.6 and 6.7). Yet the walkways do make it difficult for those with strollers, bicycles, or walking disabilities to access the lawn-seating area around the monument (the other option is to scale the four-foot-wall, not an easy task). However, plans for the other two parts of the Washington Monument security plan ran into congressional resistance as public criticism of the underground visitor centre and tunnel influenced politicians on the Hill.

Subterranean Fixes

Plans for an underground visitor centre at the Washington Monument complemented a recent trend in designing underground structures in places where space is limited. There are actually several other underground centres proposed or recently completed in Washington, D.C. The Park Service has proposed constructing an underground White House "museum and education center." The subterranean U.S. Capitol Visitors Center, completed in 2008, is a three-level underground centre of 580,000 square feet (two-thirds as large as the Capitol itself) and houses a security checkpoint, an orientation centre, a 600-seat cafeteria, gift shops, two 250-seat theatres, and congressional office space. Although the original 1999 budget was $265 million, final costs totaled $621 million.[47]

The reaction in general to underground structures has been mixed. *USA Today* eloquently declared: "Washington's bunker mentality grew after the

Figure 6.6. An aerial view of the Washington Monument's sunken sidewalks. Courtesy of Library of Congress.

Figure 6.7. A ground view of the Washington Monument's sunken sidewalks, with bollards in place. Photo by author.

September 11th events; hidden structures deep below the earth will better protect tourists, it's believed. But these subterranean spaces defile the very monuments they aim to serve. They lack the essentials of open, human structures, daylight, fresh air, outdoor views, and a sense of connection to place. Forcing visitors to burrow like groundhogs diminishes the meaning of our nation's treasured architecture."[48] Supporters counter that underground centres improve security and do not disturb landscaping; opponents called them D.C.'s version of Boston's Big Dig.

Opposition to the Washington Monument plan underscores that many see this key area of public space as the physical and symbolic expression of democracy and freedom. Critics say that security measures move towards "sterilizing a city whose landmarks and layout were intended to inspire."[49] In an interesting exchange of semantics at a panel discussion, one audience member criticized the "underground tunnel," to which one of the principle architects replied, "It's not a tunnel, it's a concourse." Robert Hershey, president of the D.C. Society of Professional Engineers, shot back: "It's a crypt."[50]

It is true that our monuments have become icons – and targets – because of their political symbolism. However, fear of terrorism should not dictate the design of structures. As Benjamin Forgey says: "What we have done in the name of security after September 11th – and even before – has done terrible damage not only to the beauty of the city but to its meanings. This is the capital of an open democracy, but it comes off as a confused, fortified compound. Security emplacements encroach upon our most hallowed monuments. They surround our most important political institutions. What we are getting is a distorted story."[51] Another *Washington Post* editorial questioned, "Of what value are the shrines if they are sealed off or made more difficult for the public to reach? Openness and public access are hallmarks of American freedom, even at the risk of enemies seeking to exploit what we hold dear."[52] While security measures may prevent some terrorism, the result is a very different Mall. It is unclear whether those who designed the security changes to the Washington Monument understood how these changes would rewrite the Mall. In the name of security, the Park Service and other federal agencies have erected bollards, bunkers, and fences that do damage not only to the beauty of the city but to its meanings. The capital is a confused, fortified compound and the Mall reflects this.

Former D.C. mayor Anthony Williams, who was at the time also a member of President Bush's Homeland Security Advisory Council, admitted that "a little

more openness is called for. I think we've struck the balance too far toward security."[53] Williams expressed concern about the potential loss of access, noting,
"We cannot allow the symbols of American freedom and democracy to be transformed into fortresses of fear."[54]

In response to increasing criticism in the fall of 2003, Senator Byron Dorgan
(D-Nebraska) sponsored an amendment (S. Ammdt. 1777) to block the funding
for the underground visitor centre and tunnel.[55] Dorgan asserted that "the question of whether this would be a necessary and important contribution or simply
a tragic waste of taxpayer money has not been answered."[56] The Senate Subcommittee on Interior Appropriations concurred with Dorgan and voted to withhold
funding for the underground centre and tunnel. Shortly after, the Park Service
announced that it had abandoned plans for the underground visitor centre and
tunnel. For now. However, with an understanding that the Mall is limited in
potential space, demands for visitor centres and museums will continue, and
architects and designers may return, again, to the idea of locating these structures
underground.

Resisting a Discourse of Fear and Retrenchment

Controversy over the fortification of the Mall can be seen as a resistance to the
power of the hypersecurity discourse that has threatened to negatively affect
public space and public access. Restrictions on public space anywhere, but particularly the Mall, are worrisome because of the historically important role of
public space a site for the formation of citizenship and a conduit for discussions
on civil society.[57] The Mall is a national park, and by law it must be accessible to
the public (what "access" means, however, is not precise). Security plans and visible fortifications reinforce fear and retrenchment and may have the potential to
restrict or make difficult public access in a space that is federally mandated to be
accessible to the public. Ironically, the language of the NCPC security plan consistently offers a discourse reaffirming the national commitment to accessibility and
openness both of the Mall and of American government while simultaneously
curtailing these very values. As one of the nation's pre-eminent stages for public
protest, security measures and CCTV may inhibit protest, free expression, and
even celebrations on the Mall. Any security plans that could impede that public-
space function need considerable discussion and debate before implementation.

Given that the public was largely ignored during the planning process (in the name of national security), debate and discussion has been ineffective.

In a post-September 11th world, the aesthetics of security communicates a message that is odds with the meaning of the Mall as public space and the stage of democracy. The rhetoric expressed in support of the numerous hypersecurity elements reveals that, since September 11th, concerns over security have trumped concerns over how implementing these security measures will affect the meaning and geography of the Mall. The security panic is not just a manifestation of the fortress-of-fear mentality; it is also another testimony to the need for developing a long-term master plan for the Mall, so that it is not subject to ad hoc planning projects that are inconsistent with the meaning and use of this public space.

Questioning security measures on the Mall might seem ill-advised during the War on Terror, but, in the long term, it is vital that we find a balance between security and access in public space. The symbolic, cultural, political, and economic importance of Washington, D.C., carries weight that is sure to affect how other cities and planners deal with security and fortification. In a new hyper-vigilant, hypersecure post-September 11th world, we have spent a lot of money trying to provide the appearance of universal protection of all the buildings and all of the people in them even though this is impossible. It is not reasonable to expect people whose job is to minimize danger to exercise moderation in their security plans, or to accept increased risk in the name of democratic access. But such measures should not proceed without genuine and thoughtful debate. In a democratic society, security should be a collaborative and public process – since 9/11, security officials seem to have not only the last word but the only word. It is possible that fortification efforts will restrict or curtail public space and express an architecture of fear and vulnerability in places that stand for democracy, freedom, and public access. These changes are often occurring without genuine public debate. Will we go too far?

PART III

PLANNING AND PUBLIC PARTICIPATION

This section focuses on trends and debates around public participation in planning, citizens asserting their "right" to use the Mall in new or creative ways, and new plans and visions for the Mall.

Chapter 7 explores the absence of public participation in planning and documents some of the obstacles to a meaningful role for the public. There are mechanisms in place for some public participation, but these are ineffectual. This chapter also discusses the way in which the District is attempting to re-engage the Mall and claim it as part of the urban fabric. These are encouraging trends, but more is needed.

Chapter 8 considers how citizens are asserting their right to determine new uses and visions or to protest Mall restrictions. The examples discussed in this chapter resonate with philosopher Henri Lefebvre's concept of the "right to the city." One example considers individual action and protest at the Jefferson Memorial. The protest took the form of a flash mob dance party. Mary Brooke Oberwetter and more than a dozen of her friends organized an expressive dance at the Jefferson Memorial. Such exuberance and noise is against the rules at the Jefferson Memorial and she was arrested. Was the protest frivolous, a misinformed view of First Amendment rights? Or was it an act of civil disobedience, an attempt to take back the Mall from a long unquestioned policy about what constitutes appropriate activity at a memorial?

A second example considers how the public might more effectively participate in visionary planning on the Mall. In 2010–12, as recounted earlier, I helped to organize an ideas competition to redesign the Washington Monument grounds. The competition encouraged the public to help shape the future through collective action, a reclaiming of the right of the public to determine the destiny of public spaces..

Chapter 9 looks at recent planning efforts for the Mall. Today, the Mall is the legacy of two great historic visions: the L'Enfant Plan of 1791 and the McMillan Plan of 1901. We are now in the Mall's third century and yet neither the L'Enfant Plan nor the McMillan Plan speaks fully to the Mall of today. The Mall lacks a comprehensive vision for the twenty-first century. The chapter begins by examining several recent planning efforts by the National Capital Planning Commission and the National Park Service. NCPC efforts have been to articulate how to better deal with development pressures, and where to locate future memorials; the Park Service has a plan that sees the Mall largely as a resource to be managed. The Park Service plan did address the issues of neglect and disrepair on the Mall, but critics say that it was fragmented in its approach. Neither of these plans was visionary, or comprehensive. The result is that the Park Service, as well as the NCPC and the CFA, lack Mall-wide standards and design principles to guide coherent decision making.

I then turn to some of the innovative ideas championed by the National Coalition to Save Our Mall. The Coalition calls for a new guiding vision, one that will incorporate the Mall's growing popularity for civic gathering and recreation and the proliferation of memorials and yet balance this with the Mall's historic integrity and symbolism. The Coalition advocates a vision that is forward-looking but simultaneously cognizant of the historical narrative. It wants to retain the Mall's national symbolism, which embodies democratic values, while embracing twenty-first-century functions. One idea proposed is to expand the Mall geographically. Supporters of an expanded Mall say that it will open up exciting opportunities for imaginative redesign of underused federal parklands. A second idea is to create a Third Century Mall Commission, much like the McMillan Commission of the early twentieth century. This commission could help craft a comprehensive, long-term vision. It might also serve to unify fragmented management on the Mall.

CHAPTER 7

Whose Mall Is It?

A day before Barack Obama was inaugurated in January 2009, he attended the concert "We Are One," and on the stage in front of the Lincoln Memorial he addressed the crowd: "What gives me that hope is what I see when I look out across this Mall. For in these monuments are chiseled those unlikely stories that affirm our unyielding faith – a faith that anything is possible in America ... And yet, as I stand here tonight, what gives me the greatest hope of all is not the stone and marble that surrounds us today, but what fills the spaces in between. It is you – Americans of every race and region and station who came here because you believe in what this country can be and because you want to help us get there." Obama understood that the power of the Mall derives not from its stoic architecture, or inspiring memorials or grassy open spaces, but from the people who visit, who use the space in celebration or protest, and who, ultimately, use the Mall as a stage for the expression of democratic ideals.

Ironically, the history of the Mall is a history of public space devoid of public participation in planning and management policy. One of the key problems is the lack of transparency and effective public participation in the planning process. There is a deeply disturbing and fundamentally anti-democratic lack of public involvement in major decisions that have long-term effects on the Mall. This premier public space has been created, not by focus groups or people's input, but by the visions of single, powerful individuals. From Peter L'Enfant's original vision, to the ambitious McMillan Plan drafted by Burnham, Olmsted, McKim and Saint-Gaudens, to the desires of senators and representatives who approve new memorials and museums, to the architects and designers of memorials and monuments, the evolution of the Mall has, in large part, been dictated by the few. The only meaningful way in which citizens have participated in writing the narrative of the Mall has been through protest and conflict, not partnerships and participation.

Such a poor record of involving the public in the planning process raises important questions. Whose Mall is it? Who is the public in federal public space? How is the public represented among the complex management structure? How is public input in planning and management policy carried out? These questions lie at the centre of the challenges the Mall confronts in the twenty-first century. The public voice should be integral to shaping the narrative of the Mall.

Public Participation in Planning

Who is the public? The "public" cannot really be equated with an individual and is only vaguely identifiable. At the federal level, the result has been a tendency to define public accountability primarily in terms of elections, rationalized bureaucracies, judicial review, and transparency.[1] Granting the public a voice is an important part of a pluralist democracy; however, the notion of the "public" or "community" is itself contentious.[2] Although scholars agree that public space and the sustaining of the public sphere are critical, it is less clear how to define and involve the public. Community can be defined descriptively in categories such as geographical, religious, ethnic, age, and so on. Defining community is even more problematic when it is federal public space, since everyone in the country is, theoretically, the "public." The concept of "public" is problematic in the case of the Mall (or any other national park) because Congress and the federal agencies that have jurisdiction over the Mall are considered to be "representatives of the public." I distinguish between the public at large (American citizens for whom these public spaces are designated and preserved) and the elected or appointed representatives of the public (Congress, Executive Branch appointees, and federal agency administrators). It is the public at large that has been denied an authentic role in shaping the Mall. Unlike other urban public spaces, where there is an identifiable local community which planners and policy makers can engage – involving the "American public" in planning on the Mall is a daunting task.

Currently, the practice of public leadership is being transformed because of many factors: transportation, communication, and information technologies have shrunk the world, resulting in changes in the public sector. At the same time, we live in an age where trust in government has eroded and this is reflected in political discourse, such as the extreme polarization that has dominated national politics recently. Such changes are forcing public leadership to move towards a model of connecting and collaborating.[3] One of the most important trends has been the emergence of innovative ways to involve citizens, both as a result of increased demand for openness and transparency and as a realization that such involvement enhances the legitimacy of the enterprise.[4] The field of urban planning embraced public participation during the 1990s, and the rhetoric of involving communities in planning and development has become embedded in government policy and local practice. Scholars have examined the ways in which the participatory turn in planning has influenced neighbourhood regeneration and revitalization.[5] Many planners and developers recognize that engaging the public in the process of planning and policy can advance social inclusion and enhance democracy. Therefore, they have developed many forms in which public participation can occur: study circles, round tables, focus groups, citizen juries, design charrettes, and visioning exercises are often used to gauge public opinion or to bring members of the public directly into the planning process. Citizen participation in planning lends legitimacy to government action.

Despite the modern embrace of "public participation in planning," achieving community involvement remains elusive, particularly on the Mall. This is because the participatory process in planning has been somewhat limited to citizens *reacting to* existing plans and programs, rather than being an integral part of the process. In reality, there are many barriers to public engagement, including poor information, a lack of resources, and a lack of trust among the public.

Planning for the National Mall

In stark contrast to trends in participatory public planning in many communities, Mall planning and management has been relatively hidden from view and public scrutiny. There are numerous challenges for including greater public participation. First is the Mall's complex management structure. Recall the torturous twenty-four-step process for the siting and design of memorials. There are numerous federal agencies, which meet at different places, at different times, and on different days. Second is a federal-agency culture that has not embraced genuine public participation. Some of that is the result of Park Service-wide culture; some stems from the way in which this specific park unit, the National Mall, is managed and its broader cultural attitude towards public participation. Add to that the reality that planning can be far more complex in Washington than in most cities because of the federal government's role, and the result is a tangle of politics – federal and local, business and civic, neighbourhood and personal.[6] This has led to an absence of public involvement.

Although it is true that many Americans rate the National Park Service highly (as compared to, say, the Internal Revenue Service), the embedded Park Service culture does not always serve its parks well. Lary Dilsaver and Bill Wyckoff have shown that the Park Service embraces a persistent set of beliefs and is reluctant to change. Three key beliefs were at the core of the Park Service when it was founded: the importance of open space and democratic access to the parks; the nation's best interests are served by average citizens visiting the parks for inspiration; and the Park Service has the responsibility to educate or "interpret."[7] These beliefs were "inculcated in employees and would come to form the agency." To this day, they "are so deeply imbued in both the agency and the public that they form a culture of management."[8] A member of the Central Park Conservancy told me: "Despite its best interests, the Park Service is scared to yield control. It is an insular culture. Park Service personnel resent change in the power structure and are often obsessed with issues of rank. This results in a lack of outreach to nonprofit partners. In addition to the foundational beliefs, the Park Service also embraced the organizational structure of the military, complete with uniforms and established hierarchies. As a result, the Park Service is a bureaucracy that is based on hierarchy, G-levels, and paying more attention to those above you on the hierarchy than to the public."[9]

Planners who have critiqued large bureaucratic planning processes have called for "transformational stewards" who value heightened creativity and initiative and have a concern for the larger public community and organizational transformation that results in better management and leadership.[10] It is not clear that the administrative leaders of the Mall have embraced that view until very recently. For example, the Park Service refused to allow the public to review the plans for the underground visitor centre and tunnel at the Washington Monument, describing "the details as security-sensitive."[11] They often exempt themselves from their own rules, or perhaps conveniently overlook them. Another obstacle is that the Park Service is part of a bureaucracy that attempts to unify the system through rules and regulations. These regulations often work well in the large nature parks, like Yellowstone or Grand Canyon, but can constrain the urban units whose use and visitors pose very different challenges. The initial objection to pedicabs and Capital Bikeshare on the Mall is an example where Park Service administrators were adhering to a formal system of regulations that did not allow for the realities of an urban location. This makes it difficult for the Park Service to "think outside the box." It is not encouraged to. Urban sites like the Mall are more the exception than the rule, and the wider bureaucracy is not flexible enough.

Along with the Park Service, the other two agencies that are charged with planning and Mall development, the NCPC and the CFA, have a similar history of a lack of public engagement, as I have noted in other examples throughout this book. Historically, the CFA and the NCPC have been the "equivalent to Aristotle's council of wise men ... this generally has meant the 'old guard' of the period in question."[12] Some CFA and NCPC administrators have been in their jobs for decades, making it difficult for others to challenge these "fiefdoms" once they have made their decision as to design and location.[13] Even those in professions that might have legitimacy to critique – such as architects – often do not. Several architects have admitted that the American Institute of Architects is afraid to express its real opinion on many Mall issues. So too are many landscape architects – they worry that their objections could damage relationships with these federal agencies and potentially derail future contracts for work with the Park Service. A bureaucratic culture has made public input in planning difficult to achieve, and public comments and reactions to draft plans are often dismissed.

Today the Mall has more stakeholders than before. The District has re-engaged with the Mall and Monumental Core, and new citizen's groups are demanding a voice. To be fair, it is difficult within any large bureaucracy to provide a full range of creativity and intimate governance. The Park Service has long recognized that it cannot do everything and must build coalitions and partnerships to achieve its mission. Some park units have done better than others at creating partnerships such as public trusts or conservancies. The Golden Gate National Parks Conservancy in San Francisco was established some twenty-six years ago, in 1981, as the official private partner of the Golden Gate National Recreation Area. In contrast, the Park Service did not establish a private partner, the Trust for the National Mall, until 2007.

A Less Than Public Process

Ironically, despite the plethora of public agencies, commissions, and congressional committees, the review of planning and changes to the Mall (such as the construction of a new memorial, or the creation of security barriers) remains a highly *unpublic* process. In the case of public involvement in decisions about the Mall, there is a difference between intention and reality. There is a legitimate concern that policy continues to be made behind closed doors, regardless of public input, and that significant barriers to genuine public participation remain entrenched in the bureaucratic structure. This has led some to wonder if the Mall is really public space after all.

The past culture of the Park Service supervisors for the Mall, and of the CFA and NCPC "fiefdoms," has established a legacy where the public has largely been absent or ignored. These agencies follow the letter of the law – by encouraging and seeking public participation – but not its spirit, since they rarely respond favourably to suggestions made by the public at large. Although they follow the process of public participation, public concerns are seldom incorporated into results and products. Some have complained that often the planning and review agencies, particularly the CFA and the NCPC, make decisions behind closed doors, and fail to adequately inform the public of its rights to attend meetings and comment on proposals. Some meetings take place at awkward hours, in difficult-to-find locations. Prior to the fight over the World War II Memorial, most meetings were announced in the Federal Register, a "publication of impeccable reputation and exceedingly limited circulation."[14] In 2010 *Washington Post* columnist and blogger Philip Kennicott wryly commented, "The trouble with socialism is that it takes too many evenings, and the trouble with democracy, as practiced by the National Park Service, is that those evenings aren't worth the bother."[15] As recently as 2010, he documented his experience at a Park Service workshop on alterations to the security design for the Washington Monument:

> I drove out to a dark and inaccessible patch of East Potomac Park to attend the NPS public meeting ... there was no access to mass transit.
>
> But the room was full, and people clearly were passionately engaged ... Much of the official presentation was a perfunctory walk through of the legal parameters for public comment. After architect Hany Hassan spoke, the Park Service announced that despite the efforts to several audience members to ask questions and make

comments at the microphone, the public was very definitely NOT going to be heard ... The NPS employees didn't even bother to take notes – and were, in fact, told not to take notes. There were no formal workshop procedures, and the groups they asked the audience to join weren't even given designated places to sit and engage.

It was a farce. The best you can say of this process is that the NPS is incompetent at public engagement and workshops. But I fear it is much worse than that, the process is designed to thwart any chance of a public back and forth between the audience and the NPS. They didn't even keep a transcript of the meeting. What's the point of coming out? The NPS should be ashamed of this kind of event, and they should change their policies to institute a clear, meaningful and effective platform for true public engagement.[16]

More troubling was that Kennicott's experience came three years after the Park Service issued a formal order to renew its commitment to civic engagement as the essential foundation and framework for creating plans and developing programs. The order stated: "True civic engagement is more than just a formal process to involve people in our NPS mission – it is a continuous, dynamic conversation with the public on many levels."[17] Perhaps the order never reached the Mall administrators. Recently, the three agencies have done better in setting times for their meetings further in advance and in noting them on their websites. Yet, according to National Coalition to Save Our Mall Chair and President Judy Scott Feldman, "it seems as if many of these agencies, including the Park Service, would prefer the public *not* be involved with decision-making on the Mall."[18] By law, these agencies must engage the public and allow for a public-review process. This is known, in shorthand, as "Section 106." Through this process, the public has access to the planning process; in some cases, this allows the public to reassert its voice, to reclaim public space.

Public Review and Section 106

In 1966 Congress passed the National Historic Preservation Act to preserve the historical and cultural foundations of the nation. It mandates the federal government to provide leadership in the preservation of America's historic resources and to "administer federally owned, administered, or controlled ... historic resources in a spirit of stewardship for the inspiration and benefit of present and future generations." Section 106 of the law requires federal agencies to consider the effects of their actions on historic properties and provide the community an opportunity to comment on federal projects prior to implementation.[19] Section 106 is the process by which federal agencies take into account the effect of changes to historic resources listed, or eligible for listing, on the National Register of Historic Places and allow the public to respond to such changes. The objective of Section 106 review is not to stop projects but to ensure that the views of the public are considered during project planning. The Advisory Council on Historic Preservation, the federal agency in charge of making sure other federal agencies comply with Section 106, states that "interactive consultation is at the heart of Section 106 review."[20]

In 1966 the National Mall Historic District was listed on the National Register and as such became subject to Section 106 requirements. Since the Mall is a historic landmark, U.S. citizens are allowed a voice when federal actions will affect it. Adverse effects could include physical destruction or damage, change in the character of the property's use or setting, or the introduction of incompatible visual elements. Because the Mall is a federal property, any new memorials, security plans, or infrastructure changes are carried out by a federal agency and hence subject to Section 106 review. The Park Service has developed guidelines implementing these responsibilities: "In planning and budgeting, the Section 106 process should be factored into Park Service project schedules and coordinated with any required NEPA consultation. Consultation must not be delayed until a proposal has become unalterable, thus foreclosing the [Advisory] Council's and [State Historic Preservation Officer's] opportunity to provide effective comment."[21]

In addition to Section 106, the National Environmental Policy Act of 1972 requires that all federal agencies review proposed changes for environmental impacts. The Council on Environmental Quality is the agency in charge of ensuring that the NEPA requirements are upheld. Together, Section 106 and the environmental-impact assessment are the two processes by which federal agencies in charge of the Mall are mandated to include public consultation. Generally, however, the "public consultation" occurs after the plans have been drafted, which is problematic since it means that the public might not have been involved with the initial planning and so are only allowed to "comment" on an existing draft plan. There is a public-review period, generally of thirty days. At the end of that period, there may be a hearing in which the public is invited to express concerns (although increasingly the Internet is used as a venue as well). It is important to distinguish here between public participation during the planning process and public reaction and response to the plan. Both have been unacceptable with regard to the Mall; the former has been totally absent while the latter has been weak and ineffectual.

The history of public involvement on the Mall has been limited in part because no public partnerships or non-profit organizations have existed until relatively recently. Several local citizen groups such as the Committee of 100 for the Federal City, the D.C. Preservation League, the D.C. Historic Preservation Office, the National Association for Olmsted Parks, the National Trust for Historic Preservation, and the Society of Architectural Historians have tried to advocate for issues on the Mall but have not achieved much influence in the decision-making process. National Coalition to Save Our Mall members have made a concentrated effort to assert the public voice. Since becoming involved with Mall planning and development in 2000, the Coalition has advocated for comprehensive planning for the entire Mall and more public representation in planning and policy making. The organization was originally founded in 2000 to protest the design and location of the World War II Memorial but evolved to challenge the planning *process* itself as being anti-public in character and contradictory to the needs of such an important public space. Coalition Chair and President Judy Scott Feldman remembers the struggle to represent an alternative public voice against the design and location of the World War II Memorial:

> Those of us who testified against the site and design – including Senator Bob Kerrey and other members of Congress, Richard Moe, President of the National Trust for Historic Preservation, and numerous professionals, citizens groups, and concerned citizens tried to add a public voice to the process. It became clear, however, that something was seriously wrong. At the so-called public meetings, Commissioners votes appeared to be already decided before public testimony was given. Repeatedly Chairmen Brown and Gantt refused to consider objections to the Rainbow Pool site, a site selected without public knowledge or input in 1995. The memorial design grew increasingly intrusive on the Mall's open spaces and grand vistas, but the Commissions approved each revision and expressed no concern about the threat to the aesthetic, historic, and cultural resource.[22]

Another Coalition member was so frustrated by this process that he made the following statement at one of the public meetings: "I realize that this is a final exercise in futility, but I still appeal to you one last time to stop this abysmal process. I only have 3 minutes, so let me review just one more new example in a sorry history of wrong decisions, unlawful actions and complete indifference to the will of the general public by this and other Commissions ... This hearing is really just one more and perhaps final public farce. The general public continues to futilely wait for responsible action from this Commission and for somebody to obey the law."[23]

George Oberlander, a retired planner and member of the Coalition board, summed up his experiences at the many Section 106 hearings he has attended over the last ten years: "They all smile when I raise issues ... they don't necessarily listen or respond. It's possible that some might agree with my ideas, but the way this process works is that their vision is inevitable. And they'd prefer it *not* be tinkered with in any way."[24] He likened these meetings to Kabuki Theatre – elaborate plans, good acting, but public participation that is more symbolic than meaningful. He also distinguished between public participation (where the public was asked to comment, submit responses) and the incorporation of those suggestions and comments. He believes that the Park Service congratulates itself on inviting and encouraging public participation, but rarely are the public's views reflected in the final plans.

During the last ten years, members of the Coalition, many of whom are retired urban planners and architects, have been the only non-profit representatives regularly attending meetings dominated by the Mall's key federal agencies: the Park Service, the CFA, and the NCPC. Coalition members attended dozens if not hundreds of Section 106 meetings about the Vietnam Visitors Center, the MLK Memorial, the Museum of African American History and Culture, and, most recently, the Park Service's 2009 National Mall Plan. In all these cases, the Coalition provided written comments and oral testimony. This is a remarkable feat in that there are numerous barriers to public involvement in both Section 106 and NEPA hearings. For example, sometimes Section 106 meetings are announced with little more than twenty-four-hours' notice, but citizens who wish to testify must call and register ahead of time; in addition, the meetings are often held during the day, making it difficult for those with full-time jobs to participate.[25] This is how agencies follow the letter but not the spirit of Section 106 consultations.

After a decade of attending countless meetings, members of the Coalition met to reconsider their role. Said Judy Scott Feldman: "The meaningful impacts of this activity are meager, except to allow agencies to boast that the public has a say.

Comments made by the public are routinely ignored or rejected. In fact, the response from the Commission of Fine Arts has been negligible, sometimes negative, never praiseworthy of the effort expended."[26] Coalition members believe that the NCPC needs to establish more effective rules for the Section 106 and NEPA process to ensure that the public process is encouraged instead of discouraged.[27] The two federal agencies with oversight over public review of the planning process, the Advisory Council on Historic Preservation and the Council on Environmental Quality, have been mostly unresponsive to public comments. Meanwhile, the relationship between the Coalition and the Park Service has become more adversarial. Coalition members believe that the Park Service interprets its mandate on public involvement in a limited way, and one result is that the secretary of interior can approve a site for a memorial prior to the first public meeting on the project being held, thus negating public input at the earliest stages.[28] More than once the Park Service has postponed the Section 106 process or other sessions to which the public is invited, opening up to public comment only when it was too late for it to have any meaningful effect.[29] Another criticism of the Park Service is that it rarely finds "adverse impacts" when conducting its EIA. Coalition members were frequently disappointed to find that the planning process would continue to move forward in a "quiet, behind-the-scenes way that encourages agency decision-making away from the public eye."[30] They expressed frustration that the Park Service would summarily dismiss their suggestions without thoughtful debate or discussion and that it acted paternalistically towards citizen groups or non-profit organizations. Their experiences have led some Coalition members to believe that the Park Service does not really seek public comment but rather makes decisions based on what it thinks the community wants and needs. They conclude that the Park Service is obstructionist when it comes to wanting and valuing public input.

Public participation in planning the Park Service 2009 National Mall Plan is another example. Feldman was critical of the ways the Park Service engaged (or didn't really engage) with the public:

Because the Mall functions today as more than a collection of monuments and memorials, or a grand landscape, the public needs to be given a meaningful role in decision making. So far, there has been a symposium where the public was only allowed to ask questions but not engage in discussion. And there have been a number of open-house type public events. But those events, where NPS officials stand

with maps and plans and invite public comment, limit input by the public to reacting to NPS concepts. They do not allow citizens to engage in discussion with NPS
planners and with one another. The NPS should provide a forum setting that allows
better dialogue.[31]

Of her experience at a 2010 Section 106 hearing on the Mall Plan, Feldman
remarked: "The hearing was a surreal experience. All the NCPC Commissioners
praised the Mall Plan, and one suggested it receive an award. All the nonprofits
that testified sounded quite different ... Public comment didn't matter. NCPC
loved the plan and the Commissioners barely mentioned that there had been
public comment by about 7 people and groups. They loved how 'open' and 'public' the process was. Curiously, however, there was no mention that even while
public, the public voice did not seem to be heard or taken into account for the
Plan decisions."[32]

Despite the Coalition's view that the "public voice" is being dismissed by government agencies, its activities have been garnering growing recognition among
print and electronic media. Since 2006 most articles and editorials about the Mall
in the *Washington Post* and the *Weekly Standard*, for example, have included the
Coalition's position on a variety of Mall-related issues. As a result, the Coalition
has been effective at being a "watchdog" group, although it aspires to something
much greater – a transformation of the planning process.

Coalition members are ambivalent about continuing to participate in Section
106 consultations. While they feel dismissed, they have also been told by agency
insiders that the cumulative impact of a persistent non-profit group has forced
the agencies to follow the letter of law in a way they had not intended. Coalition participation has also, Feldman reports, resulted in more internal discussions and debates within the agencies, although these are still behind-the-scenes
and not revealed in public consultation.[33] One federal agency appointee told
Feldman, "It's a shame that the relationship with the Coalition is adversarial,
although the CFA wouldn't be doing nearly as much as they would have without
this pressure."[34] Hence the role of the Coalition in the Section 106 process has had
an indirect impact; though weak, it is important.

Where does a citizen go when he/she is upset at a federal agency? What is the
countervailing power to the complex federal bureaucratic system that controls
the Mall? There are no clear answers. One last resort is legal. Preservation groups
or individuals can litigate in order to enforce Section 106. On 2 October 2000 the

Coalition joined with WWII Veterans to Save the Mall, the Committee of 100 on the Federal City, and the D.C. Preservation League in filing a lawsuit against the federal agencies responsible for the WWII Memorial proposed for the heart of the National Mall. Their explanation for this lawsuit was as follows:

> The government has violated its own laws and regulations in an illegal process that began back in 1995. Site selection was made by a few powerful men, without public involvement. No environmental impact statement was ever done for this sensitive and historic part of the National Mall and Lincoln Memorial grounds. Instead, the Park Service issued a finding that the proposed Memorial would have "no significant impact" on the Mall – an astonishing claim given that the Memorial would cordon off this part of the open space and transcendent vistas stretching between the Lincoln Memorial and Washington Monument with a sunken and enclosed plaza topped by 56 stone pillars.
>
> In our complaint we cite violations of the Commemorative Works Act of 1986, the National Environmental Policy Act (NEPA), and Section 106 of the National Historic Preservation Act. We concur with Cathryn Slater, Chairman of the Advisory Council on Historic Preservation, who in her September 5 letter to Secretary Babbitt lambasted the National Park Service for its handling of the memorial process and for shutting out public input, and who recommended that the current design be rejected.
>
> ... This illegal process represents nothing less than the gutting of the Commemorative Works Act which Congress passed in 1986 to protect the open public spaces and vistas of our nation's capital, and in particular the National Mall. It is an assault on environmental and historic preservation law. Above all, it is a subversion of the open and public process, the public's legitimate and legal right to know and be included in decisions affecting our public lands. If the National Mall is not protected by these laws, then no historic resource is.[35]

Although the lawsuit was eventually dismissed, this does not deny the accuracy of the claims in the lawsuit.

Reclaiming the Mall: The Disconnected District

The absence of a "public" voice in the Mall has long included a disconnected local constituency. Although the Mall is geographically located in the District of Columbia, there exists a complex relationship between the D.C. government and the federal authorities responsible for the Mall. Guy Wilson summed up this complex relationship thus: "The twentieth-century Mall resembles a geological fault line in all its movements and shifts, with layers of different thicknesses presenting competing interests or constituencies stacked in their order of impact: first, politicians; second protectors; third, users; then architects and other designers; and finally the City of Washington, D.C."[36] The Mall exists as a self-contained entity, largely independent of its city.

The Mall and the city, though having much in common, are distinct spaces. Because the Mall is federal public space, the city lacks authority over how it is used and developed. Recently, planning controversies, such as the debates over the location of the World War II Memorial and security plans for the monuments and memorials, reinforced how little influence the mayor and the D.C. Office of Planning have over the process. For example, nearly every member of the D.C. political elite (including the mayor and the D.C. congressional delegate) expressed opposition to the location of the recently completed World War II Memorial, yet they had little power to reverse the site selection or to force the federal agencies to revisit their decision during the Section 106 meetings. The disconnect between the city and federal spaces within the city is endemic to most capital cities. At the same time, however, the Mall is deeply embedded in national politics and thus subject to broader debates about what people and events should be remembered, and what should not. Thus, changes to the Mall can be seen as associated with and part of a broader national (rather than local) discourse and politics.

The Mall is not seen as a "D.C." space. It is not a vital neighbourhood where people live. Unlike Central Park or Golden Gate Park, there are no residences that surround the Mall, only federal buildings. As a result, there is no immediate constituency demanding better planning and management. At the same time, there is little incentive for D.C. to advocate for a vibrant, active Mall. For many Washingtonians, the Mall is not a place for residents, it is not a civic outdoor space; it is simply a stage for large protests or a series of stops for tour buses. Adam Irish, member of the D.C. Preservation League, wrote: "The monumentalist vision of Washington has choked nearly all urban life from the Mall and its environs. It has fashioned large sections of our city into pleasing vistas for tourists but has given the rest of us lifeless wastelands."[37] Washington, D.C., blogger David Alpert concurred: "It's sad that D.C.'s large, central part is virtually ignored by most residents ... I virtually never visit the Mall, which is unpleasantly sun-baked, too spread out, and largely devoid of convenient transportation or food. The Tidal Basin and Jefferson Memorial are wonderful, but even more distant from transportation, and crossing Independence and Maine Avenues gives pedestrians the feeling that they are unwelcome interlopers in a highway median."[38] In fairness, however, there are many recreation facilities on the Mall – including more than six volleyball courts, twenty-two baseball diamonds, two football fields, and three rugby fields – that play a significant role in D.C. recreational life.

The lack of affordable public transportation is another factor in the city/ Mall disconnect, as discussed in the previous chapter. The Metro provides public transportation to the Mall, but with only one stop, the Smithsonian; Mall visitors then must navigate another mile or so to reach the Lincoln Memorial. A private taxi is an option, but this can be expensive. The result, say many locals, is that the Mall has become an insular park in the centre of city, beyond the reach of affordable transportation for District residents.

One result of this geographic disconnect has been that city politicians and planners have been hesitant to waste political capital on the Mall. Historically, on those rare occasions when the city expressed an interest in the Mall, many of the federal agencies viewed this as a threat to their interests/jurisdiction. More recently, the city has been mostly disinterested in Mall issues. Further, many balk at criticizing the Park Service, which provides a source of local jobs. At the same time, one of the problems confronting good planning is that so much federal land needs to be supported and served by local infrastructure. This would seem to indicate the critical importance of coordinated efforts, but such efforts have not happened for the last one hundred years.

D.C. Delegate Eleanor Holmes Norton has a significant, if quixotic, role in terms of the Mall. The House defers to her to raise Mall issues; the Senate just appears uninterested in what she has to say. The D.C. Council also defers to Holmes Norton. One of her staff members said, "If the city wanted it, she'll want it. If she doesn't know the city wants it, she's not going to stick her neck out."[39] Perhaps as a result, Holmes Norton has been curiously apathetic in making big noises.

Some critics believe that Holmes Norton is protective of the federal agencies in charge of the Mall, particularly the Park Service. She appears to be comfortable with allowing the federal agencies to continue planning programs even if she is not satisfied with their management. One reason for this may be that the Park Service employs many D.C. residents.

The deeper issue is the District's relationship to the nation. The city is divided between its role as the home of the federal government and the home to 900,000 human beings. And it confronts one of the more challenging paradoxes: as the capital of democracy, the city itself is denied self-government and autonomy.

Reconnecting the District of Columbia

For some time, the Mall has been more of a physical barrier to the urban fabric of the city than an integral component. Urban renewal and the highway programs of the 1950s and 1960s created a moat around much of central Washington; freeways and a web of tunnels, bridges, and railroad tracks fractured neighbourhoods.[40] The result is that much of residential Washington, D.C., is isolated from the Mall and Monumental Core. Since 2006 the District has attempted to reengage federal agencies, in part because of several compelling issues: transportation, improving the quality of life for D.C. residents, and enhancing the tourist experience through an expansion of tourism beyond the Monumental Core. One planning effort has focused on reintegrating the Mall into the city.

In 2008 the D.C. Office of Planning unveiled its "Center City Action Agenda," which redefines central Washington and features the National Mall as its centrepiece. The plan seeks to link the downtown with the southwest waterfront, creating a more vibrant, interconnected area. It targets the area north and south of the National Mall for major residential and commercial development in the hope that this area will become an economic engine. Then Office of Planning Director Harriet Tregoning stated: ""The Mall has long been the southern boundary of the District's Downtown. With Downtown's emergence over the past 10 years as both a real residential neighborhood and entertainment district, and as the premier office location in the region, the Mall has been an important part of the area's growing vibrancy ... The Center City Action Agenda moves the center of the city south and east to include the southeast and southwest waterfronts and crosses the river into Anacostia. No longer the lower boundary of Downtown, The Mall becomes the literal center of Center City Washington."[41]

Another major planning effort focuses on the parks and open space of the federal city. The numerous squares, triangles, and small neighbourhood parks in D.C. are a legacy of L'Enfant's vision. They are part of the rich public space in the city: nearly one-quarter of the District's land area is devoted parks and open space. D.C. is home to more than 7,600 acres of parks and boasts one of the highest park-per-capita-ratios in the United States, at 12.9 acres of park per 1,000 residents.[42] And yet nearly 90 per cent of all parks and open space in D.C. is under the jurisdiction of the Park Service, not the D.C. government. It is an odd arrangement that dates back to the historic nature of L'Enfant's Plan and also the unusual relationship between the federal government and D.C. government. In 2007 the D.C. Office of Planning and the District's Department of Parks and Recreation collaborated with the Park Service and the NCPC to draft *CapitalSpace*, a plan to manage parks and open space located in the District. During the planning process, agencies admitted that there needed to be better coordination among agencies and improved information sharing with the public. As with the Mall, many of the other parks in D.C. suffer from the fragmented management structure. The Plan noted such challenges: "Because multiple government agencies manage varying responsibilities and activities on park land and open space in Washington, finding basic information for a specific park is not always easy. For example, it can be difficult to know who to contact to reserve a picnic area, find out about an upcoming event, or report a bench in need of repair."[43] The plan was adopted by the NCPC in April 2010. *CapitalSpace* points out that the quality and capacity of many of the parks within the District have failed to keep pace with the needs of local residents and visitors. It proposes to make parks in the city centre more inviting and active, to link numerous parks into a continuous greenway trail, to improve public schoolyards and playfields, to protect and restore wetlands, floodplains, and wooded areas, and to build trails for bike/pedestrian use that connect parks to the Anacostia and Potomac rivers.[44] The plan is noteworthy for its intention to better tie together the city's green spaces, public spaces, and open spaces. In this sense it provides a vision of a Mall more effectively connected to the city and a wider park network.

It is early yet to make any conclusions about the success of the District's reengagement with the Mall and the Mall's reorientation within the city psyche. It is also far too early to assess how well the federal and district agencies are working together in this new era of cooperation. However, the fact that these two recent plans have integrated the Mall into the future of the District is an important change from the past when the city was largely disconnected and disengaged from the Mall.

Whose Mall Is It?

Public spaces like the Mall are the loci of power and politics; they are spaces of representation. The Mall has the potential to be a very inclusive, representative public realm and public space but its stewards have failed to value public participation and the public voice. The vitality of this space should be a joint venture between the public stewards and the American public. To date, this has not been a genuine partnership. There are some signs that this is changing, but, so far, many obstacles to meaningful public participation remain.

Critical trends in contemporary planning call for a highly spatialized kind of social justice, one in which a true democratic public space ought to be planned and developed through *genuine* public input. It is a type of social justice different from that demanded by minority groups, transients, or others who have been marginalized and excluded from public space. Rather, it is about the democratization of planning and development that makes this social justice possible.

Many changes in the new millennium occurred without significant public participation in the planning process (security plans, new memorials) and with minimal attention during the public-consultation process. The first decade and a half of the twenty-first century has been full of debate and discussion about the future of the Mall. If federal agencies don't transform their processes, it may be up to the American people to take back the Mall.

CHAPTER 8

The Right to the Mall

A Flash Mob Dance Party

On 12 April 2008, the anniversary of Thomas Jefferson's birthday, Mary Brooke Oberwetter and seventeen of her friends met in the interior of the Jefferson Memorial to honour the former president through an "expressive dance." The dancers danced for the most part by themselves, in place, each listening to his or her music on headphones, believing that such activity expressed "the individualist spirit for which Jefferson is known."[1] This was one of the first so-called "flash mob" events organized at the Jefferson Memorial.

Shortly after Oberwetter's celebration began, an officer of the United States Park Police ordered her to stop dancing and leave the Jefferson Memorial. She refused, asking the officer to provide a lawful reason why she needed to do so. The officer did not answer and instead arrested Oberwetter for demonstrating without a permit and interfering with an agency function, citing a 1976 regulation that bars "picketing, speechmaking, marching, holding vigils or religious services that have the effect of drawing a crowd of onlookers." Oberwetter contended that the officer "used more force than was necessary, ripping apart her earbud, shoving her against a pillar, and violently twisting her arm." She took the issue to the courts, arguing that expressive dancing is protected by the First Amendment and therefore the Park Police's suppression of that activity was unconstitutional.

Figure 8.1. The Jefferson Memorial. Inside the rotunda is the statue of Thomas Jefferson. Photo by author.

The Jefferson Memorial is a circular, open-air structure topped by a domed roof (see Figure 8.1). It is surrounded on all sides by a series of Ionic columns, and to enter the Memorial visitors must climb forty steps rising from ground level to a portico. After ascending the steps, visitors travel through the portico to enter the Memorial's interior chamber. When entering the chamber, visitors pass a sign reading "Quiet Respect Please."

Since 1976, Park Service policy has prohibited demonstrations at any of the memorials on the Mall (Lincoln, Jefferson, Vietnam, Korean, and FDR). The ban does not include the grounds around the memorials, however. The Park Service's stated goal in prohibiting demonstrations at these four monuments is "protecting legitimate security and park value interests, including the maintenance of an atmosphere of calm, tranquility, and reverence in the vicinity of [these] memorials."[2]

At the heart of the Oberwetter case was the issue of whether "demonstration" encompasses expressive dancing and is therefore protected under the First

Amendment. The court also considered whether the expressive dancing took place in a *public forum*, such a sidewalk or the open grounds. Because Oberwetter's expressive conduct occurred in the interior of the Jefferson Memorial, not on the sidewalks or parkland surrounding it, the court concluded in its ruling of 2010: "The physical characteristics of the Memorial's interior indicate that it is a nonpublic forum. It is physically distinguishable from the surrounding parkland: an individual must affirmatively decide to visit the interior of the Jefferson Memorial."[3]

The court further noted that, while the Mall is a traditional public forum for purposes of the First Amendment, this is *not necessarily true for the non-open spaces of the Mall*. In addition, the court contended (based on Park Service definitions, no doubt) that "the Jefferson Memorial is *not a part of the National Mall*, and even if it were, such a general reference is insufficient to label the interior of the Memorial a public forum."[4] The court pointed to the 1976 Park Service policy that had effectively closed the interior of the Jefferson Memorial to a wide range of expressive conduct, thereby indicating that it is "public property which [is] not by tradition or designation a forum for public communication."[5] Based on this precedent, the court determined that "the characteristics of the Jefferson Memorial and its regulatory history indicate that the Memorial's interior is a nonpublic forum" and therefore not protected by First Amendment rights; in other words, Park Service policy prohibiting expressive activities in a non-public forum does not violate the First Amendment. The ruling concluded that dancing is not allowed at the memorials "because it stands out as a type of performance, creating its own center of attention and distracting from the atmosphere of solemn commemoration."[6] In short, dancing infringed on the ability – and rights – of all visitors to enjoy the memorial in peace.

Determined to protest the ruling and defy the court, on Memorial Day weekend 2011 several dozen demonstrators returned to the Jefferson Memorial to dance. U.S. Park Police and a SWAT team shut down the memorial, cleared dozens of people from the rotunda, and forcefully arrested five dancing demonstrators. YouTube videos of the event went viral. One video showed an office grabbing a dancer by the throat; another showed a demonstrator being slammed to the ground.[7] Reports in the *Washington Post* and on evening television news questioned whether officers were too aggressive in arresting demonstrators. Adam Kokesh, an Iraq War veteran and citizen activist, arrested for dancing, spoke about the irony of being arrested "for paying homage to Thomas Jefferson, America's foremost defender of freedom."

In June 2011 Kokesh then organized a follow-up "Dance Party at TJs" and encouraged other cities to hold similar "Freedom Dances" (such dances took place in Denver, San Antonio, Austin, Orlando, and Danville, Ill.). More than three thousand people signed up on Facebook to attend the D.C. event.[8] Organizers explained that those who did not want to risk arrest could show their support by dancing around (but not in) the memorial. On 3 June, about two hundred people gathered to dance.[9] Some wore tutus, one was dressed as Thomas Jefferson. Everyone danced to their own music in quiet. After about ten minutes of dancing and leaping, police began to move the crowd to the entrance of the memorial. This time, no arrests were reported; however, the memorial was shut down for about ninety minutes as officers cleared out demonstrators. The Park Service issued a statement: "Just as you may not appreciate someone using a cell phone in a movie theater or someone dancing in front of your view of a great work of art, we believe it is not appropriate to be dancing in an area that memorializes some of the most famous Americans."[10]

The issue divided some: Were the protests frivolous, a misinformed view of First Amendment rights? Or were they acts of civil disobedience, attempts to take back the Mall from a long-unquestioned policy about what constitutes appropriate activity at a commemorative site? Is the law prohibiting demonstrations in the memorial acceptable? Is the 1976 Park Service policy stating that the memorial is not a public forum just wrong? Has this policy been more rigorously enforced since 9/11 and the passage of the Patriot Act, which some claim has curtailed these freedoms? Should we allow protests at commemorative sites?

Those who saw the events as frivolous noted that they did not qualify as civil disobedience because no one had been banned from dancing in the memorial on the grounds of race, ethnicity, religion, age, gender, sexual orientation, or citizenship status.[11] Those who saw the events as significant pointed to the idea that the right to be social involves the ability to actively produce space and determine one's own vision of honouring and commemorating Jefferson.

Despite the fact that the Dance Party ultimately lost in the courts, it represents an attempt to challenge the way we use and interact with each other on the Mall and at the memorials. This example shows an attempt by individuals to deliberately use the Mall to express discontent with the restrictions on its use, thus asserting the public's right to reclaim this space.

The Rally to Restore Sanity and One-Up Glenn Beck

Two celebrity-led rallies in 2010 highlight the way in which the Mall's symbolism as a protest space continues to resonate. These rallies centred on the emergence of a highly polarized political culture. Interestingly, both were initiated by television celebrities known for their political commentary. Both argued that they were not political events (they were). Both claimed to be non-partisan (they weren't). And both sought to "reclaim" the Mall for their political causes.

In August 2010 FOX News commentator Glenn Beck held a rally to "Restore Honor to America." The rally had explicitly conservative political and religious undertones. Beck and one of his featured guests, Sarah Palin, claimed that the rally was not an official Tea Party event, saying, "There will be absolutely no politics involved."[12]According to Beck, the rally "has nothing to do with politics. It has everything to do with God, turning our faith back to the values and principles that made us great."[13] Sarah Palin, a Tea Party heroine and a former Republican vice-presidential candidate, said that she was speaking not as a politician but as the mother of a combat veteran. But signs in the crowd, which was estimated to number around eighty-seven thousand, revealed a more partisan politics: "FOX News = 21st Century Paul Revere," "Bury Obamacare with Kennedy," "Where's the Birth Certificate?" "The Anti-Christ Is Living in the White House," "We Came Unarmed This Time," and "America: Love It or Go Back to Kenya."

Beck's rally was held on the steps of the Lincoln Memorial on the 47th anniversary of Martin Luther King, Jr's 1963 "I Have a Dream Speech," leading civil rights leader Al Sharpton to organize a counter-protest in response. Some felt that the date chosen was an intentional insult to the civil rights movement. District of Columbia Delegate Eleanor Holmes Norton said: "The 'March on Washington' changed America. Our country reached to overcome the low points of our racial history. Glenn Beck's march will change nothing. But you can't blame Glenn Beck for his 'March on Washington' envy. Too bad, he doesn't have a message worthy of the place."[14] Beck countered that King's message focused on the content of a person's character and that was a direct way to restore honour.

In response to Beck's rally, along with a growing criticism that political discourse had become increasingly polarized, Comedy Central's Jon Stewart and Steven Colbert co-hosted their own "counter-demonstration" rally in October 2010. Stewart and Colbert's event, called "Rally to Restore Sanity/and or Fear," was held on the eve of mid-term elections, 30 October 2010. The rally was a critique of the conservative media and of the pervasive incivility that has become part of political discourse. Both Stewart and Colbert are known for shows that mix irony and complicated satire, attracting numerous young voters who have turned to Comedy Central's "The Daily Show" and "Colbert Report" for political news.

Although Stewart prides himself on not taking anything seriously, the rally had layers of meaning beyond comedy. It is too easy to position the event as a publicity stunt to promote two TV shows. The rally satirized what has emerged as a bitter political divide in contemporary American society. Stewart and Colbert taped into a growing contempt for "Washington," highlighting the political tension in American discourse that seemed palpable. Said one rally-goer: "More than entertainment or politics, I just think this is a release for everyone. We've had so much tension. I want to be around people who believe in civil discourse, that you can disagree respectfully."[15] Stewart told an estimated crowd of more than two hundred thousand that the politico/media culture reflects a view of America as polarized and dysfunctional, where people can't work together to get anything done. "We hear every damn day about how fragile our country is – on the brink of catastrophe – torn by polarizing hate and how it's a shame we can't work together to get things done. But the truth is, we do. We work together to get things done every damn day. The only place we don't is here," he said, pointing to the Capitol behind him, "and on cable TV."

Stewart insisted that the purpose of his rally was twofold: to have fun, and to encourage a civil tone in American politics; on the other hand, many of those in attendance on the Mall carried with them a politically liberal agenda. Admittedly, some signs asked for less anger and more thoughtful public debate; many emphasized the rally's official themes, including "Use Your Inside Voice," "Moderation or Death!" "My Other Sign Is a Ballot," "Say No to Hate, Say Yes to Pancakes," "I Could Be Wrong," "I'm Not Angry, I Just Want a Taco," and "Even My Sign Chooses Not to Yell." Other signs, however, were more political: "Palin/Voldemort 2012," "We the People' Isn't Just for People That Watch FOX News," "At My Tea Parties, We Respect Differences of Opinion," "Don't Let Glenn Beck Teabag Your Children!" and "SOCIALISM: You Keep Using That Word. I Don't Think It Means What You Think It Means." The Rally to Restore Sanity/and or Fear attempted to de-mythologize the concept of "Polarized America" (right/wrong, left/right, racist/inclusive, Christian/not) and to uncover what happens when the extremists on either side co-opt the agenda.

Figure 8.2. The 2010 Rally to Restore Sanity. Photo by Catherine Hobbins.

The location of the rally on the Mall was also symbolic. Two months earlier, Glenn Beck had held his rally on the steps of the Lincoln Memorial. Stewart and Colbert deliberately chose the opposite end of the Mall from Lincoln, representing two different television audiences and political constituencies. The sad shape of the Mall was also highlighted. On the website for the rally, Stewart urged people to donate money for the Mall's upkeep to the Trust for the National Mall: "We encourage you to make donations to the Trust for the National Mall. We feel it's important to preserve this historic site for future rallies and for future Americans to rally on! And let's face it; we're a little afraid that you might make a mess. We really, really hope you don't – we hope that, in the name of sanity and reasonableness, you won't be dicks and will actually pick up after yourselves. But just in case you accidentally, like, put a beverage down on the Mall's coffee table without using a coaster, we figure that giving a little something back to the National Mall might, at least, soften the blow. But really, mainly, it's about the 'preserving the historic site' thing."[16]

Ultimately, both rallies captured an important moment. Beck's rally highlighted an undercurrent in conservative political discourse of discontent and anger and fear of the future and used the Mall to express this. Stewart and Colbert employed the power of comedy shows to inspire political debate, political consciousness, and political action (in the form of attending the rally). Were these genuine attempts to reassert the "right" to the Mall or merely "lite" versions of protest theatre? I would argue the latter, but regardless, the public consciously joined these rallies on the Mall to express discontent with national political discourse, perhaps asserting itself in (re)claiming this space.

A New Take on an Old Monument

In the spring of 2010 several Washington-area scholars and architects, including me, formed the Steering Committee for the National Ideas Competition for the Washington Monument Grounds. WAMO Steering Committee members believed that the vast grounds were a void at the centre of the Mall's cross-axes and that the Mall desperately needed a vision for the monument grounds that responds to today's needs while also giving expression, at long last, to the great legacy of L'Enfant and McMillan.[17] Because there is no comprehensive master plan for the Washington Monument grounds, it was an opportunity for the American people to offer their own ideas for the future and to reclaim a voice about Mall planning.

At the heart of the competition was a provocative idea: What if the Washington Monument and its grounds are not yet finished? Could this be a chance to reimagine a future that both responds to modern needs and anticipates the grounds' evolving role in American democracy? What does this example show about the power of the public to envision inspirational new ideas for the Mall?

An Incomplete History of the Washington Monument

We take for granted the power and elegance of the Washington Monument, but it almost wasn't built. Following Washington's death in 1799, there was a desire to memorialize the first president, but Congress failed to appropriate money for the monument. In 1800 there was a proposal for a pyramidal mausoleum one hundred feet square at the base and of proportionate height, in lieu of the equestrian statue contemplated by a 1783 resolution and included in L'Enfant's original design.[18] The House approved the proposal but the Senate did not and the idea of a monument ran into partisan deadlock. While several different plans were suggested, nothing materialized. Congressman Robert Winthrop of Massachusetts explained, "Our beloved country, while yet in its infancy, and I may add in its indigency, with no experience in matters of art, and heavily weighted down by the great debt of the Revolutionary War, knew better how to vote for monuments than how to build them, or, still, how to pay for them."[19] These words ring true today. In contrast to congressional ambivalence, cities and states had no trouble building monuments to Washington, including a 220-foot monument in Baltimore, Maryland (1829), and a colossal equestrian statue in Richmond, Virginia (1858).[20]

Historian Kirk Savage has explored the politics behind the Washington Monument as a contest between opposing visions of Washington the man as well as competing visions of commemoration. He writes, "Both the man and his monument were once the symbolic battlegrounds for long-lasting disputes over national identity."[21] While some feared that Americans would "man-worship" Washington, others struggled with his more ambiguous legacy: he was a defender of the Union and critic of slavery, on the one hand, and a leader of rebellion and a slaveholding planter, on the other.[22] This tension would create conflict over how to complete the monument. Debates over how to commemorate Washington echoed the political divisions between the Federalists and Republicans, as well as broader debates about style, aesthetics, and even memory. It pitted those who thought that the best way to commemorate Washington was through marble and stone against those who argued that collective memory could exist only within the citizenry itself.[23] In addition to the struggle over Washington's ideological legacy, there was debate over which architectural style would best physically express his legacy. The 1783 proposal that called for Washington on a horse was, by 1800, too much in the tradition of European representation for a new democracy that sought to construct a uniquely American culture. Importantly, the struggle to realize the Washington Monument was a critical moment – it was the first *national* debate over who were our heroes, what were their ideals, how should they be commemorated, and how they would fit within the narrative of national identity.

After more than fifty years of congressional inaction, private citizens organized the Washington National Monument Society in 1833 to raise money for the monument. Chief Justice John Marshall was elected the Society's first president; later, ex-president James Madison would succeed him. Within three years, the

Society had raised $28,000 which it used to solicit designs in a contest. The chosen design was by Robert Mills, who had also designed the Treasury Building that was under construction at the time (it was completed in 1842). Mills's design was a blend of Greek, Babylonian, and Egyptian architecture. He proposed a 600-foot obelisk surrounded by an enormous circular temple at the base that included free-standing sculpture inside and out (see Plate 2). On the outside, on top of the temple, was a conspicuously large statue of Washington driving a horse-drawn carriage. In addition to the monument itself, Mills's design extended to the grounds around the monument up the entire length of the Mall to the foot of the Capitol. It was the intention of the Washington Monument Society that the monument should fill the skyline, dominating the Mall and anchoring the centre of the city. The Washington Monument was visually unambiguous in a very ambiguous pre-Civil War society. The legacy of Washington was something to which a country divided by the issue of slavery could pledge its allegiance. The design for the Washington Monument and for the Mall harkened back to the less divisive political ideologies of the Revolutionary era at a time when there was a deep intellectual chasm in American politics. It appeared to be a sign of the nation's new power and unity.[24] Savage contends that Mills's design for the first time visualized the Mall as a national symbolic space of ideal institutions and values for society.

Mills estimated that it would cost one million dollars to complete the Washington Monument. It took another ten years after the design context to raise sufficient funds to begin (some $87,000). In 1848 Congress granted the Washington Monument Society thirty-seven acres on the Mall to build the Washington Monument and construction began. The final placement of the monument was slightly off the original axes because that location was found to be unstable ground; the monument was shifted by some 317 feet to the east and 123 feet to the south. On 4 July 1848 President James Polk laid the cornerstone of the Washington Monument. Construction proceeded until 1854, when the Society ran out of funds. The 156-foot stunted shaft remained in the skyline for the next twenty years, a period that some referred to as a "disheartening pause" (see Figure 8.3). The abandoned monument caused some chagrin. Remarked Congressman Robert Winthrop: "How shall I depict the sorry spectacle which those first one hundred and fifty-six feet, in their seemingly hopeless, helpless condition, with that dismal derrick still standing as in mockery upon their summit, presented to the eye of every corner to the Capital for nearly a quarter of a century! No wonder the unsightly

Figure 8.3. The partially completed Washington Monument, circa 1860. Courtesy of Library of Congress, Prints and Photographs Division, Brady-Handy Photography Collection, http://loc.gov/pictures/resource/cwpbh.03248/.

pile became the subject of pity or derision ... That truncated shaft with its untidy surroundings looked only like an insult to the memory of Washington."[25] Indeed, the forlorn stump caught the eye of Mark Twain, who wrote: "It has the aspect of a factory chimney with the top broken off. The skeleton of a decaying scaffolding lingers about its summit, and tradition says that the spirit of Washington often comes down and sits on those rafters to enjoy this tribute of respect which the nation has reared as the symbol of its unappeasable gratitude."

After the Civil War, Congress reluctantly turned its attention again to the monument, and in 1876 it approved funds for completion of the project. But, as Kirk Savage argues, times had changed. The United States was now in the midst of Reconstruction and "the monument was not about the world of George Washington and his thirteen colonies; it was about a new nation that had split apart violently, reunified forcibly, and now stood poised to become an international power on the world stage."[26]

In the intervening years, most of Mill's concept had been criticized. The nation no longer needed Washington depicted in statue, not even in his own monument.

Several alternative designs had been proposed, including a triumphal arch and a neo-Aztec tower. Debates proceeded about whether to keep the obelisk (not American in style) and how to develop a "national style." Ultimately, since the shaft was begun as an obelisk, the monument would be built as such. Congressional refusal to make any decisions created a power vacuum into which stepped Lieutenant-Colonel Thomas Casey of the Army Corps of Engineers. Casey took charge and decided that the elaborate ornamentation of Mills's design had to go. He simplified the design. The rotunda was eliminated, as were the series of fountains that were considered too expensive. The height of the obelisk was reduced from 600 to 555 feet after Casey consulted with an expert on Egyptian architecture. Casey also conceived of the monument as a modern electrified skyscraper that included an elevator inside the shaft. The elevator to the top viewing platform gave visitors the first "bird's-eye view" of the city.

Savage contends that the design and construction changes engineered by Casey introduced a new spatial ideal: "Decades before photographers turned their cameras downward from New York City skyscrapers, tourists and professionals were doing so from the monument's eight openings."[27] The shaft's technological ingenuity, scale, and strength echoed the qualities America's modern democracy wanted to project both at home and abroad.

The result is the simple, towering obelisk completed in 1884. Its completion was a ready-made metaphor for the reunification of the country after the Civil War.[28] Today, the Washington Monument soars as a symbol of city, but its history reveals several important ideas that will echo into the twenty-first century. For some, the Washington Monument remained unfinished, at best only partially complete. This idea has inspired a series of other plans or visions over the past two centuries.

Twentieth-Century Visions for the Washington Monument

The 1901 McMillan Plan reaffirmed and expanded L'Enfant's vision for the Mall. During the planning process, the Park commissioners were challenged to deal with the changes to the Mall over the past one hundred years. They were likely influenced by wider reforms such as the urban park movement and the playground movement that stressed the moral and physical necessity of public recreation. Their report noted that "the positive dearth of means of innocent enjoyment for one's leisure hours is remarkable in Washington, the one city in the country where people have the most leisure."[29] For all of these reasons, the commissioners ultimately interpreted the Mall more as a park or garden than as an urban boulevard.[30] The McMillan Plan for the Mall is perhaps best described as the restoration of the *spirit* of L'Enfant rather than the actual park he envisioned. The commissioners' primary intention was to develop the Mall for *public use*.

The Park Commission wanted to restore L'Enfant's Grand Avenue by removing the railroad station, adding neo-classical buildings, and extending the vision of the Mall onto the newly created landfill areas of the Potomac Park, west of the Washington Monument. Beyond their plans for the Mall as a unified whole, the commissioners felt that the Washington Monument needed a more appropriate setting, referring to it as "the gem of the Mall system." The monument became the fixed point around which they centred a new Monumental Core (Figure 8.4). Their plan for the Washington Monument grounds included a sunken garden, stepped terraces, and fountains three hundred feet wide on three sides of the monument. In addition to the more formal landscape and architecture, the commissioners, influenced perhaps by the emphasis placed on recreation by a growing urban park movement, proposed a place of recreation called the Washington Common, today the Tidal Basin area. This area would contain a stadium for athletic contests and festival occasions, ball grounds, tennis courts, and playgrounds for children.[31] The Tidal Basin itself would provide facilities for boating, wading, and swimming in the summer as well as for skating in the winter.[32] In addition, the newly created West Potomac Park was programmed for recreation and leisure, with, among other things, polo fields, a bathing beach, a nine-hole golf course, volleyball courts, and baseball fields. Many of these still remain.

The Washington Monument was a key focus of the commissioners, who intended a vast transformation of the grounds. Dominating the entire District of Columbia, the monument had taken its place with the Capitol and the White House as one of the three foremost national structures.[33] One element to the plan was to restore the Washington Monument as the convergence of the two axes.[34] This involved redrawing the line from the Capitol by planting elms and other trees and shrubs and installing water fountains and statuary to give the visual appearance of these two structures being in alignment (see Figure 8.5). The monument would sit on a plaza more than forty feet above an enormous formal garden. It would reassert the centre axis, with a swatch of green carpet surrounding it and with borders of elms "marching to the Monument grounds"

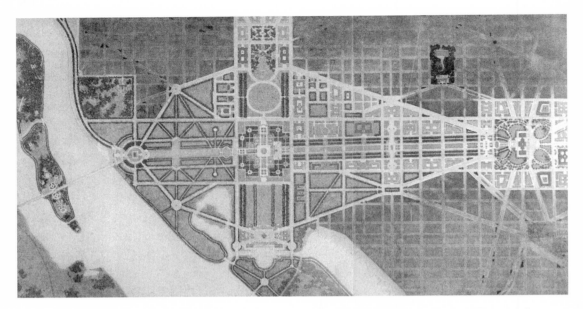

Figure 8.4. The McMillan Plan centres its design on the Washington Monument and grounds. The circles represent terraced gardens; the rectangles were to be fountains and pools. Courtesy of Library of Congress.

Figure 8.5. The McMillan Plan for Washington Monument grounds. Courtesy of Library of Congress.

to strengthen the platform of the obelisk. The plan would also enhance the "axial relations between the White House and the Monument," with the Monument Gardens, a sunken garden surrounded by terraces, small trees, hedges, and fountains, and a great round pool encircling the monument platform. Circular pools and cascading gardens would counterbalance the deviation from the Washington Monument's original axis as well as provide a visual feast of water features and landscaping. The Monument Gardens would also protect the Monument by preventing anything else to "come so near as to disturb the isolation which the monument demands." The Gardens would, hoped the Park Commission, "become the gem of the Mall system."

(Not) Implementing the McMillan Plan

The McMillan Plan was immense and sophisticated; it was patriotic and ceremonial and it resonated with the original L'Enfant Plan, all of which contributed to its public appeal. A few days after the plan went on display in Washington's Corcoran Gallery, the *New York Times* reported that "it would make Washington the most beautiful city in the world."[35]

The plan elicited generally favourable responses, although it was not without its critics.[36] There were several reasons for resistance. First, some congressmen balked at the high cost estimates, which ranged from $200 to $600 million. Secondly, there was political opposition to certain elements of the plan. For example, there were objections to specific proposals, such as the removal of the deteriorated Botanic Garden or the cutting down of existing trees to comply with the plan's call for a more open vista. There were also controversies over the width of the Mall (proposed to be 800 feet). Thirdly, there was unease with the plan's monumental character. Some felt that it was too theatrical and imperial in contrast to L'Enfant's more modest and lively Grand Avenue. Kirk Savage argues that the redesign of the Mall, the Washington Monument, the Lincoln Memorial, and the Grant Memorial (1922) was a watershed moment in our "notion of the public monument."[37] By emphasizing the idea of national unity, national identity, and commemoration, the McMillan Plan radically changed the use of the Mall – from a big, disorderly park to the nation's Monumental Core. While this might not have been evident to many, it was to those who opposed the plan.

The most pronounced failure in executing the McMillan Plan involved the Washington Monument grounds. Investigations conducted on the subsoil concluded that the sunken gardens could not be constructed without jeopardizing the foundation of the monument. The area that was of great focus for the commissioners remains untouched more than a century later (save for the security walkways). Today, the site is an open lawn with some trees clustered around the perimeter. Without the formal landscape, the Rainbow Pool at the east end of the Lincoln Reflecting Pool lost a significant portion of its purpose.[38] Given this, it seems reasonable to conclude that the Washington Monument grounds have not been completed as the 1901 McMillan Plan instructed.[39]

Many ideas have been proposed for the Washington Monument and its grounds over two centuries, but none was ever fully implemented. It appears a sad truth: our monument to George Washington has never received its intended landscape setting. This idea has been accepted by numerous scholars, so perhaps the claim that the Washington Monument and its grounds remain unfinished is not as provocative as it first appears. Consider this example. In 2011 the National Building Museum opened its "Unbuilt Washington" exhibit which catalogued lost opportunities and terrifying near-misses. The exhibit featured Robert Mills's 1846 design, the McMillan Plan, Downing's 1950 Plan, a proposal to turn the grounds into exposition space for the 1892 World's Fair (see Plate 3), and several other plans from the twentieth century. The exhibit was another reminder that various visions for the Washington Monument have been largely forgotten by most Americans, ephemeral echoes of what might have been.

WAMO: Revisioning the Washington Monument Grounds

The WAMO competition elicited hundreds of proposals, many of which were imaginative and inspired. A few are worth highlighting. The "Monument of Unity" (Plate 4) adds curves on the east and west sides of the monument mound to create generous entrances to a new central space. In addition, the design adds a layer of history to the visitor experience by revealing the now-hidden foundations of the monument. "A People's Forum" (Plate 5) refocuses attention on the neglected Jefferson Pier and calls attention to L'Enfant's original axial plan. This design creates a new 3,000-seat Washington Amphitheater as a national gathering place that also serves as a grand and fitting base for the Washington Monument.

"A Great Inclined Plane" (Plate 6) suggests extending the Mall over the two streets so people can walk to the monument without having to cross traffic.

The WAMO competition was different from traditional design competitions. First, it was an ideas competition. Secondly, it was not sanctioned by the Park Service, which meant that the winner would not necessarily see his/her idea ever implemented. An ideas competition is different from a design competition in that the most important objective is to encourage people to explore possibilities for the future. It allows people to think about larger issues, such as: Who are we as a people? How should we remember our past and tell the ongoing American story? The competition was not intended to develop a final plan for the monument grounds; rather, the purpose was to spur public involvement and begin a public conversation about what role the monument grounds should play in the life of the twenty-first-century Mall, or even if the grounds should be developed further at all. It was also about inspiring the public to become involved in discussions around use and development. Said the competition's chair, Jim Clark: "We wanted this competition to educate people from schoolchildren to design professionals about this important civic space and stimulate them to think creatively about its future. Opening up the competition to anyone 12 and up was part of that goal."[40] Initially, some people responded to the idea of the WAMO competition by saying that they would leave the grounds alone. But in the end, no one submitted such an entry. Architect Kent Cooper noted that once people started remembering their own experience using the Mall, and once they looked at the history of the monument and its grounds, nearly everyone wanted to make changes.

Another advantage to an ideas competition over a design competition is that submissions do not necessarily have to be feasible in the present (since the Park Service would not have considered for a minute the idea of implementing any of the winning ideas). This opens up the competition to the imaginative, the fanciful, and the futuristic. The public was encouraged to believe that any technological limits that exist currently might be overcome in the future. For example, several submissions suggested that an underground parking garage would solve parking issues; in reality, the high water table and the unstable soil make underground construction impossible. But only for the time being. Who know what might be possible in 2020? Or 2030?

The WAMO competition can also be seen as an act of public reclaiming of the Mall. Many committee members felt that the Park Service had consistently demonstrated a lack of creativity and public involvement in planning, and that the WAMO competition launched a conversation that engaged the public in envisioning the Mall's future. The Park Service, not surprisingly, was not supportive of the competition, quickly and emphatically distancing itself from any affiliation with it, as did the CFA and the NCPC. As an ideas competition, there was never any expectation that the winning designs would be built – that was not the point. The committee members also held out the slim hope that perhaps the Park Service would be inspired by the submissions to think more innovatively about the space and be more committed to soliciting ideas from the public at large in the future. Kirk Savage commented: "The National Ideas Competition is an ideal way to spark new thinking from citizens and professionals about this hugely important symbolic space. With fresh, visionary thought the Washington Monument grounds could one day become the real heart of the nation, not necessarily in the way L'Enfant or the McMillan planners envisioned it but in a new way that speaks to the aspirations of the 21st century."[41]

The WAMO competition encouraged the public to help shape the future through collective action, a reclaiming of its right to determine the destiny of open spaces and an empowering of ordinary Americans. The re-visioning of the Washington Monument grounds shows that there is a need for the public to reassert itself in Mall issues. When they do, some interesting and creative ideas are born.

CHAPTER 9

Envisioning the Twenty-First-Century Mall

Every one hundred years or so the Mall has been recast as the physical embodiment of the currents influencing national identity. It is the legacy of two great historic visions: the L'Enfant Plan of 1791 and the McMillan Plan of 1901. The former vision created the "Grand Avenue" and connected the U.S. Capitol to the Washington Monument on the banks of the Potomac River, where it intersected the axis of the White House and President's Park. The 1901 McMillan Plan incorporated triangular areas north and south of the Mall for new federal buildings, and extended the Mall west and south onto landfill beyond the original banks of the Potomac, creating sites for the Lincoln and Jefferson memorials. The McMillan Plan also reclaimed land for new waterfront parks, parkways, and new memorials and re-landscaped the ceremonial core of Washington. L'Enfant's Plan set a grand vision for the first one hundred years of the city; the McMillan Plan updated that vision for the twentieth century. "L'Enfant could not have foreseen the AIDS Quilt stretched from the Washington Monument to the Capitol, but surely he would have approved; similarly, folk fairs, fireworks and public protests are all latter day uses of the Mall that were not envisioned two centuries ago."[1] During the twentieth century, citizen action made the Mall a stage for our democracy, a place to play, celebrate, remember, seek redress, and even raise consciousness on pressing issues. The public has come to see and use the Mall as more than monuments and green space. It is a vital public space that comes from the many uses that continually revitalize and reshape both its meaning and its function.

More than a hundred years have passed since the McMillan Plan and the Mall has continued to grow without a guiding vision for its third century. Many of the changes and challenges discussed in this book require thoughtful public discussion – the lack of a comprehensive vision is one.

Ten years ago, a 2005 Senate subcommittee hearing was pivotal in the process of reimagining the Mall. Typically, congressional hearings are held to consider legislative matters; however, this hearing was about broader issues of planning and fragmented management on the Mall. Senator Craig Thomas (R-WY), then chairman of the Senate Subcommittee on National Parks, opened the hearing with these words: "The National Mall stands at the door of its Third Century. All must work together. We have an opportunity to plan a vision for the Mall for the 21st century. I'm looking forward to receiving the testimony and working toward a plan of action that maintains the integrity of this incredible part of the park system." Much of the hearing focused on two ideas. The first idea was to establish a planning group similar to the McMillan Commission of 1901 to envision how the Mall should evolve over the next one hundred years. The second idea was more radical and intriguing: to expand the Mall geographically. The hearing forced, perhaps for the first time, the Park Service, the Commission of Fine Arts, and the National Capital Planning Commission to address emerging Mall "problems," including the definition of the Mall, memorial pressure, security issues, problems of jurisdiction and interagency cooperation, and the lack of a comprehensive plan. The hearing confirmed that the most recent Mall master plan by the Park Service had been completed in 1972 and was hopelessly out of date. Then Director of Planning for the Park Service Capital Region John Parsons admitted that "we acknowledge that there is no single current plan focus on Park Service Management of the National Mall. This is something the National Park Service intends to rectify."[2] As a result of this hearing, in 2006 the Park Service launched the National Mall Plan, a planning process that would take four years to complete.

This chapter examines competing visions for the twenty-first-century Mall. I first examine planning efforts by the NCPC to deal creatively with development pressures, including where to locate future memorials. I then turn to the 2010 National Mall Plan as drafted by the Park Service, before concluding with an exploration of the ideas championed by the National Coalition to Save Our Mall, which continues to advocate for a much larger comprehensive vision and thinking "outside the box."

The National Capital Planning Commission's Legacy Plan

Although it is almost twenty years old, one vision for the twenty-first-century Mall and the Monumental Core is the NCPC's 1997 report *Extending the Legacy: Planning for America's Capital for the 21st Century* (hereafter the Legacy Plan). Adopted by both the NCPC and the Park Service, the Legacy Plan provides planning guidance over federal lands in Washington and its surrounding areas (this includes the Mall, but it is not the exclusive focus). The Legacy Plan was the result of concern about overbuilding on the Mall. The NCPC called this plan "the third act in a continuing planning drama that began over 200 years ago, when President George Washington commissioned Pierre L'Enfant to lay out the new capital. Like the L'Enfant and McMillan plans, it looks ahead 50 to 100 years. And like them, it offers a framework for future development."[3]

The Legacy Plan is not intended to be a blueprint that plans the future in precise and immutable detail but "is more like a map with a few dramatic highlights. It is both a guide to the big picture and a defense against the myopic quick fix."[4] NCPC Executive Director Patricia Gallagher called the Legacy Plan "bold and ambitious in the tradition of the L'Enfant and McMillan plans, and like its predecessors, it expresses many of the civic and national values of contemporary American society."[5] In reality, the plan reflects what many cities have learned in the past decades: that civic beautification can stimulate economic development and help catalyse private investment.

The NCPC predicted that dozens of new memorials and monuments would be proposed between 1997 and 2050. Accordingly, it suggested that these projects be redirected to areas immediately around the Mall (but not on it), including the White House and President's Park, Pennsylvania Avenue, the Capitol, East and West Potomac Parks, the Southwest Federal Center, and parts of the southwest waterfront area. The plan re-centres the city's Monumental Core on the Capitol (instead of the Washington Monument) and emphasizes areas for new memorials and museums north, south, and east of the Capitol. This re-centring also reclaims the Anacostia River to the east, historically neglected by the city. By reclaiming the river, the Legacy Plan will build on the example of the McMillan Plan in expanding the "cross-axis" of the city.

The plan proposes to redistribute federal investment to all quadrants of the city, not just the city centre, which is where most of this investment has concentrated until now. It calls for the creation of three "lively" corridors of federal and private development radiating from the Capitol and suggests potential attractive sites elsewhere in the city. It also redirects development away from the Mall and to other areas of the city.[6] The plan calls for a mix of federal offices, housing, open civic spaces, and retail and commercial activities. By mixing commercial, private, and government uses, the NCPC hopes that neglected areas of the city will become new destinations for tourists. It also envisions the redevelopment of the southwest waterfront. The waterfront, much of which is publicly owned, is an under-utilized neighbourhood. The plan proposes to transform this area into a continuous band of open space from Georgetown to the National Arboretum with a new networks of parks, plazas, trails, and marinas. Construction on the southwest waterfront began in 2014 and continues.

In 2001 the NCPC followed up the more general Legacy Plan with the Memorials and Museums Master Plan in partnership with the Commission of Fine Arts and the National Capital Memorial Commission. This plan identifies 100 specific sites for future memorials and museums. These sites are more widely distributed within the city in areas away from the Mall. The plan has guided the placement of several new memorials, including those honouring American Disabled Veterans, the U.S. Air Force, President John Adams, and President Dwight D. Eisenhower. Yet shortcomings remain. Many of the potential sites for monuments and memorials suffer from neglect or inaccessibility or inadequate connections to the most visited areas of the city.[7]

Both NCPC plans are notable for acknowledging that the Mall can no longer be the sole destination for new memorials, and for diverting future development away from the Monumental Core. The Park Service and the NCPC believe that the Legacy Plan is a vision for the twenty-first century.[8] At the same time, both have acknowledged that the Mall still needs a comprehensive master plan. This is because the Legacy Plan does not address detailed or site-specific design and management concerns. In contrast, a master plan for the Mall should include land-use guidelines for future additions as well as plans for physical modifications, vehicular and pedestrian circulation, visitor facilities and services, public recreational uses, public celebrations and gatherings, physical security, and temporary events. John Cogbill, NCPC chairman, explained: "A new Mall master plan would be a valuable tool in preserving its historic landscapes, managing its physical development, and improving its maintenance and service for visitors and residents alike. NCPC supports and encourages the National Park Services' requests for funds for such a master plan. NCPC's unique mission as the federal government's central planning agency ... makes us a natural, necessary and willing partner with the National Park Service and others to undertake a master planning effort."[9]

There has been some criticism about the Legacy Plan and the Memorials and Museums Master Plan. Architectural historian Norma Evenson noted that it was difficult to criticize the plans because the proposals were vague and "inoffensive and the illustrations were generalized to the point that you really can't talk about the design, because it's not meant to be specific ... At any rate, it's a nice plan. I just don't think it's very important, because it doesn't touch on any really major urban issues. If the city of Washington continues the way it's going, the Plan is going to be like putting a band-aid on a corpse."[10] Another critic noted that memorials and museums are not a real estate problem: they are really about how we tell our national narrative, something *not* addressed in either NCPC plan. Treating memorials and museums as ad hoc additions to the memorial land-scape, to be located on "available" real estate, is not crafting a coherent national narrative.[11]

The Park Service's National Mall Plan

In 2006 the Park Service launched its National Mall Plan to envision and define the future of the Mall. The Park Service said its intention was to create "a long-range vision plan focused on improvements related to pubic use, health, appear-ance and preservation of the historic National Mall."[12]

A well-publicized goal of the Park Service was to seek broad public input in the planning process. In November 2006 the Park Service launched the planning process with a public symposium; however, the symposium consisted mostly of prepared presentations by Park Service officials and offered little opportu-nity for public discussion and input.[13] Park Service planners from the Denver Office and the National Capital Parks proceeded with months of planning. They issued periodic media releases and newsletters (posted online and distributed to visitors at parks) that provided updates on the planning process and focused on specific themes, such as commemoration. The public was encouraged to comment through a dedicated website and by e-mail and surface mail. Over the course of the four-year planning effort, the Park Service received approxi-mately thirty thousand comments, from every state in the union. Three planned public meetings and three Section 106 meetings were held but only after the initial stages of planning. This is not surprising given how the Park Service had dealt with issues of public input in the planning process previously. However, its efforts represent an improvement over past practices.

In November 2006 the Park Service posted fifteen open-ended questions on its website for public comment. The comment period ran through 16 March 2007 and generated about five thousand responses. In addition to the comments received from the general public, five organizations submitted extensive feedback, namely the American Society of Landscape Architects, the Downtown D.C. Business Improvement District, the National Coalition to Save Our Mall, the National Parks Conservation Association, and the Tour Guide Guild of Washington, D.C. The issues raised included:

- lack of a purpose or identity for the National Mall;
- landscape: poor condition and aesthetics;
- sustainable practices: no recycling, little evidence of conservation;
- sub-par facilities (insufficient restrooms drinking fountains, cooling stations, benches, tables, chairs, and shelter; inadequate lighting; poorly maintained walkways);
- services: poor quality and quantity of food services, inadequate information in signs and maps, lack of a visitor centre, and insufficient recreational opportunities (kayaks, rowboats, model boats were requested);
- transportation: inadequate parking and onsite public transit, no bike lanes or bike racks.[14]

In short, the public noted many of the same problems I discussed in chapters 2 and 3.

The Park Service planning team, based in Denver, included public input as well as the Park Service's own landscape studies in preparing a draft plan around four themes. In 2007 it released its preliminary ideas and invited public comment. Most Park Service plans follow a fairly specific formula: there are several plans (called alternatives), a "preferred alternative," which is usually the most ambitious, and a "take no action" alternative. The no-action plan is common to all Park Service plans since it outlines the existing conditions and serves as the baseline against which to measure the other alternatives. Every Park Service plan consists of a "preferred alternative" and several other alternatives that differ mostly by the constraints of a proposed budget. Generally, the preferred alternative includes all of the major objectives of the planners, while the other alternatives offer variations of the major objectives.

The draft plan featured several alternative plans. Alternative A focused on the historic landscape design of the Mall, as well as increasing educational materials and opportunities. Alternative B focused on national civic space for public gatherings and events, reinforcing other high-use opportunities such as demonstrations. Alternative C focused on urban open space, urban ecology, recreation, and healthy lifestyles. The fourth theme was a "no-action" alternative, a scenario in which current management continues without major changes.

The most immediate feedback came from those concerned that changes might compromise First Amendment rights. This was due to an unfortunate statement in the draft that "preserving historic resources, providing for public enjoyment, and accommodating First Amendment demonstrations are potentially contradictory purposes of the National Mall." Why the Park Service made this statement is not clear, but the result was that thousands of people interpreted it as a potential assault on, or the beginning of limitations to, First Amendment rights on the Mall. Some feared that the Park Service meant to restrict future protests and other First Amendment activities on the Mall. In all, about 16,500 comments (92 per cent of the comments submitted) pertained to the concern that the National Mall Plan might curtail the right to freedom of speech and assembly. A sampling of comments specific to First Amendment rights is given in Table 9.1 below.

Thus began the first kerfuffle in the planning process. The Park Service called the overwhelming concern over First Amendment rights a "widespread misunderstanding that the National Mall would change these fundamental rights." Said Park Service Superintendent Margaret O'Dell: "At no time has the NPS entertained the possibility of limiting First Amendment demonstrations."[15] The winter 2009 newsletter highlighted unequivocally, in large, bold type, the message that "First Amendment Demonstration Rights Will Not Change Under Any Alternative ... This vital and essential role will not change under any alternative being considered for the National Mall plan. A primary, fundamental purpose of the National Mall will always be to provide a venue for First Amendment demonstrations."[16] In addition, the Park Service updated the National Mall Plan website to reflect and reinforce the commitment to First Amendment rights.[17] Finally, at the request of some members of Congress, the Park Service drafted a

Table 9.1 Concerns about First Amendment Rights

Preserve the exercise of First Amendment rights of free speech, association, and to petition our government for redress of grievances; need more restroom facilities and access to the disabled.	The ideal balance is to allow Americans to use these grounds as they see fit, as often as they wish. This is a historically significant location for demonstrations and should be maintained with that same spirit in mind. Free speech and assembly should not be curbed, restrained, or otherwise stifled in any manner. Concerns regarding maintaining the grounds, for example, for any of the listed parks is not a sufficient reason to curb assembly and/or speech.
The lawn is not important. Free speech is. There should be no government-designated protest pit or zone to stage-manage or channel free-speech activity to suit the government, or to stifle or abridge our rights to expression in the public forum that is the National Mall	Do not make it more difficult to hold protests on the Mall. Spaces for dissent in this country are rapidly closing, and I beg you to stand up for free speech and the right to peaceably assemble to bring our grievances to the attention of the government.
Please maintain the right to express opinion publicly, including the use of organized demonstrations, in each of these areas. The public spaces of the Capitol [sic] are essential in guaranteeing that both minority and majority opinion can be made public without media control or government limitation.	It is essential that we maintain the National Mall as a civic space, and not allow a plan to be implemented which could be interpreted as leaving the door open to restricting protests. Please don't shut down the National Mall for mass protests! It's one of the few large, centrally located and richly symbolic spaces that Americans still have to express themselves as mass movements.

Source: "Public Comments Report: Newsletter 3, Alternatives: A Background Report for the National Mall Plan Prepared by the School of Recreation, Health, and Tourism George Mason University for the National Mall & Memorial Parks," April 2008.

response to constituents' concerns, stating that the Park Service was committed to protecting First Amendment rights.

A second "crisis" was anger over the proposal to ban public events under the elm trees that line the Mall between the museums and open greensward. The Park Service reasoned that this was necessary to protect tree roots in the compacted soils. Many felt that the ban would apply to the Smithsonian Institution's annual Folklife Festival. Letters of protest went to the Park Service, and several *Washington Post* editorials criticized the proposal; within several weeks, the Park Service reversed the ban.

Although the Park Service was active in engaging public participation in this planning process, there were still some criticism about how meaningful the process really was. Early on there was a symposium where the public was allowed to ask questions but not engage in discussion. There were a number of open-house-type public events, but those events also limited the public to reacting to Park Service concepts; citizens were not allowed to engage in discussion with Park Service planners and with one another.[18]

The final six-hundred-page draft was released in December 2009. The plan proposed to "respectfully rehabilitate and refurbish the National Mall so that very high levels of use can be perpetuated. The needs of all visitors and users will be met in an attractive, convenient, high-quality, energy-efficient, and sustainable manner." Several elements of the plan are worth discussing. First, the plan pays particular attention to improving facilities and infrastructure for events. These included adding separate bicycle lanes and bike racks and improving tour bus drop-off locations; widening or paving many walkways to enhance the visitor experience; providing better signage for intersections; including permanent trash/recycling containers; and improving restroom facilities. The Mall plan also focused on addressing the significant backlog of deferred maintenance and repairs. Highlights of the National Mall Plan include:

- better meet the needs of visitors of all ages and ability levels, including tourists and local recreation users, groups and individuals, and visitors who speak English as well as languages from around the world.
- meet recreation needs, including surfaces for jogging and walking; provide separate bicycle lanes or trails; upgrade fields for softball, soccer, kickball, and other active sports; and improve conditions for passive recreation like picnicking and walking.
- improve the appearance and health of soils, vegetation, and the overall landscape; improve water quality and storm-water management; and enhance the Mall as a healthy and well-functioning urban ecosystem.
- provide convenient and appropriately sized visitor facilities.
- improve basic services such as restrooms, water, information, and refreshment locations, with conveniently located seating and facilities.
- provide spaces designed for cultural activities and for capturing iconic photographic images.
- achieve the highest standards of accessibility and universal design.
- provide areas where groups can meet, find shelter, sit, gather for educational programs, or eat without affecting other visitors.

- improve circulation and amenities for pedestrians, bicyclists, and other visitors.
- incorporate sustainability into designs.
- facilities: replace gravel walkways with new paving, implement deferred maintenance on resources.
- redesign specific areas:
    – restore the D.C. World War I Memorial;
    – restore the Grant Memorial at the foot of the Capitol;
    – remove the Capitol Reflecting Pool between 1st and 3rd streets, and instead lay out as a civic square with new concession stands;
    – remove the Sylvan Theater (near the Washington Monument) and replace it with a new structure for food service, retail, information, exhibits, restrooms, and Park Service operations space; and
    – build a new Welcome plaza and facilities at the Smithsonian Metro entrance.[19]

In short, most of the plan aimed to improve the facilities and solve the existing maintenance problems, providing for, at long last, the rehabilitation of the D.C. War Memorial, the restoration of the Lincoln Reflecting Pool, and the repair of the sinking sea walls at the Jefferson Memorial (all of which have been since restored and rehabilitated).

On 9 November 2010 Department of Interior Secretary Ken Salazar and Park Service Director Jon Jarvis signed a Record of Decision, thereby officially accepting the National Mall Plan. The NCPC also approved the plan in December 2010. The Park Service and the Trust for the National Mall are currently working together to raise money to implement the plan fully. Because the plan rectifies well-catalogued problems, it is difficult to conclude that this is "visionary."

Critiquing the Mall Plan

The Park Service calls the plan "a practical, ambitious but achievable vision for a sustainable National Mall where visitors feel welcomed and proud of this space that symbolizes our nation."[20] However, the National Coalition to Save Our Mall criticized the plan for not being a "vision" at all but mostly a management plan for grass and plants and restrooms. Other non-profit groups, including the National

Association for Olmsted Parks, the D.C. Preservation League, the National Trust for Historic Preservation, the Committee of 100 on the Federal City, the Society of Architectural Historians, and the National Parks Conservation Association, agreed with the Coalition. In a joint letter to the Park Service, these seven organizations wrote that, while they supported the management plan for the Mall, it was not possible to develop a bigger vision for the Mall solely within the parameters of the Park Service's jurisdiction. As previously discussed, this is because the Mall is not just the responsibility of the Park Service but rather includes areas that fall under the jurisdiction of other agencies, including the Smithsonian, the National Gallery of Art, the Architect of the Capitol, and D.C. government. In a separate letter to the Park Service, Nell Ziehl, program officer for the National Trust for Historic Preservation, said: "We believe that the National Mall is such a complex and overwhelmingly significant historic resource that 1) any master planning project should involve a coordinated, multi-agency approach ... and 2) that any major design changes should derive from a unified vision for the National Mall."[21] In the Commemorative Works Act, Congress defined the Mall as "the great cross axis," but some of the cross-axis was not included in the Park Service's National Mall Plan boundaries. The groups pointed to the existence of multiple planning efforts (including the NCPC's Legacy Plan and Memorials and Museums Plan, the D.C. government's Center City Action Agenda, the Architect of the Capitol's Capitol Complex Master Plan, and various Smithsonian undertakings) that lack an overall, unifying vision.[22] Under the Park Service's National Mall Plan, the Mall will be restored piece by piece rather than as a single entity. Plate 7 shows how the plan divides the Mall into a series of separate "cultural landscapes." This seems to be fragmented planning, not comprehensive planning, and it is the outcome of the divided Mall management discussed previously. The National Mall Plan focuses on projects that are under Park Service jurisdiction only and makes no mention of any that might require multi-agency, multi-jurisdictional cooperation. The Park Service clarified that "the NPS *National Mall Plan* is a long-term plan to guide resource conservation and management and operations on portions of the National Mall under NPS jurisdiction."[23] Critics contend that the plan, along with others recently drawn up, could lead to piecemeal planning of the worst sort. The Coalition's Judy Scott Feldman said: "We can't call this a vision for the National Mall if it doesn't encompass the museums and iconic buildings like the White House and Capitol."[24] The National Mall Plan treats the Mall as a collection of separate and sometimes unrelated memorial landscapes; however, visitors don't distinguish between the property of the Park Service and that of the Architect of the Capitol. Visitors see the Mall as a whole, from the Capitol to the Lincoln Memorial. Thus, the approach of the National Mall Plan is a continuation of the jurisdictional "silos" that have characterized Mall management. Several groups noted that the Park Service had conflated planning for specific sites on the Mall with developing a larger vision.

In addition, the scope of the Park Service planning effort was a matter of some confusion and concern; it is not clear how the National Mall Plan relates to the historic L'Enfant and McMillan plans. These two plans received scant attention or discussion in the National Mall Plan. Instead, the Park Service focused on planning for individual "cultural landscapes" such as the Washington Monument grounds or the Lincoln Memorial grounds. Discrete areas are thus treated as separate parkland instead of as integral components of a larger, unified Mall that has evolved from the visions of L'Enfant and McMillan.[25] Without identifying the legacy of the two earlier plans, the National Mall Plan fails to provide a larger context. Some worried that the Park Service's management priorities could set in motion changes that could enshrine the status quo and inhibit needed improvements.

This raises the question: What is the difference between a vision and a plan? The term "vision" is often used in planning, but few plans are genuinely visionary. A plan is essentially a detailed statement of physical facilities and how these will be altered and managed. For example, a Park Service management plan involves primarily minor changes, while a "master plan" implies the development of a larger-picture vision. A vision is a general concept of what you want to accomplish in a particular place – it is more a philosophical statement. A management plan deals with repairing problems and infrastructure; a vision rethinks these problems. A vision for the Mall should discuss and account for its nationally symbolic and narrative qualities; the National Mall Plan does not address these. Architect and Coalition board member Kent Cooper explained that "the Park Service has a plan. But it is not vision. The Park Service is focused on a management plan – as it is required to do, but we should not confuse this with creating a new vision for the 21st century."[26]

Critics of the National Mall Plan say that, without a larger vision, seemingly minor choices such as lighting, paving materials, signage, and landscaping will have an impact on the design integrity of the entire Mall. Absent a comprehensive vision, the Park Service, the NCPC, and the CFA lack Mall-wide standards and design principles to guide coherent decision making. Because the Park Service limits the National Mall Plan to the management concerns under its jurisdiction, it fails to take into account the larger context. It thus replicates a planning and management structure that has consistently viewed the Mall as a fragmented landscape. So, too, does the NCPC Framework Plan, which addresses opportunities for future museums and memorials *off* the Mall but not on the Mall itself. Neither constitutes a large, comprehensive vision of the Mall's future. Planner George Oberlander noted: "There is the NCPC *Legacy Plan*, the NCPC *Memorial and Museums Plan*, the City Center Plan and now the Park Service *National Mall Plan*. There's a lot of planning going on these days, but that doesn't necessarily add up to a comprehensive plan for the capital city and the Mall as a whole."[27] The Legacy Plan, for example, has many elements that are very useful, but it stops short of providing an adequate vision for the twenty-first century because it is incomplete. Similarly, the Memorials and Museums Master Plan suggests new memorial and museum sites but does not take into account the fact that meaningful memorials and museums are highly dependent on being located in relevant cultural contexts.[28] Ultimately, all of these plans exist as fragments, a continued "Balkanization" of competing agencies that reflects a failure to coordinate and meaningfully interact with each other and with the public. The example of the McMillan Plan shows that assembling the best creative minds can create a plan that has the vision to expand and rejuvenate the Mall. A larger inclusive vision would serve the American public, not just government agencies. Planning by federal agencies only for their own jurisdiction cannot create a vision for the future.

The Coalition called the National Mall Plan a "concept" document because it did not include actual plans or drawings or scientific studies or even general design principles to guide a coherent, unified Mall-wide design. Coalition Chair and President Judy Scott Feldman asked: "Why, after three years in development, does the Plan not include a more detailed transportation plan, a sustainability plan, and a landscape plan so the public knows what the Park Service has in mind and can comment intelligently? Aren't we putting the cart before the horse by leaving what should be critical public decision making now to NPS and its contractors at some future date?"[29] The Park Service counters that these missing elements will be addressed in the future. Coalition members suggested that the name of the plan be changed to represent more accurately its Park Service-centred scope and purpose, something like "National Park Service Concept Plan for Its Holdings on the National Mall."

A Competing Vision for the Mall

The Coalition has called for something more visionary than the Park Service's National Mall Plan and something more comprehensive than the NCPC's Legacy Plan and Memorials and Museums Master Plan. "The fear is that we are in danger of losing the Mall's democratic heart and spirit if we don't take action to monitor development and plan for the National Mall's next 100 years."[30] Coalition members contend that the existing plans lack a coherent narrative and thus fail to address how to incorporate and tell contemporary and American history. As an independent citizens' organization, the Coalition is not bound by congressional or D.C. policies and priorities. It therefore has the ability to critique agency efforts and also to offer other suggestions and solutions. Among the critical goals the Coalition has identified are the following:

1   establish meaningful and continuous public participation in planning, management, and financing of the Mall;
2   create an updated, comprehensive vision and design framework that includes Mall expansion;
3   integrate the Mall with the city's neighbourhoods and circulation and transportation systems;
4   expand the Mall to provide much needed space for public activities and future memorials and museums; and
5   develop programs to maximize the value of public uses of the Mall, by local citizens and national and international visitors, for building awareness of our democracy.[31]

Different from a traditional master plan, a broader vision would show what the Mall might look like in the years ahead. It would capture the Mall's modern quality as a stage for democracy and national commemoration, and the ambiguity, contradiction, and messiness that entails. The Coalition describes its concept as a "citizens' vision" for the Mall. It calls for a new guiding vision, one that will incorporate the Mall's growing popularity for civic gathering and recreation and the proliferation of memorials and yet balance this with the Mall's historic integrity and symbolism.[32] It wants to retain the Mall's national symbolism, which embodies democratic values, while embracing twenty-first-century functions, and argues that such an undertaking goes far beyond the mandate of the Park Service alone.

Creating a Third Century Mall Commission

The Coalition advocates the creation by Congress of a "Third Century Mall Commission," modelled on the McMillan Commission of 1901. The Third Century Commission (like the McMillan Commission) could be a temporary body that creates an updated master plan for the Mall as a whole and provides a blueprint for all plans developed by the various Mall management and review agencies. Or such a commission could be permanent, similar to the Library of Congress. In this model, the Third Century Mall Commission would be an independent office in the congressional branch of the federal government and would have the authority both to undertake comprehensive long-term planning and to implement it.[33] It would become *the* authority on the Mall, perhaps reducing the problem of fragmented management. Whatever form it takes, a Third Century Commission would not be a typical planning commission in that the most critical questions before it would not necessarily be about architecture or design but rather about re-visioning the national narrative for this public space. A compelling reason to re-vision the national narrative on the Mall is that eventually there will be proposals to erect war memorials for the first and second Gulf Wars and perhaps a memorial to the War on Terror. There are likely to be more proposals for monuments to presidents, and probably suggestions for new museums. Reconsidering the narrative of national identity and rethinking how to express that narrative is one challenge that a commission could undertake (and something that was completely absent in the Park Service's National Mall Plan). For example, a commission might suggest that, instead of building yet more war memorials, there could be a U.S. Military History Museum that tells the story of *all* military actions in the larger context of our nation's history. It might also rethink the architecture of commemoration: Is it possible to tell history with plaques and markers? Can some memorials be virtual? Finally, a commission might consider the wider context of national history: Where on the Mall should we honour our poets, scientists, and ordinary Americans, whose lives, dreams, and struggles have shaped and strengthened our democracy?[34] A commission would focus on the Mall as unified public space, not simply as a collection of museums and memorials: "Mall planners need to rethink the basic approach to the Mall's narrative landscape. Instead of leaving memorial decisions to private interests, they can develop a set of narrative goals and principles – a national curriculum for the Mall – to guide what stories are told, where new elements are best located to create a coherent

narrative, and what forms new narrative components could take. These principles should include contemporary interpretative techniques that do not require
new education centers at each memorial."[35]

The members of the Third Century Mall Commission would be charged with
articulating the symbolism and narrative that is the basis of the Mall's national
significance and public function as a stage for American democracy, and with
recommending a *public process* by which to consider, review, and approve new
facilities, museums, memorials, and other development.

To attract broad support in Congress and the public, the Mall commission
could be composed of nationally esteemed leaders in the fields of design, geography, history, education, historic preservation, environmental science, business,
development, and other relevant fields. In addition, to ensure that the public
voice is heard, the Coalition calls for including on the commission at least two
members of non-profit, public-interest citizen organizations with a demonstrated
record of advocacy on behalf of the Mall.

In order to avoid the problem of fragmented management, congressional oversight of the Third Century Mall Commission could be placed under the House
Government Reform Committee and the Senate Committee on Homeland Security and Government Affairs, or better yet, a Joint Committee or Subcommittee
on the National Mall. The commission would report to Congress annually on the
state of the Mall. It would not add another layer of management because it would
be given more authority. The commission would also be able to reach beyond the
limited authority and jurisdiction of any of the existing federal or city agencies.

To date, federal government representatives have balked at the concept of con-
solidating Mall management, each wary of relinquishing turf and power. Former
Park Service official John Parsons criticized the Coalition for "its misguided effort
to convince others of the wisdom of establishing a new commission to examine
the future of the Mall."[36] Not surprisingly, he recommended that, despite other
federal agencies that have a presence on the Mall, "the Park Service should
clearly remain in charge of the day-to-day management and long-term vision
for this precious resource."[37] Of course, this negative response towards thoughtful public involvement is precisely why the Coalition supported an independent
Mall commission. Before a Senate hearing on "The Future of the National Mall"
in 2005, Chairman Craig Thomas said that he intended to create a Mall commission, "but then he changed his mind after the Park Service, the NCPC and
Commission of Fine Arts discouraged him, claiming that it would simply add

another layer of bureaucracy. And besides, they would do the visionary planning themselves."[38] Today, no one in Congress has championed the idea of the Third Century Commission.

Growing the National Mall?

I want to revisit briefly an important piece of legislation. In 2003 Congress amended the 1986 Commemorative Works Act in part to address the continued pressure for new memorials. The 2003 law declared the Mall "a substantially completed work of civic art." To preserve its integrity, it designated a "Reserve Area" within the core of the great cross-axis where the siting of new commemorative works is prohibited.[39] The area designated "no build reserve" was now off-limits to any future memorials, monuments, and museums[40] (Figure 5.5). The idea that a space can be "completed" raises interesting questions. Geographers who study public space say that public space is a process, never a complete project. If national identity is always fluid and changing, the Mall is also changing and becoming – how can it be "completed?" As one commentator noted, "the Mall is both a living monument and a work in progress."[41] There remains a lot of American history that yet needs to be told. Where will we tell the stories important to the twenty-first or twenty-second centuries? Are we comfortable with the idea that the Mall should not reflect the national narrative beyond the twentieth century? Will Congress really enforce the idea of the "Reserve Area" or will it find ways to allow more memorials to be built in the Mall's core? Congress has already demonstrated its own ambivalence about applying the act: it exempted the World War II Memorial from it in 2000, exempted a planned Vietnam visitor centre from it in 2003, and authorized the Smithsonian to choose a site on the Mall for the Museum of African American History and Culture.[42] While Congress and the federal agencies have attempted to protect the Mall with laws, plans, and policies, these measures appear weak and not enforceable. Is the "No Build Reserve" moratorium unrealistic?

Elizabeth Meyer has criticized the use of the concept of "work of art" as an argument against changing a designed landscape. She notes that the fallacy behind the idea of a landscape as a completed work of art "precludes the opportunity for a designed landscape to evolve, to be reinterpreted through design, and to acquire the rich layering that comes with respecting something or some place through design tactics. Instead, we turn landscapes into mummies."[43]

She maintains that, if we recognize that designing a landscape is intrinsically the art of reading and interpreting a site, distilling its actual or latent essence, and amplifying its characteristics, then there are alternatives to declaring the Mall as a reserve or filling it up with new memorials.[44]

Despite a moratorium on new commemorative works on the "no build reserve" of the Mall's cross-axis, there remains constant pressure for new memorials and exceptions are continually being made. As Thomas Luebke, secretary for the Commission on Fine Arts admitted: "We've got marching orders from Congress that we can't put new commemorative memorials on the Mall. But the Mall provides a forum for a national narrative, so we have to find a way to *grow that quality* elsewhere as well."[45] The dilemma may appear to have only two outcomes: either more and more monuments, memorials, and museums will be crammed onto the Mall, or worthy projects will be forced to accept what their proponents consider second-class locations elsewhere in the District. For at least a decade, the NCPC Legacy Plan has been trying to steer future monuments to off-Mall locations, but few memorial and museum sponsors want to accept sites scattered across the city. They want the Mall. Is there a third possibility?

One intriguing solution to dealing with the Mall's increased popularity and use is to expand it geographically. Growing the Mall by physically increasing its geography has historic precedence. The McMillan Plan did just that when it called for new memorials to be located on newly dredged land south and west of the Washington Monument. In this case, Congress could incorporate already existing parks and green areas into the legal definition of the Mall. By claiming lands that include East Potomac Park, L'Enfant Promenade and Banneker Overlook, the South Capitol Street corridor, the John F. Kennedy Center for the Performing Arts, and public parkland on the D.C. and Virginia sides of the Potomac, the Mall would expand figuratively. An expanded Mall would then encompass a three-mile-long waterfront park, thus growing by 50 per cent. Figure 9.1 shows the boundaries of an expanded "Third Century Mall." It might seem a game of semantics, since the Mall would absorb existing lands. In 1900 doubters predicted that no one would venture into the "swampland," but the Lincoln and Jefferson memorials have proven otherwise.[46] Supporters of an expanded Mall say that a new geography would create room for many new memorial projects and museums, along with better parking.

With little traction in Congress for the idea of expanding the Mall, Coalition members took matters into their own hands and sponsored a series of public

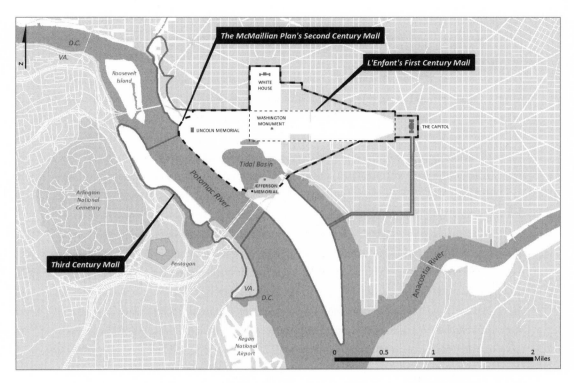

Figure 9.1. Imagining an expanded Mall for the twenty-first century. Map by author based on ideas from the National Coalition to Save Our Mall.

forums and meetings to elicit ideas for redesigning and expanding the Mall, and, in partnership with the Corcoran Gallery of Art, they organized a design charrette with regional planners and architects.[47] Participants in the latter included distinguished architects Arthur Cotton Moore, Don Hawkins, and W. Kent Cooper. The purpose was to begin to reimagine the Mall.

The idea of an expanded Mall opens up exciting opportunities for imaginative redesign of underused federal parklands. The Corcoran forum showcased designs for waterfront museums, marinas and water taxis, inland canals, and the conversion of East Potomac Park into a vibrant place of recreation, plazas, and beaches. New pedestrian and bike bridges would link the Mall to underutilized parts of the city, reintegrating the Mall's public open space into the city's neighbourhoods. Architect W. Kent Cooper, who organized the forum, noted that the enlargement, unlike that proposed in the McMillan Plan, did not need to be rigidly linear. He envisioned ceremonial avenues and new bridges that would reconnect seemingly disparate areas and create new circulation patterns at the memorials.

A design by architect Arthur Cotton Moore extends the Mall south from the Jefferson Memorial onto new land, with the Supreme Court as its centerpiece (Plate 8). He calls the area Judiciary Hill. Moore's reasoning for this idea harkens back to L'Enfant design, which geographically separated Congress from the White House to represent the separation of branches of government. At the time, the Supreme Court was the only branch of government whose obligations and organizational structure were not specifically set out in the constitution, and its wanderings reflected its early lack of power and how it evolved.[48] Now, however, the third branch of government could be situated along the axis of the Mall, completing the north-south cross-axis of White House→ Jefferson → Supreme Court. The Supreme Court's new location as the anchor of an expanded Mall would actually complete the symbolism of planning, balancing the Executive Branch at the north end of the Monumental Core, the legislature at the east end, and the judiciary at the south end. Moore explained that "the main driver for the expansion of the Mall on the north/south axis is to provide space for the apparently insatiable desire for memorials and museums on the Mall. The Mall, as presently configured, is in danger of becoming cluttered, and such an expansion would allow for considerably more of these commemorative works, including possibly a Washington version of the Statue of Liberty at the tip of the expansion, welcoming water-borne visitors to the Capital."[49] His idea of completing the Mall's symbolism of the separation of powers and forming a triangular composition is just one way to reimagine the Mall.

An expanded Mall would have room for more memorials. It could also provide a hub that would include services such as visitor centre, Metro access, parking, and public transportation. An expanded Mall would have increased water frontage and increased reaction.

The idea of expanding the Mall has not been without critics. There is some legitimate concern about balancing the need to preserve and improve existing public open spaces (such as East Potomac Park) with new uses. Running and cycling advocacy groups worry that an expanded Mall would "adulterate the peaceful, pristine three-mile loop … we do not need additional monuments and memorials and traffic. We need to protect and treasure our green space and to encourage people to exercise."[50] Another letter notes that East Potomac Park is a gem of greenery and should not be turned into a parking lot with concession stands that would deprive District residents of opportunities for walking, running, inline skating, tennis, and golf.[51] But some of these reactions miss the point of the Corcoran forum: most of the visions proposed would enhance public use for runners, golfers, and boaters and create an East Potomac Park more in line with what Congress originally intended when it designated those three-hundred-plus acres in the late nineteenth century. Back then, the Army Corps of Engineers planned recreational complexes along the Washington Channel shoreline, but the plans were never carried out, nor were bridges built to connect the island to the southwest waterfront.

To envision an expanded Mall is to reject the declaration that the Mall is a "finished work of civic art." It is hard to imagine that L'Enfant's did not envision the city of Washington adapting to conditions and opportunities over the centuries. History cannot be stopped, which means that there will always been a need for new memorials, monuments, and museums. Seemingly insurmountable challenges can be met while respecting the legacy of the L'Enfant and McMillan plans. An expanded Mall could do more to meet the civic and cultural needs of the twenty-first century.

The Coalition has worked to advance the idea of a Third Century Commission and an expanded Mall, meeting with hundreds of organizations and government representatives – from various House and Senate staff, to newspaper journalists and National Public Radio, to the League of Women Voters and local Rotary Clubs. The idea for an expanded Mall was taken up briefly in Congress. As chair of the Senate Subcommittee on National Parks, Senator Thomas declared that "it's time we take another serious look at the Mall as was done in 1901 ... In 1901 Senator McMillan responded to concerns over development that resulted in a plan for the Mall as we know it today. The Mall has outgrown its britches and it will take more than a new belt and suspenders to fix it."[52] But, as with other attempts to rethink the Mall, this idea was also met with resistance from both the Park Service and the NCPC, which contend that the Commemorative Works Act of 2003 defined the Mall as completed and with fixed boundaries.[53] So far, Congress seems reluctant to overturn this act and so the idea of an expanded Mall remains just that – an idea.

Conclusion

Interesting challenges and new debates are changing the way we use and interpret the Mall as public space. As a national park, the Mall is a federal public space, under the stewardship of the National Park Service. But there are also other federal agencies that have jurisdiction on the Mall, and this has led to chronic management challenges such as neglect (primarily due to deferred maintenance) and fragmented and confusing planning. These problems are the failures of both Congress and the Executive Branch to provide clear management structures that ensure the Mall is effectively managed. The rise of public-private partnerships like the Trust for the National Mall may help with the maintenance backlog by raising money for the Park Service. But this also raises questions about why such an important public space is not properly funded by the government in the first place. Congress needs to do better by the Mall.

Demands for new memorials have also introduced debates about how new memorials add to or change the narrative of the Mall, about the high price of memorials and the need for corporate sponsorship, and about the loss of open space. Although Congress has passed a law stating that the Mall is "completed," tremendous pressure continues for new memorials. And there are still silences on the Mall – events and individuals that are not represented in the form of monuments and memorials but perhaps ought to be. It is hard to believe that there will not be another memorial built on the Mall. Meanwhile, security and fortification measures have had an impact on use, public access, and the symbolism. These remain a highly visible part of the twenty-first-century Mall.

Although many Americans see the Mall as the nation's front yard, there has been a lack of public participation in planning and development on the Mall. Perhaps because of recent attempts to reclaim the Mall by the public, there is some evidence that federal agencies are beginning to value the public voice and to make public involvement meaningful. But the Mall's fragmented management structure and the complexity of planning and development processes are bound to ensure that the public will continue to struggle to make its voice heard. There is no one single organization in charge, no one entity in charge of all decisions regarding the Mall. This makes it difficult for the public to know to whom to go to with petitions, suggestions, and innovative ideas. Despite the status of the Mall as a premier public space, there is little genuine public voice in the planning process for the Mall. The good news is that there have been a number of recent plans for improving the Mall; the bad news is that there is still no comprehensive long-term vision. The lack of a comprehensive plan makes dealing with demands for new memorials, fortifications, and other development pressures difficult to resolve.

This book raises more questions than it answers. These questions should stimulate a public dialogue as we debate about how to shape the use and meaning of this special public space:

- How can the Mall be better managed? What would better management look like?
- Will there be enough resources to ensure that the Mall is kept to the standards befitting one of the nation's most valued public spaces? How can the public ensure that Congress provides these resources?
- Are public-private partnerships in public space a solution to management challenges, or are we letting government off the hook for resources it should spend on public services and public spaces?
- Will security measures prevent public access? Will we over-fortify public spaces, like the Mall, and what will this symbolize?
- What are the consequences of corporate sponsorship for memorials and monuments?
- Will continued pressure for commemoration result in the loss of other valuable uses of the Mall, such as open space and recreation?
- How can we more creatively envision commemoration on the Mall in a way that does not consume significant areas of land?

- How can there be more meaningful public participation in planning?
- How do we comprehensively plan for a twenty-first-century Mall?

The Mall is no ordinary public space. As this book has suggested, the history of the Mall has been ever-changing. The Mall has never been a static place. It is a living, public space. The Mall cannot be completed any more than our history is completed.

We need a public discussion about how the Mall can accommodate new uses and anticipate new demands. How we treat our capital city and the Mall speaks to the nation and the world about the value we place on our founding ideals and history as well as what we aspire to in the future. Let's talk about it.

Notes

Introduction

1 The terms National Mall and the Mall are often used interchangeably, but I will refer to the National Mall as the Mall for the rest of this book.

2 M. Bednar, *L'Enfant's Legacy: Public Open Spaces in Washington, D.C.* (Baltimore, MD: Johns Hopkins University Press 2006), 2.

3 M. Carmona, T. Heath, T. Oc, and S. Tiesdell, *Public Places – Urban Spaces: The Dimensions of Urban Design* (Oxford: Architectural Press 2003).

4 L. Bondi, "Gender, Class, and Urban Space: Public and Private Space in Contemporary Landscapes," *Urban Geography* 19 (2) (1998): 160–85.

5 D. Thompson, *An Ancient Shopping Center: The Athenian Agora* (Lunenburg, VT: Stinehour Press 1993).

6 J. Habermas, *The Structural Transformation of the Public Sphere: Inquiry into a Category of Bourgeois Society* (Boston, MA: Polity Press 1962). See also J. Habermas, *The Structural Transformation of the Public Sphere* (trans. T. Burger and F. Lawrence) (Cambridge, MA: MIT Press 1989).

7 In ancient Greece and Rome, for example, many public spaces were open only to freeborn male landowners; see, for example, M. Carmona, *Public Space: The Management Dimension* (New York: Routledge 2008), 24.

8 See S. Low, *On the Plaza: The Politics of Public Space and Culture* (Austin: University of Texas Press 2000); S. Low and N. Smith, eds., *The Politics of Public Space* (New York: Routledge 2006); D. Mitchell, *The Right to the City: Social Justice and the Fight for Public Space* (New York: Guilford Press 2003).

9 S. Benhabib, *Models of Public Space: Hannah Arendt, the Liberal Tradition, and Jurgen Habermas* (Boston, MA: MIT Press 1992).

10 M. Gardiner, *After Habermas: New Perspectives on the Public Sphere* (Malden, MA: Blackwell Publishing 2004), 29.

11 Low and Smith, eds., *The Politics of Public Space.*

12 W. Adams, D. Brockington, J. Dyson, and B. Vira, "Managing Tragedies: Understanding Conflict over Common Pool Resources," *Science* 302, no. 5652 (2003): 1915–16.

13 C. Hess and E. Ostrom, "Ideas, Artifacts and Facilities: Information as a Common-Pool Resource," *Law and Contemporary Problems* 66 (111) (2003): 111–45, https://law.duke.edu/search/google/journals%2066LCPHess/.

14 13 Stat. 325. Emphasis added.

15 17 Stat. 32

16 L. Dilsaver, *Cumberland Island National Seashore: A History of Conservation Conflict* (Charlottesville: University of Virginia Press 2004); J. Ridenour, *The National Parks Compromised: Pork Barrel Politics and America's Treasures* (Merriville, IN: ICS Books 1995).

17 Habermas, *The Structural Transformation of the Public Sphere* (trans. Burger and Lawrence): D. Mitchell, "The End of Public Space? People's Park, Definitions of the Public, and Democracy," *Annals of the Association of American Geographers*, 85 (1) (1995): 108–33; Mitchell, *The Right to the City*; and K. Mitchell, "Conflicting Geographies of Democracy and the Public Sphere in Vancouver, BC," *Transactions of Institute of British Geographers* 22 (New Series) (1997): 162–79.

18 Low and Smith, eds., *The Politics of Public Space*, 33–5.

19 According to Low, there are several types of protests that take place in public space: manifest protest (such as public demonstrations by marginal or outcast groups), latent protest (such as the symbolic struggle for representation in the form of memorials or other forms of architecture), and ritual protest (fiestas, parades, and carnivals that temporarily invert the everyday social structure and hegemonic meanings of the public space). All three of these types of protest occur on the National Mall. Low, *On the Plaza.*

20 Bondi, "Gender, Class, and Urban Space." See also J. Schmelzkopf, "Urban Community Gardens as Contested Space," *Geographical Review* 85 (3) (1995): 364–81.

21 L. Barber, *Marching on Washington: The Forging of an American Political Tradition* (Berkeley: University of California Press 2002).

22 D. Mitchell and L. Staeheli, "'Permitting Protest': Parsing the Fine Geography of Dissent in America," *International Journal of Urban and Regional Research* 29 (2005): 802.

23 Mitchell, *The Right to the City*; G. Valentine, "Children Should Be Seen and Not Heard: The Production and Transgression of Adults' Public Space," *Urban Geography* 17 (1996): 205–20.

24 M. Sorkin, "Introduction," and M. Davis, "Fortress Los Angeles: The Militarization of Urban Space," in M. Sorkin, ed. *Variations on a Theme Park: The New American City and the End of Public Space* (New York: Hill and Wang 1992).

25 Mitchell, "The End of Public Space."

26 Mitchell, "Conflicting Geographies of Democracy and the Public Sphere in Vancouver, BC," 165.

27 S. Carr, M. Frances, L. Rivlin, and A. Stone, *Public Space* (New York: Cambridge University Press 1992).

28 Ibid.

29 F. Lisk, ed., *Popular Participation in Planning for Basic Needs: Concepts, Methods and Practices* (Hampshire, UK: Ashgate 1985).

30 S. Luria, *Capital Speculations: Writing and Building Washington, D.C.* (New Hampshire: University of New Hampshire Press 2006), 155.

31 K. Savage, *Monument Wars: Washington, D.C., the National Mall and the Transformation of the Memorial Landscape* (Berkeley: University of California Press 2009), 4.

32 Mitchell, *The Right to the City*.

33 In the summer of 2015, the National Coalition to Save Our Mall changed its name to the National Mall Coalition. It did so because its advocacy efforts had evolved over the fifteen years since its founding, from a more reaction-oriented organization focused on threats to the Mall to one that is more actively promoting thoughtful and collaborative long-term planning. Throughout this book I will use the former name, the National Coalition to Save Our Mall. Unfortunately, the name change also meant a new website, and some of the documents included on the old website were not transferred to the new one as this book went to press. In these cases, I draw upon copies of the documents that I have in my possession.

1 From Grand Avenue to Public Space

1 B. Forgey, "The French Heart of Washington: A Book Review of Scott Berg's Grand Avenues," *Book World*, 1 April 2007, 3.

2 S.W. Berg, *Grand Avenues: The Story of the French Visionary Who Designed Washington, D.C.* (New York: Pantheon 2007), 13.

3 Ibid., 4.

4 National Archives Trust Fund Board, 1972, *Washington: The Design of the Federal City* (Washington, D.C.: GSA, National Archives Publication, no. 73–1).

5 After the war, and having become a citizen, he changed his name to the more American-sounding Peter.

6 F. Newell, *Planning and Building the City of Washington*, vol. 1 (Washington, D.C.: Ransdell 1932), 11.

7 I. Miller, *Washington in Maps 1606–2000* (New York: Rizzoli International Publications 2002), 20.

8 National Archives Trust Fund Board, *Washington*, 9.

9 Scott Berg notes, however, that L'Enfant thought Philadelphia too simple and uninspiring; he aspired to design something much more monumental and grand. Berg, *Grand Avenues*, 14.

10 Richard Stephenson, *"A Plan Whol[l]y New": Pierre Charles L'Enfant's Plan of the City of Washington* (Washington, D.C.: Library of Congress 1993), 13.

11 Miller, *Washington in Maps*, 18.

12 Ibid.

13 Ibid.

14 Berg, *Grand Avenues*, 112.

15 According to Kenneth Bowling, personal communication, 12 October 2010.

16 K. Bowling, *The Creation of Washington, D.C.: The Idea and Location of the American Capital* (Fairfax, VA: George Mason University Press 1991), 224.

17 P. Scott, "This Vast Empire: The Iconography of the Mall, 1791–1848," in Richard Longstreth, ed., *The Mall in Washington, 1791–1991* (New Haven, CT: Yale University Press 2002), 39.

18 S. Luria, "Designing Washington," *AAG Newsletter*, 44 (7) (2009): 6.

19 Berg, *Grand Avenues*, 84.

20 Luria, "Designing Washington," 6.

21 Luria, *Capital Speculations*, 6.

22 C.M. Harris, "Washington's Gamble, L'Enfant's Dream: Politics, Design and the Founding of the National Capital," *William and Mary Quarterly*, 3rd series, 56 (3) (1999): 527–64.

23 Berg, *Grand Avenues*, 103.

24 F. Bordewich, *Washington: The Making of the American Capital* (New York: Amistad 2008), 6.

25 Luria, *Capital Speculations*, xxi.

26 Ibid., 12.

27 Berg, Grand Avenues, 106–7.

28 Bednar, *L'Enfant's Legacy*, 1.

29 Each reservation was numbered and is still referred to by its reservation number today.

30 Bednar, *L'Enfant's Legacy*, 1.

31 Savage, *Monument Wars*, 30.

32 Pierre Charles L'Enfant, "Plan for the City of Washington," 1791, Library of Congress, https://www.loc.gov/exhibits/treasures/tri001.html (accessed 11 March 2106).

33 Historian Kenneth Bowling suggests that one reason why L'Enfant proposed an equestrian statue of George Washington in his plan dates back to August 1783 when Congress appropriated money to erect such a statue at the seat of government, whenever that was chosen.

34 Bordewich, *Washington*, 81–2.

35 Ibid., 100.

36 J. Reps, *Washington on View: The Nation's Capitol since 1790* (Chapel Hill: University of North Carolina Press 1991), 20.

37 Luria, *Capital Speculations*, 30.

38 M. Coit, ed., *The History of the United States: Volume 3 1789–1829: The Growing Years* (New York: Time 1963).

39 Ibid.

40 When the federal government moved permanently to Washington, D.C., no provision was made for housing the Supreme Court, so Congress resolved to let the court use a room in the Capitol. Over the years, the court used various rooms until it moved to its own building in 1935.

41 Scott, "This Vast Empire," 39.

42 H. Smith, *Washington, D.C: The Story of Our Nation's Capital* (New York: Random House 1967), 13.

43 Attributed to Stephen Hallet, L'Enfant's draftsman, and quoted in C. Abbott, *Political Terrain: Washington, D.C. from Tidewater Town to Global Metropolis* (Chapel Hill: University of North Carolina Press 1999), 34.

44 Smith, *Washington, D.C.*, 13.

45 Scott, "This Vast Empire," 43.

46 Savage, *Monument Wars*, 33.

47 Experts say that L'Enfant's ideas for the Grand Avenue were more akin to the Tulileries Gardens and the Champs-Élysées. Berg, *Grand Avenues*, 109–10.

48 Bednar, *L'Enfant's Legacy*, 1.

49 By the time the Tiber reached the Capitol Hill area, however, it became a series of springs. The land at the western area of Jenkins Hill was and sometimes still is under water. This would later prove problematic.

50 G. Olszewski, *History of the Mall: Washington, D.C.* (Washington, D.C.: United States Department of Interior 1970), 5.

51 Scott, "This Vast Empire."

52 Abbott, *Political Terrain*, 115.

53 McMillan Report, 24, National Park Service online, http://www.nps.gov/parkhistory/online_books/mcmillan/index.htm (accessed 11 March, 2016).

54 Olszewski, *History of the Mall*, 41.

55 As quoted in D. Streatfield, "The Olmsteds and the Landscape of the Mall," in Longstreth, ed., *The Mall in Washington*, 122.

56 P. Penczer, *The Washington National Mall* (Arlington, VA: Oneonta Press 2007), 21.

57 Olszewski, *History of the Mall*, 43.

58 J.W. Reps, *Monumental Washington: The Planning and Development of the Capital Center* (Princeton, NJ: Princeton University Press 1967).

59 T. Hines, "The Imperial Mall: The City Beautiful Movement and the Washington Plan of 1901–1902," in Longstreth, ed., *The Mall in Washington*, 79–100.

60 Olszewski, *History of the Mall*, 45.

61 Ibid. (quoted from the McMillan plan notes written by Charles Moore).

62 McMillan Report, 25.

63 Penczer, *The Washington National Mall*, 23.

64 McMillan Report, 25.

65 Miller, *Washington in Maps*, 119. The report is officially known as Senate Doc. 166, 57th Congress, 1st Session.

66 Abbott, *Political Terrain*, 117.

67 Streatfield, "The Olmsteds and the Landscape of the Mall."

68 Savage, *Monument Wars*, 161.

69 Olszewski, *History of the Mall*, 51.

70 E. Peets, *On the Art of Designing Cities: Selected Essays of Elberts Peets* (P. Spreiregen, ed.) (Cambridge MA: MIT Press 1968), 96–7.

71 Luria, *Capital Speculations*, 145.

72 Ibid.

73 Savage, *Monument Wars*, 152.

74 J. Carson, "Position Paper for the Commission of Fine Arts: World War II Memorial: Response," 1997 (personal archives). Courtesy of National Coalition to Save Our Mall.

75 Penczer, *The Washington National Mall*, 28.

76 National Capital Planning Commission, *Extending the Legacy: Planning America's Capital for the 21st Century* (Washington, D.C., 2003).

77 P. Lewis, "Axioms for Reading a Landscape," in D. Meinig, ed., *The Interpretation of Ordinary Landscapes* (New York. Oxford University Press 1979).

78 National Capital Planning Commission, *Extending the Legacy*.

79 N. Glazer, "Introduction," in N. Glazer and C. Field, eds., *The National Mall: Rethinking Washington's Monumental Core* (Balitmore, MD: Johns Hopkins University Press 2008), 3.

80 Scott, "This Vast Empire."

81 Barber, *Marching on Washington*.

82 Ibid., 228.

83 Mitchell and Staeheli, "'Permitting Protest,'" 802.

84 G. Cranz, *The Politics of Park Design: A History of Urban Parks in America* (Cambridge, MA: MIT Press 1989), 77–9.

85 R.G. Wilson, "High Noon on the Mall: Modernism versus Traditionalism, 1910–1970," in Longstreth, ed., *The Mall in Washington*, 147.

86 R. Stern and R. Gastil, "A Temenos for Democracy: The Mall in Washington and Its Influence," in Longstreth, ed., *The Mall in Washington*, 263.

2 Neglecting the Mall

1 D.C. Preservation League, "Most Endangered Places for 2006," http://www.D.C.preservation.org (accessed March 2008).

2 Smith, *Washington, D.C.*, 31.

3 Berg, *Grand Avenues*, 204.

4 D. Meinig, *The Shaping of America. Volume I: Atlantic America, 1492–1800* (New Haven, CT: Yale University Press 1986).

5 Luria, *Capital Speculations*.

6 Savage, *Monument Wars*, 13.

7 Berg, *Grand Avenues*, 203.

8 Savage, *Monument Wars*, 35.

9 Smith, *Washington, D.C.*, 38.

10 Berg, *Grand Avenues*, 204.

11 Olszewski, *History of the Mall*, 9.

12 Ibid., 9.

13 Abbott, *Political Terrain*, 62–3.

14 T. O'Malley, "A Public Museum of Trees: Mid-Nineteenth Century Plans for the Mall," in Longstreth, ed., *The Mall in Washington*, 62.

15 Abbott, *Political Terrain*, 58–62.

16 O'Malley, "A Public Museum of Trees," 61.

17 Ibid.

18 As quoted in Penczer, *The Washington National Mall*, 11.

19 John Kelly, "John Kelly's Washington: A Fool's Monumental Errand, in More Ways Than One," *Washington Post*, 1 April 2010, B02.

20 O'Malley, "A Public Museum of Trees," 63.

21 Olszewski, *History of the Mall*, 20.

22 Meinig, *The Shaping of America*, 480.

23 Abbott, *Political Terrain*, 40.

24 Olszewski, *History of the Mall*, 22.

25 Ibid., 23.

26 Ibid.

27 Abbott, *Political Terrain*, 68.

28 Olszewski, *History of the Mall*, 24.

29 Abbott, *Political Terrain*, 68.

30 National Archives Trust Fund Board, *Washington*, 41.

31 Ibid., 55.

32 Berg, *Grand Avenues*, 268.

33 Olszewski, *History of the Mall*, 42.

34 Report of the Park Commission to the Senate Committee on the District of Columbia, 1902.

35 N. Ouroussoff, "Tradition and Change Battle on the Mall," *New York Times*, http:// www.nytimes.com/glogin?URI=http%3A%2F%2Fwww.nytimes.com%2F2009%2F0 1%2F16%2Farts%2Fdesign%2F16mall.html%3Fref%3Darts%26_r%3D0 (accessed 11 March 2016).

36 Bednar, *L'Enfant's Legacy*, 22.

37 Olszewski, *History of the Mall*, 89.

38 Ibid.

39 Ibid., 91.

40 Ibid., 98–9. Emphasis added.

41 One of the most ambitious parts of the SOM plan was the banishment of automobiles from the Mall. All of the cross streets were be carried through tunnels; tourists would park at remote locations or in new underground garages. Community opposition prevented the burying of cross streets because these would link with a new set of planned inner beltways which were seen as destructive by many neighbourhood groups, leading to what became known around the United States as the "Freeway Revolt." The SOM plan also proposed tripling the number of trees on the Mall, but this was later rejected for making the plantings too dense overall.

42 Olszewski, *History of the Mall*, 102–3.

43 Wilson, "High Noon on the Mall," 147.

44 World War I Memorial Foundation, http://www.wwimemorial.org/.

45 S. Donnell, "D.C. War Memorial to Get Makeover," NBC Washington, 16 July 2010, http://www.nbcwashington.com/the-scene/events/DC-War-Memorial-to-Get-Makeover-98639214.html (accessed 11 March 2016).

3 Managing the Mall

1 As quoted in CNN, "National Mall in Monumental Disrepair, Activists Say," 4 July 2008, http://www.cnn.com/2008/US/07/04/national.mall/index.html (accessed 6 July 2008).

2 J. Parsons, "Responses to Questions for the Record Submitted by Senator Craig Thomas during the Oversight Hearing on the National Mall, April 12, 2005."

3 E. Holmes Norton, "Testimony for House Natural Resources Subcommittee on National Parks, Forests and Public Lands, Tuesday May 20, 2008."

4 C. Goodsell, *The Case for Bureaucracy*, 4th ed. (Washington, D.C.: CQ Press 2004), 3.

5 G. Hardin, "The Tragedy of the Commons," *Science* 162 (3859) (1968): 1234–48.

6 E. Ostrom, *Governing the Commons: The Evolution of Institutions for Collective Action* (New York: Cambridge University Press 1990).

7 G. Kaedekodi, *Common Property Resource Management: Reflections on Theory and the Indian Experience* (Dehli: Oxford University Press 2004), 18.

8 E. Blackmar, "Appropriating 'the Commons': The Tragedy of Property Rights Discourse," in Low and Smith, eds., *The Politics of Public Space*, 51.

9 National Park System Advisory Board Science Committee, *Revising Leopold: Resource Stewardship in the National Parks*, 2012, National Park Foundation, 3, http://www.nps.gov/calltoaction/PDF/LeopoldReport_2012.pdf.

10 B. McCay, "Emergence of Institutions for the Commons: Contexts, Situations and Events," in E. Ostrom, ed., *Drama of the Commons* (Washington, D.C.: National Academies Press 2002), 362.

11 Adams, Brockington, Dyson, and Vira, "Managing Tragedies."

12 C. Hess and E. Ostrom, "Ideas, Artifacts and Facilities: Information as a Common-Pool Resource," *Law and Contemporary Problems* 66 (2003): 111–45, https://law.duke.edu/search/google/journals%2066LCPHess/ (accessed 11 March 2016).

13 Ostrom, *Governing the Commons*.

14 Constitutionally, national parks are one of the few properties that are "owned" by the entire public (unlike state parks or municipal parks). As such, this study may offer an interesting angle on "who is the public" and "who are its users." In the case of the Mall, the entire U.S. population is legally entitled to this commons. The idea of "the public" and "the users" of the CPR is worthy of more development, but it is beyond the scope and limits of this book.

15 Ostrom, *Governing the Commons*, 21

16 See ibid.; E.W. Pinkerton and M. Weinstein, *Fisheries That Work: Sustainability through Community-Based Management* (Vancouver: David Suzuki Foundation 1995); and R. Wade, *Village Republics: Economic Conditions for Collective Action in South India* (Cambridge: Cambridge University Press 1988).

17 Parsons, "Responses to Questions."

18 This schematic diagram suggests the hierarchical ideal of the authority structure, but the influence and information flows in multiple directions.

19 For most of the nation's national parks, this would be the only oversight committee with jurisdiction.

20 Congressional Research Service, "National Mall Jurisdiction," 2005, a report prepared for the Senate Energy and Natural Resources Committee (personal archives). Courtesy of National Coalition to Save Our Mall.

21 J. Parsons, "Statement of John Parsons, Associate Regional Director for Lands, Resources and Planning, National Capital Region, National Park Service, Department of Interior, before the Subcommittee on National Parks, Senate Committee on Energy and Natural Resources, Concerning the Oversight of the National Mall," 12 April 2005 (personal archives).

22 J. Feldman, "Testimony before the Senate Committee on Energy and Natural Resources, Subcommittee on National Parks," 12 April 2005 (personal archives). Courtesy of National Coalition to Save Our Mall.

23 Ridenour lamented that on occasion high-ranking members of appropriations committees will bypass the proper authorizing committees in order to ensure that projects such as the inclusion of new park units in their districts or states will be passed, a violation of the formal processes of the system. Yet he also admits that courting friendly relationships with ranking members on certain committees such as House Interior Appropriations or the House Subcommittee on National Parks was instrumental in ensuring favourable outcomes in terms of budgets and other issues. Ridenour, *The National Parks Compromised*, 77.

24 H. Kaufman, *The Administrative Behavior of Federal Bureau Chiefs* (Washington, D.C.: Brookings Institution 1981), 166.

25 M. Dowdle, *Public Accountability: Designs, Dilemmas and Experiences* (Cambridge, New York: Cambridge University Press 2006), 3.

26 J. Kee, K. Newcomer, and M.S. Davis, "Transformational Stewardship," in Ricardo Morse, Terry Buss, and C.M. Kinghorn, eds., *Transforming Public Leadership for the 21st Century* (Armonk, N.Y., London: M.E. Sharpe 2007), 174.

27 In March 1933 Congress passed Public Law no. 428, 47 Stat. 1517. Section 16 of this act required the president to investigate and determine what reorganizations were necessary and to implement reorganizations by executive order. Executive Order 6166, issued in June 1933, was the response. At this time, the executive order created an Office of National Parks, Buildings and Reservations, which was later changed to National Parks. The order also abolished various commissions that at that time had jurisdiction over parks and other federal areas in the District, including the Arlington Memorial Bridge Commission, the Public Buildings Commission, the Public Buildings and Public Parks of the National Capital, the National Memorial Commission, and the Rock Creek and Potomac Parkway Commission. See National Park Service, "Legislative History of National Capital Parks and Description of the Seventeen Original Reservations," http://www.archives.gov/federal-register/codification/executive-order/06166.html (accessed 11 March 2016).

28 As quoted in Olszewski, *History of the Mall*, 72.

29 C. Heine, *A History of National Capital Parks*, U.S. Department of Interior, 1953, http://www.nps.gov/parkhistory/online_books/nace/adhi.htm (accessed 11 March 2016).

30 Olszewski, *History of the Mall*, 72.

31 Ibid., 73.

32 According to Susan Kohler, President Theodore Roosevelt created by executive order the Council on Fine Arts, a permanent body to advise the government on matters pertaining to the arts and particularly the architectural development of Washington. However, several years later, President William Howard Taft decided that such a role should be commissioned by Congress. S. Kohler, *The Commission of Fine Arts: A Brief History, 1910–1995* (Washington, D.C.: U.S. Government Printing Office / Commission on Fine Arts 1996), 3.

33 T. Luebke [CFA secretary], "Testimony before the Senate Committee on Energy and Natural Resources, Subcommittee on National Parks," 12 April 2005.

34 Kohler, *The Commission of Fine Arts*, 7–8.
35 The original plans for the Reflecting Pool called for a long rectangular pool with two cross arms as shown in the McMillan Commission drawings. However, by the time construction began, there were several large, temporary buildings on the site where the northern arm was to be placed. Although the CFA would have preferred the "horrid Government buildings" to go, they ultimately omitted the cross arms and instead created an oval pool, the Rainbow Pool. Ibid., 14–15.
36 Ibid., 68–9.
37 Ibid., 7.
38 Ibid., 33.
39 Streatfield, "The Olmsteds and the Landscape of the Mall," 130.
40 National Capital Planning Commission. "History of NCPC," http://www.ncpc.gov/ncpc/Main(T2)/About_Us(tr2)/About_Us(tr3)/History.html (accessed 11 March 2016).
41 Wilson, "High Noon on the Mall," 161.
42 J.C. Brown, "The Mall and the Commission of Fine Arts," in Longstreth, ed., *The Mall in Washington*, 255.
43 Ibid., 258–9.
44 Ibid., 259.
45 There are others who may influence the outcome, including political executives and career personnel in departments and agencies, interest groups, and political parties that see appointments as a patronage process.
46 G.C. Mackenzie, *The Politics of Presidential Appointments* (New York: Free Press 1981), 6.
47 J. Feldman, personal communication, 16 May 2008.
48 Wilson, "High Noon on the Mall," 148.
49 Y. Rydin and E. Falleth, *Networks and Institutions in Natural Resource Management* (Cheltenham, U.K.: Edward Elgar 2006), 9.
50 Ibid.
51 Congressional Research Service, "National Mall Jurisdiction."
52 National Park Service, "History," http://www.nps.gov/nationalmallplan/History.html (accessed 11 March 2016).
53 National Park Service, "Glossary." This definition taken from http://www.nps.gov/nationalmallplan/Documents/Symposium%20Papers/Glossary.pdf (accessed 11 March 2016.
54 Parsons, "Responses to Questions," 1.
55 J. Feldman, 12 March 2007, letter to Susan Spain, project executive for the National Mall Plan (personal archives). Courtesy of National Coalition to Save Our Mall.
56 Starting around 2005, the Park Service defined the Mall as "encompassing the area east/west from the Capitol Grounds to the Lincoln Memorial and north/south form the White House to the Jefferson Memorial." These boundaries were partly the result of the 2004 Commemorative Works Clarification and Revision Act, and hence became the legal definition. See Parsons, "Responses to Questions."
57 National Park Service, "History," http://www.nps.gov/nationalmallplan/History.html (accessed 11 March 2016).

58 Various testimony of National Park Service administrators, senators, representatives, and other expert witnesses.

59 K. Barker, "Ad Rules Relaxed for NFL Bash," *Washington Post*, 4 September 2003, B01.

60 Ibid.

61 E. Fisher, "Live Show Kicks off NFL Year," *Washington Times*, 3 September 2003, http://www.washingtontimes.com/news/2003/sep/3/20030903-115907-9991r/ (accessed 9 September 2003).

62 A. Eisele, "Desecration of the Mall," *The Hill*, 3 September 2003, 10.

63 "Senate Aims to Curb Mall's Commercial Use," *New York Times*, 23 September 2003, http://www.nytimes.com/glogin?URI=http%3A%2F%2Fwww.nytimes.com%2Faponline%2Fnational%2FAP-Selling-The-Mall.html%3F_r%3D0 (accessed 12 March 2016).

64 Letter and e-mail from Betty McCollum, Donna Christensen, and Eleanor Holmes Norton to House colleagues, 10 September 2003 (personal archives). Courtesy of National Coalition to Save Our Mall.

65 L. Hales, "NFL's Civic Fumble on Mall Tarnishes Museum's Honor," *Washington Post*, 13 September 2003, C1–2.

66 J. Bingaman, remarks on "Recent Events on the National Mall" to the Senate, 15 September 2003, S11429, http://thomas.loc.gov/cgi-bin/query/F?r108:8:./temp/~r108qgokh7:e794 (accessed 20 September 2003).

67 M. Reel, "Measure Would Limit Ads on the Mall," *Washington Post*, 24 September 2003, A04.

68 This is according to the Gibson, Dunn and Crutcher's ("GDC") investigation into and analysis of Contract No. CC-NACC004–89 (the "Contract") between the National Park Service and Landmark Services Tourmobile ("Tourmobile"). The analysis is based primarily on documents received in response to several Freedom of Information Act requests. The GDC investigation was conducted on behalf of the National Coalition to Save Our Mall. Its report noted that information obtained from Freedom of Information Act requests showed that the Park Service received $332,198 per year on average over the five-year period 2004–8.

69 George Mason University School of Public Policy Transportation Policy, Operations and Logistics, "A Review of Access and Circulation on the National Mall in Washington, D.C.," 7 May 2008 (personal archives). Courtesy of National Coalition to Save Our Mall.

70 J. Gould, "Park Service Can't Advertise D.C. Circulator," *The Current*, 15 July 2009, 3, 20.

71 See n.68.

72 U.S. Department of the Interior, Office of Inspector General, *Evaluation Report, Sole Source Contracting: Culture of Expediency Curtails Competition in Department of the Interior Contracting* (Report No. W-EV-MOA-0001-2007). Washington, D.C., 2008. Emphasis added.

73 It should be noted, however, that problems with sole-source concessions are not limited to the National Capital Parks. This is a system-wide issue. A 2000 report by the Government Accountability Office (GAO) stated that "for many years, concerns have been raised by the Congress, the Park Service, and GAO about the need to reform existing concessions law and the need for better management of the agency's

concessions program." The report also noted that "the Park Service's concessions contracting practices are out-of-date and do not reflect the best practices of the federal government, the private sector, or other contracting practices within the agency. For example, contracting staff in other agencies throughout the federal government are encouraged to write contracts that are performance based – meaning that the contracts contain incentives for good performance and disincentives for performance that falls below expectations. However, the agency's concessions program is not using performance-based contracts; and according to several senior Park Service concessions program officials, the agency has no plans to do so. Furthermore, for about 10 years, the agency has had difficulty addressing its contracting workload in a timely manner, resulting in chronic backlogs of expired concessions contracts" (6). A third issue with concessions is lack of accountability. The GAO report pointed out that superintendents are not being evaluated on the results of their concessions programs, and, as a result, the lack of accountability is not surprising (7). See GAO, "Park Service: Need to Address Management Problems that Plague Concessions Program," March 2000, http://www.gao.gov/archive/2000/rc00070.pdf. (accessed 10 March 2016)

74 D. Alpert, "The Grand Canyon or Logan Circle? It's All the Same to the Park Service," *Washington Post Local Opinions*, 24 July 2011.

75 Deferred maintenance is not solely an issue for the National Mall; the Park Service estimates that national parks across the country need $6 billion in deferred maintenance. And some acknowledge that the Park Service has been chronically underfunded. In 2006 the Bush administration launched the Centennial Initiative. The goal was to generate a combination of federal money and private donations to meet Park Service needs. The proposal included $100 million in federal money to be spent annually in the park system for ten years. It was hoped that this initiative would generate $3 billion for maintenance in time for the Park Service to celebrate its 100th anniversary in 2016. Issues of adequate funding for the national parks also predate the 21st century. Funding for the national parks failed to keep pace with increased visitors in the immediate post-World War II years, and maintenance of roads, rails, and structures – which had been abandoned during the war – stagnated and funds were instead diverted to handle increased crowds. In 1956 the Park Service launched Mission 66 to deal with housing, camping facilities, and resource projection. L. Dilsaver and W. Wyckoff, "Agency Culture, Cumulative Causation and Development in Glacier National Park, Montana," *Journal of Historical Geography* 25 (1) (1999): 84.

76 J. Ackridge, III [chair, Trust for the National Mall], "Testimony before the Subcommittee on National Parks, Forests and Public Lands, Committee on Natural Resources, Tuesday May 20, 2008," 1–2.

77 As quoted in CNN, "National Mall in Monumental Disrepair."

78 M. Ruane, "America's Unkempt Front Yard," *Washington Post*, 18 June 2008, A1.

79 Examples include the *Kansas City Star*, which ran a story on 29 June 2008 titled "In a City That Treasures Its Past, the National Mall Has Become a Monument to Neglect"; and the *Dallas Morning News*, which, on 4 July 2008, had a story headlined "The Washington Mall Deserves a Better Look."

80 Ruane, "America's Unkempt Front Yard."

81 L. Dilsaver, personal communication, 19 June 2008.

82 Ridenour, *The National Parks Compromised*, 79–81.

83 Ibid., 93.

84 Ibid., 114.

85 Goodsell, *The Case for Bureaucracy*, 61.

86 D. Rettie, *Our National Park System: Caring for America's Greatest Natural and Historic Treasures* (Urbana and Chicago: University of Illinois Press 1995), 182–3.

87 Ibid., 174–5.

88 Ibid., 176.

89 Ibid., 166–7.

90 Ibid., 163.

91 Ridenour, *The National Parks Compromised*.

92 B. Westley and B. Zongker, "National Mall in Disrepair after Years of Neglect," *Washington Times*, 23 July 2009, http://www.washingtontimes.com/news/2009/jul/23/national-mall-disrepair-after-years-neglect/ (accessed 25 July 2009).

93 Ibid.

94 N. Cordes, "National Mall Showing Its Age: Price Tag on Maintenance of Nation's Front Yard Is Causing Budget Controversy," CBS News broadcast, 4 July 2009, http://www.cbsnews.com/news/national-mall-showing-its-age/ (accessed March 10, 2016).

95 Trust for the National Mall, e-mail newsletter, 3 July 2008 (personal archives).

96 R. Vogel, "Welcome," in *Covering More Ground. Trust for the National Mall 2013 Annual Report* (3), http://nationalmall.org/annual-reports/2013/#4. (accessed 10 March, 2016)

97 Blackmar, "Appropriating the Commons," 71.

98 Ibid.

99 Ibid., 72–3.

100 According to the newsletter of the Trust for the National Mall, http://go.nationalmall.org/webmail/68172/81188233/3bd2b1e1aa33ac0622c462be49c1dcf7 (accessed 2 October 2015).

101 S. Higham, "A Music Festival Holds Part of the Mall for Big-Dollar Attendees. Is That Okay?" *Washington Post*, http://www.washingtonpost.com/lifestyle/this-music-festival-will-reserve-part-of-the-national-mall-for-big-dollar-ticket-buyers-is-that-okay/2015/09/22/617f7a4e-5afb-11e5-9757-e49273f05f65_story.html (accessed 2 October 2015).

102 Goodsell, *The Case for Bureaucracy*, 3.

103 Ostrom, *Governing the Commons*, 17.

104 For example, Park Service administrators at the Presidio, part of the Golden Gate National Parks in San Francisco, have examined a variety of management structures that incorporate the Park Service mission while addressing the unique challenges of this park unit. The Presidio, once an Army Post, was rapidly converted into a national park and had numerous re-use issues confronting both historic and non historic structures. In addition, the legislation creating the Presidio required this particular park unit to become economically self-sustaining. These challenges

required a management structure that could combine National Park Service and private-sector expertise. In 1992 McKinsey and Company evaluated these alternative management structures in a report titled "Defining a Viable Management Structure for the Presidio after 1995." The report recommended a congressionally authorized entity. Congress authorized the Presidio Trust in 1995.

Part Two: Use and Development Pressures

1 E. Doss, "War, Memory, and the Public Mediation of Affect: The National World War II Memorial and American Imperialism," *Memory Studies* 1 (2) (2008): 227–50.
2 M. Sturken, *Tourists of History: Memory, Kitsch, and Consumerism from Oklahoma City to Ground Zero* (Durham, N.C., and London: Duke University Press 2007), 13.
3 D. Walkowitz and L. Knauer, eds., *Memory and the Impact of Political Transformation in Public Space* (Durham, N.C., and London: Duke University Press 2004), 2.
4 Sturken, *Tourists of History*.
5 See, for example, S. Graham, "Special Collection: Reflections on Cities, September 11th and the 'War on Terrorism' – One Year On," *International Journal of Urban and Regional Research* 26 (3) (2002): 589–90.
6 For example, the University of California's Peoples Park controversy as documented by Don Mitchell in "The End of Public Space?"; or the conflict over residential "monster houses" in Vancouver and the perception of a loss of socio-economic "exclusivity" as examined by Katharyne Mitchell in "Conflicting Geographies of Democracy and the Public Sphere in Vancouver, BC."

4 Making Space for the Dream

1 The official dedication had been scheduled for 28 August 2011 to mark the 38th anniversary of King's 1963 "I Have a Dream Speech." The threat of Hurricane Irene cancelled the dedication and it was rescheduled for September. The memorial, however, had been opened to the public early that week so that D.C. residents could enjoy a "sneak peek." It remained open to the public despite the lack of an official dedication ceremony.
2 O. Dwyer and D. Alderman, *Civil Rights Memorials and the Geography of Memory* (Chicago, IL: Center for American Places at Columbia College, Chicago, 2008), 5.
3 R. Romano and L. Radford, eds., *The Civil Rights Movement in American Memory* (Athens: University of Georgia Press 2006).
4 M. Azaryahu, "The Power of Commemorative Street Names," *Environment and Planning D: Space and Society* 14 (1996): 311–30.
5 Dwyer and Alderman, *Civil Rights Memorials and the Geography of Memory*, 36–7.
6 K. Savage, *Standing Soldiers, Kneeling Slaves: Race, War, and Monument in Nineteenth-Century America* (Princeton, NJ: Princeton University Press 1997); also R. Schein, ed., *Landscape and Race in the United States* (New York: Routledge 2006).
7 J. Leib, "Separate Times, Shared Spaces: Arthur Ashe, Monument Avenue and the Politics of Richmond, Virginia's Symbolic Landscape," *Cultural Geographies* 9 (2002): 286–312.

8 O. Dwyer, "Interpreting the Civil Rights Movement: Place, Memory and Conflict," *Professional Geographer* 52 (2000): 660–71.

9 D. Alderman, "Street Names as Memorial Arenas: The Reputational Politics of Commemorating Martin Luther King, Jr. in a Georgia County," *Historical Geography* 30 (2002): 99–120.

10 Dwyer and Alderman, *Civil Rights Memorials and the Geography of Memory*, 7.

11 Ibid., 5.

12 B. Zongker, "Construction to Begin on King Memorial in D.C.," Associated Press, 29 October 2009, http://www.mlkmemorial.org (personal archives). At some point after the completion of the memorial, the MLK Memorial Association established a new website (http://www.thememorialfoundation.org/), and many of the documents and press releases found at the earlier website did not migrate. In these cases, I have again drawn upon copies of the documents in my personal possession.

13 Dwyer and Alderman, *Civil Rights Memorials and the Geography of Memory*.

14 K. Foote, *Shadowed Ground: America's Landscapes of Violence and Tragedy*, 2nd ed. (Austin: University of Texas Press 2003).

15 C. Thomas, *The Lincoln Memorial and American Life* (Princeton, NJ: Princeton University Press 2002), 168.

16 National Capital Planning Commission, "Martin Luther King, Jr. Memorial," *NCPC Quarterly*, January 1999, 4.

17 National Capital Planning Commission, "Memorializing Martin Luther King, Jr.," *NCPC Quarterly*, spring 2001.

18 Quoted in M. Neibauer, "King Memorial Inches Closer to $100M," *Examiner*, 8 May 2007, http://www.mlkmemorial.org (accessed 20 April 2010).

19 M. Preston, "The King Memorial: A Shared Dream," *Urban Influence Magazine*, February/March 2006, http://www.mlkmemorial.org (accessed 20 April 2010).

20 Quoted in E. O'Keefe, "Interior Department Gives Final OK for MLK Memorial," *Washington Post*, 26 October 2009, Metro Section, http://www.Washingtonpost.com.

21 Washington, D.C. Martin Luther King Jr. National Memorial Project Foundation, "Mission and Vision Statement of the Memorial Project," 2010 (personal archives).

22 H. Johnson, Sr, "Remarks," 2009 (personal archives).

23 Washington, D.C. Martin Luther King Jr. National Memorial Project Foundation, "About the Memorial," 2016, http://www.thememorialfoundation.org/content/facts-about-memorial (accessed 15 March 2016).

24 Ibid.

25 Savage, *Monument Wars*.

26 Zongker, "Construction to Begin on King Memorial in D.C."

27 The website is no longer active.

28 Quoted in P. Polston, "Delegation in Vermont Protests Outsourcing of MLK Memorial," *Seven Days*, 7 November 2007, http://www.sevendaysvt.com/vermont/Redirect?url=http://www.7dvt.com/2007/delegation-vermont-protests-outsourcing-mlk-memorial (accessed 1 April 2010).

29 M. Fisher, "Sculpting Martin Luther King, Jr.," *Washington Post*, 11 May 2008, http://voices.washingtonpost.com/rawfisher/2007/08/sculpting_martin_luther_king_j.html (accessed 1 April 2010).

30 Monument Builders of North America, "Monument Builders Association Forms Task Force to Study Outsourcing of King Memorial to China," 2008 (personal archives).

31 Quoted in E. Robinson, "King as He Was," *Washington Post*, 20 May 2008, A13.

32 National Public Radio, "Some Say Memorial Design Misrepresents MLK Jr.," 5 December 2007, audio/transcript at http://www.npr.org/templates/story/story. php?storyId=16918803 (accessed March 2010).

33 Robinson, "King as He Was."

34 Ibid.

35 Dwyer and Alderman, *Civil Rights Memorials and the Geography of Memory*, plate 15.

36 Ibid., plate 14.

37 E. Blair, "Quote on MLK Memorial to Be Fixed, but How?" 23 February 2012, http:// www.npr.org/2012/02/24/147301301/quote-on-mlk-memorial-to-be-fixed-but-how.

38 G. Weingarten and M. Ruane, "Maya Angelou Says King Memorial Inscription Makes Him Look 'Arrogant,'" *Washington Post*, 30 August 2011, https://www. washingtonpost.com/local/maya-angelou-says-king-memorial-inscription-makes-him-look-arrogant/2011/08/30/gIQAlYChqJ_story.html (accessed 11 March 2016).

39 G. Oberlander, personal communication, 7 May 2014.

40 An off-the-record conversation with a Park Service administrator.

41 The process is so detailed that it is difficult to create a flow diagram that would fit on one page. Instead, I provide a brief synopsis of a multiple-step process.

42 National World War II Memorial Foundation, 2010, "Fundraising," http://www. thememorialfoundation.org (accessed 11 March 2016).

43 Quoted in W. Koch, "Organizers of MLK Memorial Quicken Pace to Get Slain Leader among Greats," *USA Today*, 12 January 2006, http://usatoday30.usatoday.com/ news/nation/2006-01-12-mlk-memorial_x.htm (accessed 1 April 2010).

44 The Memorial Foundation, http://www.thememorialfoundation.org/content/press-release/125-million-letter-credit-wal-mart-foundation-expedite-construction-martin (accessed 11 March 2016)

45 See, for example, Dwyer, "Interpreting the Civil Rights Movement"; Leib, "Separate Times, Shared Spaces"; Schein, *Landscape and Race in the United States*.

5 The Brawl on the Mall

1 Bednar, *L'Enfant's Legacy*, 37.

2 See, for example, Dwyer, "Interpreting the Civil Rights Movement"; N. Johnson, "Cast in Stone"; Heffernan, "For Ever England"; and Withers, "Place, Memory, Monument."

3 Y. Whelan, "The Construction and Destruction of a Colonial Landscape: Commemorating British Monarchs in Dublin before and after Independence," *Journal of Historical Geography* 28 (2002): 508–33.

4 N. Johnson, "Sculpting Heroic Histories: Celebrating the Centenary of the 1798 Rebellion in Ireland," *Transactions of the Institute of British Geographers* 19 (1994): 78–93; N. Johnson, "Cast in Stone."

5 B. Osborne, "Constructing Landscape of Power: The George Etienne Cartier Monument, Montreal," *Journal of Historical Geography* 24 (1998): 431–58.

6 Leib, "Separate Times, Shared Spaces."

7 J. Bodnar, *Remaking America: Public Memory, Commemoration, and Patriotism in the Twentieth Century* (Princeton, NJ: Princeton University Press 1992); also D. Hayden, *The Power of Place: Urban Landscapes as Public History* (Cambridge, MA: MIT Press 1995)

8 See, for example, G.J. Ashworth, "From History to Heritage – From Heritage to Identity: In Search of Concepts and Models," in G.J. Ashworth and P.J. Larkham, eds., *Building a New Heritage: Tourism, Culture and Identity in the New Europe* (London: Routledge 1994); S. Graham, G.J. Ashworth, and J.E. Tunbridge, *A Geography of Heritage* (London: Routledge 2000); E. Linenthal, *Preserving Memory: The Struggle to Create America's Holocaust Museum* (New York: Viking 1995).

9 M. Glantz and R. Figueroa, "Does the Aral Sea Merit Heritage Status?" *Global Environmental Change* 7 (4) (1997): 359.

10 Graham, Ashworth, and Tunbridge, *A Geography of Heritage*.

11 K. Mitchell, "Monuments, Memorials, and the Politics of Memory," *Urban Geography* 24 (5) (2003): 442–59.

12 Ashworth, "From History to Heritage."

13 Johnson, "Sculpting Heroic Histories."

14 Some important contributions to geographic scholarship include: S. Daniels and D. Cosgrove, "Spectacle and Text: Landscape Metaphors in Cultural Geography," in J. Duncan and D. Ley, eds., *Place/Culture/Representation* (London: Routledge 1993), 57–77; J. Donald, "Metropolis: The City as Text," in R. Bobcock and K. Thompson, eds., *Social and Cultural Forms of Modernity* (Cambridge: Polity Press 1992), 417–61; J. Duncan, *The City as Text: The Politics of Landscape Interpretation in the Kandyan Kingdom* (Cambridge: Cambridge University Press 1990); J. Short, *Imagined Country* (Oxford: Blackwell 1991).

15 Bednar, *L'Enfant's Legacy*, 39.

16 D. Kiley, "A Critical Look at the McMillan Plan," in Longstreth, ed., *The Mall in Washington*, 297.

17 In 2001 Congress considered H.R. 452, which would have established the Ronald Reagan Memorial "somewhere between the Capitol and the Lincoln Memorial." Although the bill failed, it has been sponsored several more times in subsequent sessions of Congress.

18 See Mitchell, *Monuments, Memorials, and the Politics of Memory*.

19 J. Gillis, ed., *Commemorations: The Politics of National Identity* (Princeton, NJ: Princeton University Press 1994).

20 See Mitchell, "The End of Public Space?"

21 D. Alderman, "New Memorial Landscapes in the American South," *Professional Geographer* 52 (4) (2000): 659; also, N. Mills, *Their Last Battle: The Fight for the National World War II Memorial* (New York: Basic Books 2004).

22 See, for example, M. Bogart, "Public Space and Public Memory in New York's City Hall Park," *Journal of Urban History* 25 (2) (1999): 226–57; K. Till, "Places of Memory," in J. Agnew, K. Mitchell, and G. Toal, eds., *A Companion to Political Geography* (Oxford, UK: Blackwell 2003), 289–301.

23 Public Law 103–32.

24 R. Lewis, "Pedantry Spoils the World War II Memorial," *Weekly Standard*, 17 February 1997, 34.
25 M. Fisher, "A Scourge of War Not Worthy of This Battlefield," *Washington Post*, 14 November 2000.
26 As quoted in J. Fishkin, "Monumental Error: Anatomy of an Eyesore," *New Republic* 25 September 2000, 14–15.
27 *Los Angeles Times*, "Wrong Thing, Wrong Time," 10 July 2000.
28 "WWII Memorial Misplaced," *USA Today*, 20 July 2000.
29 Quoted in Fishkin, "Monumental Error."
30 C. Knight, "DC Follies," *Los Angeles Times*, 20 September 2000.
31 M. Fisher, "A Memorial, Yes, but What about Its Message?" *Washington Post*, 22 July 2000, B1.
32 Many misread the design as a sarcophagus – it was actually a cenotaph, a "stand-in" for those who were not buried there.
33 J.C. Brown, remarks made during a panel session on the WWII Memorial at the American Studies Association Annual Conference, 10 November 2001 (my personal notes).
34 J.C. Brown to Tersh Boasberg, chairman of Committee of 100 on the Federal City, 8 October 1999, Archives of the National Coalition to Save Our Mall.
35 G. Hanson, "War and Remembrance: Big Battle of Words about World War II Monument," *Washington Times*, 12 May 1997.
36 G. Mosse, *Fallen Soldier: Reshaping the Memory of the World Wars* (New York: Oxford 1990). Emphasis added.
37 D.K. Dietsch, "Capital Offense," *Architecture* 86 (March 1997): 62–3.
38 K. Haas, "Pandering to Anxiety: The National WWII Memorial," paper presented at the American Studies Association Annual Conference, 9 November 2001.
39 Fisher, "A Memorial, Yes, but What about Its Message?"
40 B. Ladd, *The Ghosts of Berlin* (Chicago, IL: University of Chicago Press 1997).
41 Foote, *Shadowed Ground*. See also Mitchell, "Monuments, Memorials, and the Politics of Memory"; Johnson, "Sculpting Heroic Histories."
42 Brown died in 2002 and did not live to see the memorial completed.
43 C. Knight, "Planned Memorial Would Damage Prime Piece of Real Estate," *Los Angeles Time*s, 19 July 2000; also, Feldman, personal communication, 14 July 2003.
44 E. Meyer, "From Urban Prospect to Retrospect: Lessons for the World War II Memorial Debates," *Journal of Architectural Education*, 2008, 57.
45 Quoted in J. Yardley, "Ambush on the Mall," *Washington Post*, 10 July 2000, C02.
46 Brown, remarks, 2001.
47 W. Jones, "The Battle of the Mall Is Not over Yet," *San Diego Union-Tribune*, 21 January 2001 (personal archives). Courtesy of National Coalition to Save Our Mall.
48 J. Feldman, "The Changing Face of National Public Space," 2000 (personal archives).
49 C. Knight, "Opponents Find a Hitch in WWII Memorial Plans," *Los Angeles Times*, 19 July 2000.
50 "Mauling the Mall," *Wall Street Journal*, 15 September 2000.
51 "WWII Memorial Misplaced," *USA Today*, 20 July 2000.
52 "Wrong Thing, Wrong Time," *Los Angeles Times*, 10 July 2000.

53 L. Wheeler, "WW II Memorial's Site in Middle of Mall is under Attack," *Washington Post*, 6 June 2000, B01.

54 Knight, "Planned Memorial Would Damage Prime Piece of Real Estate."

55 R. Lewis, "World War II Memorial Plan Needs Revision," *Washington Post*, 17 May 1997, E1.

56 Dietsch, "Capital Offense."

57 Quoted in Hanson, "War and Remembrance."

58 See Johnson, "Sculpting Heroic Histories."

59 P. Goldberger, "Not in Our Front Yard," *New Yorker*, 7 August 2000.

60 C. Krauthammer, "The WWII Memorial: Inadequate and Out of Place," *Washington Post*, 28 July 2000.

61 J. Feldman, "Memorial Mistake," *Washington Post*, 4 July 1999, B8.

62 Quoted in J. Walsh, "Design Panel Approves WWII Memorial for National Mall Site," *Boston Globe*, 21 July 2000.

63 Quoted in Fisher, "A Scourge of War Not Worthy of This Battlefield."

64 C. Cassell to Committee of 100 on the Federal City, July 1999 (personal archives). Courtesy of National Coalition to Save Our Mall.

65 Barber, *Marching on Washington*.

66 "New Site for War Memorial," *Hartford Courant*, 12 October 2000.

67 Quoted in L. Wheeler, "World War II Memorial Clears Key Hurdle," *Washington Post*, 21 July 2000, A01.

68 G. Garcia, "USA's 'Front Yard' Is Veteran's Latest Battleground," *USA Today*, 27 October 2000.

69 Committee of 100 on the Federal City, "Testimony before the Joint Task Force on Memorials," 29 September 1999 (personal archives). Courtesy of National Coalition to Save Our Mall.

70 Quoted in J. Tolson, "Scenes from the Mall," *US News & World Report*, 18 September 2000.

71 "How Many Memorials Are Enough?" NBC Nightly News, 26 May 2003, transcript (personal archives). Courtesy of National Coalition to Save Our Mall.

72 Quoted in M. Kilian, "Controversial WWII Memorial Clears Hurdle," *Chicago Tribune*, 21 July 2000.

73 Goldberger, "Not in Our Front Yard."

74 T. Illia, "Desecrating a Landmark to Build a Memorial," *San Francisco Chronicle*, 8 October 2000.

75 J. Yang, "Memorial under Fire," ABS World News Tonight, 4 June 2000.

76 "Honor WWII Vets, but Not on Mall," *Atlanta Constitution*, 20 September 2000.

77 J. Yardley, "The Battle of the Mall," *Washington Post*, 3 July 2000, C02.

78 R. Hampson, "17 Years in the Making, WWII Shrine Is a Reality," *USA Today*, 19 April 2004, A1, A5.

79 "WWII Memorial – Let's Reconsider the Site in the Nation's Capital," *Fort Worth Star-Telegram*, 23 October 2000.

80 Brown to Boasberg, 1999.

81 B. Forgey, "A Fitting Memorial in Every Way: World War II Monument Would Add to the Emotional Power of the Mall," *Washington Post*, 15 July 2000, C01.

82   Hanson, "War and Remembrance."

83   "Don't Mar the Mall," *New York Times*, 24 September 2000.

84   National Park Service, *World War II Memorial Brochure* (Washington, D.C.: Government Printing Office 2004)

85   Brown to Boasberg. Emphasis added.

86   J. Feldman, personal communication, 14 July 2003.

87   C. Knight, "A Memorial to Forget," *Los Angeles Times*, 23 May 2004.; also P. Goldberger, "Down at the Mall," *New Yorker*, 31 May 2004.

6 Securing the Mall

1   Security costs for the inauguration ran approximately $17.5 million.

2   George Will was an on-air commentator for Fox News.

3   J. Cienski, "Washington's Ugly New Look," *National Post*, 29 June 2002.

4   D. Montgomery, "Christmas at the People's House (Restrictions May Apply)," *Washington Post*, 18 December 2008, C12.

5   The literature is rich with important contributions including: M. Davis, *City of Quartz: Excavating the Future in Los Angeles* (London: Verso 1990); M. Davis, *Ecologies of Fear: Los Angeles and the Imagination of Disaster* (New York: Metropolitan Books 1998); N. Fyfe, ed., *Images of the Street: Planning, Identity, and Control in Public Space* (London: Routledge 1998); M. Sorkin, ed., *Variations on a Theme Park: The New American City and the End of Public Space* (New York: Hill and Wang 1992); J.R. Gold and G. Revill, eds., *Landscapes of Defense* (London: Prentice Hall 2000); D. Gregory and A. Pred, eds., *Violent Geographies: Fear, Terror, and Political Violence* (New York: Routledge 2007).

6   See Davis, *Ecologies of Fear*; J. Coaffee, "Rings of Steel, Rings of Concrete and Rings of Confidence: Designing out Terrorism in Central London pre and post September 11," *International Journal of Urban and Regional Research* 28 (1) (2004): 201–11; and M. Pawley, *Terminal Architecture* (London: Reaktion Books 1998).

7   N. Fyfe and J. Bannister, "The Eyes upon the Street: Closed-Circuit Television Surveillance and the City," in Fyfe, ed., *Images of the Street*.

8   J. Coaffee, *Terrorism, Risk and the City* (Aldershot, U.K.: Ashgate 2003).

9   S. Brown, "Central Belfast's Security Segment – an Urban Phenomenon," *Area* 17 (1) (1985): 1–8.

10 For example, wrought-iron security gates were installed at Downing Street in London in 1989. It wasn't until after a small private plane crashed on the south area of the White House grounds in 1994 that Pennsylvania Avenue in front of the White House was closed to vehicular traffic.

11 Coaffee, "Rings of Steel, Rings of Concrete and Rings of Confidence."

12 Ibid.

13 National Capital Planning Commission, *The National Capital Urban Design and Security Plan* (Washington, D.C., 2002), iii.

14 L. Wheeler, "A Subtler Approach to Security on Mall," *Washington Post*, 21 December 2001.

15 *The Hill*, May 2000.

16 H. Stuever, "Don't Go There" *Washington Post*, 17 January 2005, C1.

17 B. Forgey, "A Good Neighbor's Monumentally Bad Fence," *Washington Post*, 13 August 2001, C01.

18 Ibid.

19 NCPC, *The National Capital Urban Design and Security Plan*, ii. Besides the NCPC, the agencies and commissions that worked on the security design included: General Services Administration, National Park Service, Architect of the Capitol, D.C. Office of Planning, Secret Service, D.C. Department of Transportation, and Homeland Security Council.

20 U.S. Park Service estimated that in 2003 some 489,000 visitors arrived via the Metro in 2003 and likely another 150,000 using other forms of transportation.

21 "Mall Eyes," *Washington Post*, 4 July 2002, A22.

22 Quoted in T Metaska, "Candid Cameras in Washington, D.C.," *FrontPageMagazine.com*, 26 March 2002.

23 J. Parsons, "Statement of John Parsons, Associate Regional Director for Lands, Resources, and Planning, National Capital Region, National Park Service, Department of the Interior, before the Subcommittee on the District of Columbia of the House Committee on Government Reform, Regarding Electronic Surveillance in the Nation's Capital," 22 March 2002.

24 Ibid.

25 Metaska, "Candid Cameras in Washington, D.C." see also http://www.cnsnews.com/news/article/most-americans-support-government-surveillance-poll-says (accessed 10 March 2016).

26 See H. Koskela, "The Gaze without Eyes: Video-Surveillance and the Changing Nature of Urban Space," *Progress in Human Geography* 24 (2) (2000): 243–65.

27 Quoted in D. Farhrenthold and D. Nakamura, "Council Attacks D.C. Surveillance Cameras," *Washington Post*, 8 November 2002, B1.

28 Quoted in ibid.

29 "Big Brother and the Park Service," *Washington Times*, 23 March 2002.

30 National Coalition to Save Our Mall, *Mall Watch* (personal archives). Courtesy of National Coalition to Save Our Mall.

31 Ibid.

32 Ibid.

33 NCPC, *The National Capital Urban Design and Security Plan*, 5.

34 In cases where buildings were close to major roads and intersections and hence creating a stand-off distance of 100 feet is impossible, the plan recommended creating a perimeter of at least 50 feet. Most of the critical federal buildings (the Capitol, White House, the memorials, most museums on the Mall) have at least 100 feet of room to establish the security zone.

35 NCPC, *The National Capital Urban Design and Security Plan*, 33. Emphasis added.

36 J. Yardley, "On the Mall, Entrenched Thinking," *Washington Post*, 6 May 2002, C2.

37 The security-oriented landscape design was conceived by Philadelphia landscape architect Laurie Olin.

38 C. Leigh, "Subterranean Blues," *Weekly Standard* 8 (17) (2003).

39 Yardley, "On the Mall, Entrenched Thinking."

40 B. Forgey, "Washington's Tunnel Vision for Tourists," *Washington Post*, 18 May 2002.

41 B. Forgey, "Public Spaces, Still under Siege," *Washington Post*, 10 September 2002, A1.

42 As quoted in S. Hsu, "Arts Panel Cools on Underground Visitor Center," *Washington Post*, 17 May 2002, B8.

43 As quoted in A. Santana, "Experts Say the Mall Can't Be Invulnerable," *Washington Post*, 20 March 2003, B05.

44 National Coalition to Save Our Mall, Press Release, "Controversial Monument Tunnel None of Public's Business, National Park Service Says," 29 April 2003 (personal archives). Courtesy of National Coalition to Save Our Mall.

45 Interview with Judy Scott Feldman, chair of the National Coalition to Save the Mall, 20 July 2004.

46 A. Hargrove, Committee of 100 on the Federal City, to John V. Cogbill, III, chairman of the NCPC, 20 September 2002 (personal archives). Courtesy of National Coalition to Save Our Mall.

47 C. Lee, "Digging Deep for Capitol Visitors," *Washington Post*, 11 November 2003, A1. This article notes that the plan, first proposed in 1990, was to cost $71 million. It languished without funding until the 1998 killing of two Capitol police officers by an intruder raised new concerns about security and prompted Congress to allocate $100 million towards the costs. After the September 11th attacks, President Bush and congressional leaders appropriated another $275 million for security enhancements and to build more office space.

48 D. Dietsch, "New Bunker Mentality Will Mar Washington," *USA Today*, 29 July 2002, 13A.

49 S. Hsu, "Park Service Plan to Add Mall Security Hits Resistance," *Washington Post*, 1 January 2005, B01.

50 In April 2003 I attended a planning meeting that included officials from the NCPC, the CFA, and the NPS. This exchange took place during the panel discussion.

51 Forgey, "Public Spaces, Still under Siege."

52 "A Pall over the Mall," *Washington Post*, 4 January 2005, A14.

53 T. Dwyer and S. Hsu, "Security Measures Removed, Reviewed," *Washington Post*, 22 January 2005, B1.

54 Quoted in "Fortresses of Fear," *Washington Post*, 4 August 2004, A18.

55 Dorgan was then and still serves on the Interior Appropriations Subcommittee.

56 Quoted in M. Reel, "Washington Monument Entry Tunnel Plan Dies," *Washington Post*, 23 October 2003.

57 Habermas, *The Structural Transformation of the Public Sphere*; L. Staeheli, "Citizenship, Community and Struggle for Public Spaces," *Professional Geographer* 49 (1) (1997): 28–38.

7 Whose Mall Is It?

1 Dowdle, ed., *Public Accountability*, 3–4.

2 Ibid.

3 R. Morse and T. Buss, "The Transformation of Public Leadership," in Morse, Buss, and Kinghorn, eds., *Transforming Public Leadership for the 21st Century*, 10.

4 Ibid., 7–9.

5 See, for example, S. Hill and M. Salter, "Planning and Inclusion: A Discussion Paper for the RTPI" (London: RTPI 2004).

6 Bednar, *L'Enfant's Legacy*, 29.

7 Dilsaver and Wyckoff, "Agency Culture, Cumulative Causation and Development in Glacier National Park, Montana."

8 Ibid., 76.

9 Anonymous member of the Central Park Conservancy, interview with author, 15 March 2008.

10 James Edwin Kee, Kathryn Newcomer, and Mike S. Davis, "Transformational Stewardship," in Morse, Buss, and Kinghorn, eds., *Transforming Public Leadership for the 21st Century*, 154.

11 National Coalition to Save Our Mall, "Press Release April 29: Controversial Monument Tunnel None of Public's Business, National Park Service Says," 2003 (personal archives). Courtesy of National Coalition to Save Our Mall.

12 Wilson, "High Noon on the Mall," 154–5.

13 J. Feldman, personal communication, 7 April 2004.

14 Yardley, "Ambush on the Mall."

15 P. Kennicott, "The National Park Service 'Workshop,'" blog, 2010, http://www.philipkennicott.com/2010/11/10/the-national-park-service-workshop/ 2010.

16 Ibid.

17 National Park Service Director's Order 75A, "Civic Engagement and Public Involvement" (personal archives).

18 J. Feldman, personal communication, 17 June 2007.

19 Advisory Council on Historic Preservation, "Protecting Historic Properties: A Citizen's Guide to Section 106 Review," 2002, http://www.achp.gov/citizensguide.html (accessed 10 January 2008).

20 Ibid., 14.

21 National Park Service, *Cultural Resource Management Guidelines*, 1997, as reported in the National Coalition to Save Our Mall, "The Legal Battle," 2000 (personal archives). Courtesy of National Coalition to Save Our Mall.

22 Ibid.

23 N. Feldman, "Testimony," 14 December 2000 (personal archives). Courtesy of National Coalition to Save Our Mall.

24 Anonymous member of National Coalition to Save Our Mall, 2010. Remarks made during a Coalition board meeting (personal archives).

25 For example, this August 20 e-mail was sent from the National Park Service to other participating agencies and two members of NSCOM: "Dear Consulting Party Representatives, due to an unforeseen conflict, the Section 106 consultation meeting has been rescheduled to Thursday, August 23 from 9:00am to noon ... For those unable to attend we will provide you with the proposal to review and you will have 30 days to submit your comments" (personal archives). Courtesy of National Coalition to Save Our Mall.

26 J. Feldman, remarks made during a Coalition board meeting, 2010. I was in attendance.

27 J. Feldman, e-mail to Advisory Council on Historic Preservation, 27 August 2007 (personal archives). Courtesy of National Coalition to Save Our Mall.

28 J. Feldman, "Letter of Senator Craig Thomas, Committee on Energy and Natural Resources Subcommittee on National Parks," 12 April 2005 (personal archives). Courtesy of National Coalition to Save Our Mall.]nalDraftCapitalSpacePlan.pdf (aion to Save Our Mall (personal archives)] t. and launched a new web site. Much of the old mate

29 Feldman, e-mail, 27 August 2007, to Advisory Council on Historic Preservation (personal archives). Courtesy of National Coalition to Save Our Mall.

30 J. Feldman, personal communication, 24 July 2010.

31 J. Feldman to Susan Spain, project executive for the National Mall Plan, U.S. Park Service, 12 March 2007 (personal archives). Courtesy of National Coalition to Save Our Mall.

32 J. Feldman, "NCPC NPS Mall Plan Update," 5 March 2010 (personal archives). Courtesy of National Coalition to Save Our Mall.

33 J. Feldman, personal communication, 24 July 2010.

34 Ibid.

35 National Coalition to Save Our Mall, "The Legal Battle" (personal archives). Courtesy of National Coalition to Save Our Mall.

36 Wilson, "High Noon on the Mall," 147.

37 A. Irish, "Why D.C. Streetcars Are 'Preservationist,'" *Washington Post*, 18 April 2010, http://www.washingtonpost.com/wp-dyn/content/article/2010/04/14/AR2010041404364.html.

38 D. Alpert, "'Monumentalism' Puts Postcard D.C. above Human D.C.," in Greater Greater Washington Blog, 19 April 2010, http://greatergreaterwashington.org/post/5568/monumentalism-puts-postcard-dc-above-human-dc/ (accessed 12 March 2016).

39 Off-the-record conversation with author, 2010.

40 National Capital Planning Commission, *Extending the Legacy*, 5.

41 H. Tregoning, "City Center Action Agenda," 29 November 2008, http://planning.dc.gov/page/center-city-action-agenda-2008 (accessed 12 March 2016).

42 National Capital Planning Commission, Government of the District of Columbia, and National Park Service, "CapitalSpace: Ideas to Achieve the Full Potential of Washington's Parks and Open Space," 2010, 19, http://www.ncpc.gov/DocumentDepot/Publications/CapitalSpace/FinalDraftCapitalSpacePlan.pdf (accessed 12 March 2016).

43 CapitalSpace Plan, "Moving the Plan Forward," 2010, 93, http://www.ncpc.gov/DocumentDepot/Publications/CapitalSpace/FinalDraftCapitalSpacePlan.pdf (accessed 12 March 2016).

44 "CapitalSpace," 2010. http://www.ncpc.gov/DocumentDepot/Publications/CapitalSpace/FinalDraftCapitalSpacePlan.pdf (accessed 12 March 2016).

8 The Right to the Mall

1 John D. Bates, judge, U.S. District Court for the District of Columbia, "Mary Brooke Oberwetter, Plaintiff, v. Civil Action No. 09–0588 (JDB), Kenneth Hilliard and Kenneth L. Salazar, Defendants," Memorandum Opinion, 25 January 2010, 4–5.

2 Ibid., 17, according to 41 Fed. Reg. 12879, 12880 (29 March 1976).

3 Ibid., 14–15.

4 Ibid., 15. Emphasis added.

5 Ibid., 16–17.

6 Ibid.

7 See, for example, http://www.youtube.com/watch?v=uLw2ISUusz4 and http:// www.youtube.com/watch?v=lHD6Bm7cVUQ.

8 http://www.jeffersondanceparty.info/.

9 For a video of the dancing, see http://www.informationliberation.com/?id=35523.

10 L Arantani, "Dancers Shimmy at the Jefferson Memorial," *Washington Post*, 6 June 2011, n.p.

11 "Dancing at a National Memorial Isn't Civil Disobedience," *Washington Post*, 2 June 2011, htpp://www.washingtonpost.com/opinions/dancing-at-a-national-memorial-isnt-civil-disobedience/.

12 http://www.media.glennbeck.com/828/828kit.pdf.

13 A. Gardner, K. Thompson, and P. Rucker, "Beck, Palin Tell Thousands to Restore America," *Washington Post*, 29 August 2010, http://www.washingtonpost.com/wp-dyn/content/article/2010/08/28/AR2010082801106.html.

14 Ibid.

15 J. Horowitz, J. Hesse, M. and D. Zak, "Sanity and Fear; Meeting in the Middle," *Washington Post*, 31 October 2010, A1.

16 http://www.rallytorestoresanity.com/faq.

17 J. Feldman, "A Lack of Vision on the Mall," *Washington Post*, 7 April 2010, http:// www.voices.washingtonpost.com/local-opinions/.

18 Recall that the Continental Congress adopted a resolution in August 1783 which ordered that "an equestrian statue of General Washington be erected at the place where the residence of Congress shall be established." Washington was to be in Roman dress, holding a truncheon in his right hand.

19 Robert C. Winthrop and John Daniel, *The Dedication of the Washington Monument* (Washington, D.C.: Government Printing Office 1885, 44.

20 K. Savage, "The Self-Made Monument: George Washington and the Fight to Erect a National Memorial," in H. Senie and S. Webster, eds., *Critical Issues in Public Art: Content, Context and Controversy* (New York: Harper Collins 1992), 6.

21 Ibid., 5.

22 Ibid., 13.

23 Savage, *Monument Wars*.

24 Ibid., 140.

25 Winthrop and Daniel, *The Dedication of the Washington Monument*, 48.

26 Savage, *Monument Wars*, 117.

27 Ibid., 133.

28 Ibid., 140.

29 McMillan Report, 49.

30 Streatfield, "The Olmsteds and the Landscape of the Mall," 123.

31 Bednar, *L'Enfant's Legacy*, 50.

32 McMillan Report, 49.

33 Ibid., 48.

34 As pointed out in chapter 2, the monument was built off-axes because of the instability of the soil.

35 As quoted in J. Peterson, "The Mall, the McMillan Plan, and the Origins of American City Planning," in R. Longstreth, ed., *The Mall in Washington, 1791-1991* (New Haven: Yale University Press) 110.

36 This also includes contemporary critics such as Daniel Kiley, who has argued that the McMillan Plan's continuation of the Mall's axis beyond the Washington Monument was redundant and inappropriate. D. Kiley, "A Critical Look at the McMillan Plan," in Longstreth, ed., *The Mall in Washington*, 297.

37 Savage, *Monument Wars*.

38 Carson, "World War II Memorial."

39 As has been true in the past, the death of a planning visionary or an influential advocate has thwarted the realization of the plan for the Mall. In late 1902 Senator James McMillan, a staunch advocate of the plan that bears his name, died. Although the Senate had quickly passed and adopted the plan, it had done so without the support of the House, a politically egregious error that earned the enmity of Congressman Joseph Cannon, the powerful chairman of the Appropriations Committee. It also did not carry the force of law. With McMillan dead, the implementation of the McMillan Plan was subject to political delays and a protracted struggle. The commission members continued to advocate for the plan in an unofficial capacity. Initially, there was reason for optimism. In 1904 construction began on the National Museum (now the National Museum of Natural History). This was the first building to respect the new alignment of the Mall's main axis. In 1908 the Russell Senate and Cannon House office buildings were completed, conforming to the plan as well. And, while in general the McMillan Plan was accepted, like the L'Enfant Plan before it, the McMillan Plan faced many obstacles (as explained in chapter 2). Indeed, it would seem that completing plan elements was often spurred by specific celebrations of anniversaries – the 1900 capital centennial, the 1909 celebration of the centennial of Lincoln's birth, the bicentennial of 1976 – rather than by a commitment to the plan itself.

40 National Ideas Competition for the Washington Monument Grounds, Press Release, 19 September 2011, http://www.wamocompetition.org/whats-new (accessed 10 March 2016).

41 K. Savage, National Ideas Competition for the Washington Monument Grounds, 2012, http://www.wamocompetition.org/about. (accessed 10 March 2016).

9 Envisioning a Twenty-First-Century Mall

1 National Coalition to Save Our Mall, "The Future of the National Mall," October 2004 report, 3–4 (personal archives). Courtesy of the National Coalition to Save Our Mall.

2 J. Parsons, "Statement of John Parsons ... before the Subcommittee on National Parks of the Senate Committee on Energy and Resources, Concerning the Oversight of the National Mall," 12 April 2005.

3 NCPC, *Extending the Legacy*, 5.

4 Ibid., 6.
5 P. Gallagher, "Planning Beyond the Monument Core," in Glazer and Field, eds., *The National Mall*, 161.
6 Ibid., 163.
7 Ibid., 169.
8 J. Cogbill, "Testimony on Issues Related to the Future of the Mall under Subcommittee on National Parks of the Senate Committee on Energy and Resources," 12 April 2005 (personal archives).
9 Ibid.
10 N. Evenson, "Comments in a Panel Discussion for a Forum Presented by the Committee of 100 on the Federal City," Occasional Paper of the Committee of 100 on the Federal City, June 1996 (personal archives). Courtesy of the National Coalition to Save Our Mall.
11 K. Cooper, remarks made during a National Coalition to Save Our Mall Meeting, October 2008.
12 M. O'Dell, "Statement of Margaret O'Dell, Superintendent, National Mall & Memorial Parks, National Park Service, Department of the Interior, before the subcommittee on National Parks, Forests and Public Lands, of the House Committee on Natural Resources, Concerning the Future of the National Mall," 20 May 2008. Testimony distributed at hearing, 1–3.
13 I attended. Most of the day consisted of prepared presentations. Questions were taken at the end, but any question that challenged the Park Service received the briefest of answers.
14 George Mason University, "Public Scoping Comments Report: A Background Report for the National Mall Plan Prepared by the School of Recreation, Health, and Tourism George Mason University for the National Mall & Memorial Parks," April 2007.
15 O'Dell, "Statement," 5.
16 National Park Service, *National Mall Plan Newsletter* 4 (winter 2009).
17 "Public Comments Report: Newsletter 3 Alternatives: A Background Report for the National Mall Plan Prepared by the School of Recreation, Health, and Tourism George Mason University for the National Mall & Memorial Parks," http://www.nps.gov/nationalmallplan/Documents/News3Report_Sept2008_post.pdf (accessed 12 June 2010).
18 National Coalition to Save Our Mall to Susan Spain, project executive, the National Mall Plan, 12 March 2007 (personal archives). Courtesy of the National Coalition to Save Our Mall.
19 National Park Service "The National Mall Plan," http://www.nps.gov/nationalmallplan/FEISdocs.html (accessed 14 March 2016).
20 National Park Service, "Update on the National Mall Plan," 2010, http://www.nps.gov/nationalmallplan/ParkCommunications.html (accessed 17 July 2010).
21 N. Ziehl, National Trust for Historic Preservation, to Susan Spain, 29 April 2008 (personal archives). Courtesy of the National Coalition to Save Our Mall.
22 National Coalition to Save Our Mall to Susan Spain, project executive, the National Mall Plan, 29 May 2008 (personal archives). Courtesy of the National Coalition to Save Our Mall.

23 National Park Service, Press Release, 17 February 2010.

24 As quoted in M. Neibauer, "Park Service Offers Long-Term Mall Overhaul Plans," *Washington Examiner*, 30 December 2009, http://www.washingtonexaminer.com/local/Park-Service-offers-long-term-Mall-overhaul-plans-8697098-80298122.html.

25 J. Feldman, "Testimony before the House Committee on Natural Resources Subcommittee on National Parks, Forests & Public Lands on the Future of the National Mall," 20 May 2008, transcript (personal archives).

26 K. Cooper, comments made during a Coalition board meeting, 5 February 2008.

27 J. Feldman, "Reconnecting the National Mall to the Capital City in the 21st Century," paper given at Framing a Capital City Symposium, sponsored by the National Capital Planning Commission, National Building Museum, Washington, D.C., 11 April 2007, 2.

28 K. Cooper, personal communication, 28 April 2005.

29 National Coalition to Save Our Mall, "Update: March 4th Review of NPS Mall Plan," 2 March 2010 personal archives, Courtesy of the National Coalition to Save Our Mall.

30 J. Feldman, "National Mall Initiative Launches with Forum on GWU Campus," press release, 27 January 2003 (personal archives). Courtesy of the National Coalition to Save Our Mall.

31 Draft document, National Coalition to Save Our Mall, February 2006 (personal archives). Courtesy of the National Coalition to Save Our Mall.

32 National Coalition to Save Our Mall, "A Third Century National Mall Commission," 2007 (personal archives). Courtesy of the National Coalition to Save Our Mall.

33 Ibid.

34 J. Feldman, "Talking Points," 2006 (personal archives). Courtesy of the National Coalition to Save Our Mall.

35 National Coalition to Save Our Mall, "Renewing American Democracy on the 3rd Century Mall: A Vision for the National Mall," 2009 (personal archives). Courtesy of the National Coalition to Save Our Mall.

36 J. Parsons, "The Future of the History Beneath Our Feet," *Washington Post*, 18 January 2009, B08.

37 Ibid.

38 J. Feldman, "Testimony before the House Committee on Natural Resources Subcommittee on National Parks, Forests & Public Lands on the Future of the National Mall," 20 May 2008, transcript (personal archives).

39 Public Law 108–126, title II, 17 November 2003.

40 Ibid.

41 J. Cooper, "Foreword," in Glazer and Field, eds., *The National Mall*, vii.

42 J. Feldman, "The Problematics of Building on the Mall Today," in Glazer and Field, eds., *The National Mall*, 149.

43 Meyer, "From Urban Prospect to Retrospect," 61.

44 Ibid., 62.

45 Quoted in K. Paul, "A Mall Overhaul: Why a Major Facelift Is in Store for America's Front Yard," *Newsweek*, 26 July 2008, http://www.newsweek.com/id/146735/page/1. Emphasis added.

46 F. Hiatt, "Let the Mall Grow," *Washington Post*, 21 March 2005.

47 The National Coalition to Save Our Mall convened five public forums in 2004 out of which ideas about expanding the Mall grew into the Corcoran event. These meetings were held on the campus of George Washington University in conjunction with the GW Center for Urban Environmental Research. On 7 December 2005 the symposium "Designing for Democracy: The Third Century Mall" was held at the Corcoran Gallery of Art, Washington, D.C.

48 Indeed, for some 140 years or so, the court moved about, meeting briefly in two spaces in the Capitol. In 1929 President Taft proposed building a separate court building. But today's Supreme Court sits in the shadow of the Capitol, between the Library of Congress and the Methodist Building.

49 Arthur C. Moore to author, e-mail, 16 October 2016.

50 S. Nearman, "East Potomac Park Doesn't Need to Feel Like Mall, *Washington Times*, 12 December 2005.

51 A. Morris, "Letter to Editor," *Washington Times*, 12 December 2005.

52 C. Thomas, "Opening Statement Legislative Hearing on S. 1870, S. 1913, S. 1970, S.J. Res. 28, H.R. 318, and H.R. 562," 16 February 2006.

53 Comments of John V. Cogbill, III, Chairman of the National Capital Planning Commission, as quoted in T. Illia, "Citizens Group Lobbying to Expand Washington, D.C. Mall," *Architectural Record*, 13 September 2005, http://archrecord.construction.com/news/daily/archives/050913D.C..asp (personal archives). Courtesy of the National Coalition to Save Our Mall.

Index